Operational Research
Society Library
at
Brunel Library
Brunel University
Uxbridge UB8 3PH

Offshore Outsourcing of IT Work

TECHNOLOGY, WORK AND GLOBALIZATION

The Technology, Work and Globalization series was developed to provide policy makers, workers, managers, academics and students with a deeper understanding of the complex interlinks and influences between technological developments, including information and communication technologies, work organizations and patterns of globalization. The mission of the series is to disseminate rich knowledge based on deep research about relevant issues surrounding the globalization of work that is spawned by technology.

Also in this series:

GLOBAL SOURCING OF BUSINESS AND IT SERVICES
Leslie P. Willcocks and Mary C. Lacity

ICT AND INNOVATION IN THE PUBLIC SECTOR
Francesco Contini and Giovan Francesco Lanzara

EXPLORING VIRTUALITY WITHIN AND BEYOND ORGANIZATIONS
Niki Panteli and Mike Chiasson

KNOWLEDGE PROCESSES IN GLOBALLY DISTRIBUTED CONTEXTS
Julia Kotlarsky, Ilan Oshri and Paul C. van Fenema

GLOBAL CHALLENGES FOR IDENTITY POLICIES
Edgar Whitley and Ian Hosein

E-GOVERNANCE FOR DEVELOPMENT
Shirin Madon

Offshore Outsourcing of IT Work

Client and Supplier Perspectives

Mary C. Lacity
and
Joseph W. Rottman

© Selection and editorial matter © Mary C. Lacity and Joseph W. Rottman 2008
Individual chapters © individual contributors 2008

All rights reserved. No reproduction, copy or transmission of this publication may be made without written permission.

No paragraph of this publication may be reproduced, copied or transmitted save with written permission or in accordance with the provisions of the Copyright, Designs and Patents Act 1988, or under the terms of any licence permitting limited copying issued by the Copyright Licensing Agency, 90 Tottenham Court Road, London W1T 4LP.

Any person who does any unauthorised act in relation to this publication may be liable to criminal prosecution and civil claims for damages.

The authors have asserted their rights to be identified as the authors of this work in accordance with the Copyright, Designs and Patents Act 1988.

First published in 2008 by
PALGRAVE MACMILLAN
Houndmills, Basingstoke, Hampshire RG21 6XS and
175 Fifth Avenue, New York, N.Y. 10010
Companies and representatives throughout the world.

PALGRAVE MACMILLAN is the global academic imprint of the Palgrave Macmillan division of St. Martin's Press, LLC and of Palgrave Macmillan Ltd. Macmillan® is a registered trademark in the United States, United Kingdom and other countries. Palgrave is a registered trademark in the European Union and other countries.

ISBN-13: 978–0–230–52185–8
ISBN-10: 0–230–52185–1

This book is printed on paper suitable for recycling and made from fully managed and sustained forest sources. Logging, pulping and manufacturing processes are expected to conform to the environmental regulations of the country of origin.

A catalogue record for this book is available from the British Library.

A catalog record for this book is available from the Library of Congress.

10 9 8 7 6 5 4 3 2 1
17 16 15 14 13 12 11 10 09 08

Printed and bound in China

CONTENTS

LIST OF TABLES

LIST OF FIGURES

ACKNOWLEDGMENTS

First and foremost, we sincerely thank the 232 people who participated in our research study. Due to the sensitive nature of offshore outsourcing, we promised participants anonymity and thus we cannot individually acknowledge each person. Participants who did not request anonymity are acknowledged in the appropriate places throughout this book.

We thank all the great folks at Palgrave. Stephen Rutt, our UK publishing director, provides sharp vision and strong commitment to the Palgrave Series on Technology, Work, and Globalization. Alexandra Dawe has been a tremendous assistant editor by keeping our projects on track and facilitating the publishing process. Vidhya Jayaprakash and her entire team at Newgen in Chennai, India professionally and speedily copyedited the manuscript.

We also wish to acknowledge the supportive research environment at the University of Missouri, St. Louis. We thank Vice Chancellor Nasser Arshadi because his Office of Research provided two research grants to support this work. We are grateful to our Dean of the College of Business Administration, Dr. Keith Womer, for his financial support and continued recognition of our research. We thank Dr. Joel Glassman, Director of the Center for International Studies, for providing travel funds to Asia and Europe. We also thank our colleagues in the IS area, including Dr. Marius Janson, Dr. Kailash Joshi, Dr. Dinesh Mirchandani, Dr. Rajiv Sabherwal, Dr. Vicki Sauter, and Dr. Ashok Subramanian.

We would like to thank our circle of family and friends. Mary thanks her parents, Dr. and Mrs. Paul Lacity, and her three sisters: Karen Longo, Diane Iudica, and Julie Owings. She apologizes that this book interfered with her usual summer visit but thanks them all for their support and understanding. She thanks her closest friends, Jerry Pancio, Michael McDevitt, Beth Nazemi, Val Graeser, Katharine Hastings, and Leslie Willcocks. The St. Louis crew was tremendously helpful in accommodating her inflexible writing schedule. Because Jerry Pancio teased her for categorizing him as a "friend" in her last book, she here acknowledges his special place in her life as "a sole sourced partner." (Is that label better or worse?) Finally, to her son, Michael Christopher Kuban, to whom this book and all things in her life are dedicated.

Joe thanks first and foremost, his wife Pam. He deeply appreciates and treasures 20 years of love, support and friendship, the effort and dedication needed to carry the family on her back while he taught, traveled and wrote, and for convincing the kids that he had "gone to work" when he was really writing in the basement. He also thanks Dr. and Mrs. Ted Rohr for filling in and doing all the hard work while he was "gallivanting" around the world. This book is dedicated to Pam, Laura, Patrick, and Nicholas.

SERIES PREFACE

Technology is all too often positioned as the welcome driver of globalization. The popular press neatly packages technology's influence on globalization with snappy sound bites, such as "any work that can be digitized, will be globally sourced." Cover stories report Indians doing US tax returns, Moroccans developing software for the French, Filipinos answering UK customer service calls, and the Chinese doing everything for everybody. Most glossy cover stories assume that all globalization is progressive, seamless, intractable, and leads to unmitigated good. But what we are experiencing in the 21st Century in terms of the interrelationships between technology, work and globalization is both profound and highly complex.

We launched this series to provide policy makers, workers, managers, academics, and students with a deeper understanding of the complex interlinks and influences between technological developments, including in information and communication technologies, work organizations and patterns of globalization. The mission of this series is to disseminate rich knowledge based on deep research about relevant issues surrounding the globalization of work that is spawned by technology. To us, substantial research on globalization considers multiple perspectives and levels of analyses. We seek to publish research based on in-depth study of developments in technology, work and globalization and their impacts on and relationships with individuals, organizations, industries, and countries. We welcome perspectives from business, economics, sociology, public policy, cultural studies, law, and other disciplines that contemplate both larger trends and micro-developments from Asian, African, Australia, and Latin American, as well as North American and European viewpoints.

The first book in the series, *Global Sourcing of Business and IT Services* by Leslie Willcocks and Mary Lacity is based on over 1000 interviews with clients, suppliers, and advisors and fifteen years of study. The specific focus is on developments in outsourcing, offshoring, and mixed sourcing practices from client and supplier perspectives in a globalizing world. We found many organizations struggling. We also found other practitioners adeptly creating global sourcing networks that are agile, effective, and cost efficient. But they did so only after a tremendous amount of trial-and-error and close attention to details. All our participant organizations acted in a context of fast moving technology, rapid development of supply side offerings, and ever changing economic conditions.

Knowledge Processes in Globally Distributed Contexts by Julia Kotlarsky, Ilan Oshri, and Paul van Fenema, examines the management of knowledge processes of global knowledge workers. Based on substantial case studies and interviews, the authors – along with their network of co-authors – provide frameworks, practices, and tools that consider how to develop, coordinate, and manage knowledge processes in order to create synergetic value in globally distributed contexts. Chapters address knowledge sharing, social ties, transactive memory, imperative learning, work division and many other social and organizational practices to ensure successful collaboration in globally distributed teams.

Offshore Outsourcing of IT Work by Mary Lacity and Joseph Rottman examines the practices for successfully outsourcing IT work from Western clients to offshore suppliers. Based on over 200 interviews with 26 Western clients and their offshore suppliers in India, China, and Canada, the book details client-side roles of chief information officers, program management officers, and project managers and identifies project characteristics that differentiated successful from unsuccessful projects. The authors examine ten engagement models for moving IT work offshore and describe proven practices to ensure that offshore outsourcing is successful for both client and supplier organizations.

Exploring Virtuality within and Beyond Organizations by Niki Panteli and Mike Chiasson argues that there has been a limited conceptualization of virtuality and its implications on the management of organizations. Based on illustrative cases, empirical studies and theorizing on virtuality, this book goes beyond the simple comparison between the virtual and the traditional to explore the different types, dimensions and perspectives of virtuality. Almost all organizations are virtual, but they differ theoretically and substantively in their virtuality. By exploring and understanding these differences, researchers and practitioners gain a deeper understanding of the past, present and future possibilities of virtuality. The collection is designed to be indicative of current thinking and approaches, and provides a rich basis for further research and reflection in this important area of management and information systems research and practice.

ICT and Innovation in the Public Sector by Francesco Contini and Giovan Franceso Lanzara examines the theoretical and practical issues of implementing innovative ICT solutions in the public sector. The book is based on a major research project sponsored and funded by the Italian government (Ministry of University and Research) and coordinated by Italy's National Research Council and the University of Bologna during the years 2002–2006. The authors, along with a number of coauthors, explore the complex interplay between technology and institutions, drawing on multiple theoretical traditions such as institutional analysis, actor network theory, social systems theory, organization theory and transaction costs economics. Detailed case studies offer realistic and rich lessons. These cases studies include e-justice in Italy and Finland, e-bureaucracy in Austria, and Money Claim On-Line in England and Wales.

In addition to these first five books, several other manuscripts are underdevelopment. These forthcoming books cover topics of ICT in developing countries, global ICT standards, and identity protection. Each book uniquely meets the mission of the series.

We encourage other researchers to submit proposals to the series, as we envision a protracted need for scholars to deeply and richly analyze and conceptualize the complex relationships among technology, work and globalization.

LESLIE P. WILLCOCKS
MARY C. LACITY
November 2007

Jim Fox is the founding partner of ValueStream Advisors, a firm specializing in business value enhancements for finance and administration processes. Jim has extensive international finance experience and is a recognized speaker on finance process automation and sourcing. Previously, Jim served as a partner with DataServ and was responsible for Business and Product Development. Prior to DataServ, Jim held various financial management positions for global services and technology companies and served multinational companies as a senior manager for Deloitte in St. Louis, New York and Brussels. He holds a BSc with majors in both Accounting and Finance.

Vidya Iyer is a third-year PhD student of Information Systems at the University of Missouri, St. Louis. She obtained an MBA in Information Systems from Indore University in India and an MS in Information Systems from Texas A&M International University, Laredo. She worked as a software programmer for two years for Sonata Software in Bangalore, and Ruchi Software in Indore. She has also taught graduate level MBA courses at Prestige Management Institute, Indore, before joining the PhD program at the University of Missouri, St. Louis. Her research interests include outsourcing of information systems, turnover among IS employees, and computer-mediated education and e-mentoring.

Hao Lou is a professor of Management Information Systems at Ohio University. Since 1999, he has served as the Coordinator of College of Business' Hubei (China) Executive MBA program in the Center for International Business Education and Development (CIBED). His publications have appeared in *European Journal of Information Systems, Journal of Association for Information Systems, Journal of Organizational Computing and Electronic Commerce, Journal of Information Systems Resource Management, Journal of End-User Computing,* and *Journal of Global Information Management.*

Prasad S. Rudramuniyaiah is a doctoral student in Information Systems at the University of Missouri, St. Louis. Prasad holds a Bachelors' degree in Mechanical Engineering from Bangalore University, and a MSc from Middlesex University, London. Prasad started his career as a first-generation entrepreneur and subsequently worked in the IT industry in Bangalore in various positions before joining the doctoral program. His research interests include outsourcing, knowledge management, organization behavior, e-commerce, and logistics and supply chain management.

CHAPTER 1

Offshore outsourcing of IT work

Mary Lacity and Joseph Rottman

The promise of global sourcing

Global sourcing of information technology (IT) is the idea that IT work can be seamlessly distributed anywhere in the world to the best source in terms of overall value.[1] The "best source" can include combinations of in-house provision, offshore captive centers, outsourcing to multiple suppliers, and even joint ventures.[2] Senior executives dream of creating agile global IT networks to lower costs, increase quality, realize seamless sunrise-to-sunrise production, deliver faster, and disperse risks. We present evidence in this book, based on 232 interviews with people from 68 companies, that some companies are indeed achieving these business benefits from global IT sourcing.

Companies of any size can benefit from global sourcing. Some of the largest client organizations we studied have very nimble global IT sourcing networks. For example, a US-based financial services company has captive centers in Manila and Mumbai, and various joint ventures and fee-for-service relationships with 14 Indian suppliers. This level of global reach allows the company to efficiently distribute immense volumes of IT and business process work. Even some of the smallest companies we studied are benefiting from global sourcing. One small, US-based company that builds business intelligence software has quite an advanced global IT network for a company with only 43 employees. The American CEO and founder located 33 of his 43 employees in Hyderabad and three employees are located in rural Oklahoma. The CEO says that his global sourcing model is the only way he can compete with large software companies on price and quality. Six of his Indian managers frequently visit the US to keep close tabs on client requirements. The Indian managers' equity position in the company highly motivates them to succeed. Among the Indian developers, turnover is low because the employees are thrilled to be developing a complex product and the CEO pays them more money than large Indian suppliers. The CEO is growing a captive center in Oklahoma because Oklahoma is giving tax breaks and incentives like free rent to have companies hire new students out of college. Ironically, these rural employees have been Indian students from Oklahoma University!

But juxtaposed to our success stories, many IT executives we interviewed struggle to realize the full potential of global IT sourcing. Although global sourcing is technically possible because any work that can be digitized can be moved, there are many managerial challenges. One common complaint was that overall cost savings was less than anticipated due to the high transaction costs associated with finding suppliers (or erecting captive centers), coordinating, and monitoring work done offshore.[3] Other common complaints were that quality was initially poor, delivery was slow, and personnel issues such as high supplier turnover interfered with success. Our mixed findings are consistent with other practitioner surveys. Some practitioner outlets report high success rates with offshore outsourcing:

- A survey of 38 companies in North America and Europe, of which eighty-five percent were involved in offshore outsourcing of IT work, found that 89% were satisfied with their offshore outsourcing initiatives.[4]
- A DiamondCluster survey of 210 buyers found that offshore outsourcing satisfaction rates were high, but falling from 79% to 62% between 2004 and 2005.[5]

In contrast, some practitioner outlets report low success rates with offshore outsourcing:

- A Gartner survey found a 50% failure rate for offshore outsourcing initiatives.[6]
- A survey of 204 software developers found that 46% viewed the work performed by the offshore teams to be of poor quality.[7]
- Ventoro's survey of over 5200 executives from North America and Europe found that nearly 28% of respondents experienced cost *increases* and another 25% did not generate any cost savings with offshore outsourcing.[8]

How can these mixed experiences be reconciled? Our research found that global IT sourcing can deliver on its promises only if both clients and suppliers diligently manage the details. In this book, we detail the best, worst, and emerging practices to ensure offshore outsourcing success for both the clients and their offshore suppliers. We do not offer platitudes such as or "secure top management support" but rather we provide specific practices that managers can use. To understand how these practices were identified, we next explain the research base.

The research base

Between 2004 and 2007, we interviewed 232 people from 68 companies (see Table 1.1) on the topic of global IT sourcing. Most participants were interviewed in-person on the client site in the US or at supplier sites in India, China, or Canada. Most interviews were tape recorded and transcribed, allowing us to sprinkle the participants' rich quotes throughout the book. The sample is diverse in that we solicited insights from 25 client organizations, 33 supplier organizations, and 10 offshore advisor firms.

The client organizations

Half of the participants (n=97) represent client organizations from 15 different industries, with financial services organizations being the best represented industry. Twenty-four of these client organizations are based in the US and one organization is based in the United Kingdom. The size of the client organizations in terms of annual revenues ranged from $6 million to $117 billion. The mean revenue among the client firms was $32.2 billion, and the median revenue was $15.7 billion. The size of the client organizations in terms of employees ranged from 43 people to 327,000 people. The mean number of employees in the client firms was 74,852 people and the median number of employees was 38,000 people.

Above we explained that many clients in our sample, such as the large financial services firm and small business intelligence software company, are realizing the full benefits of global sourcing. However, not all client organizations we studied achieved success. For example, a biotechnology company (assigned the pseudonym "Biotech") had mixed results when it outsourced IT work to six Indian suppliers. Its story is the topic of Chapter 2. Biotech presents a highly realistic and typical picture of a client's experiences with offshoring of IT work for the first time and how best and worst practices quickly emerge.

A manufacturing company provides another example of mixed results. This company engaged 15 offshore suppliers yet only has a total offshore headcount of 300 IT employees! Their global IT supply network is not very agile or efficient. In this company, powerful decentralized business units selected offshore suppliers, so there were no synergies or integration across the IT supply network. In fact, some units were paying drastically different prices to the same supplier! Moving forward, the company's centralized Program Management Office (PMO) will play a greater role in reducing the number of suppliers, renegotiating contracts, and managing the offshore program.

Table 1.1 Research participants

Company role in offshore outsourcing	Company description	Number of research participants
US-based clients (except as noted)	1. Aerospace	3
	2. Beverage	3
	3. Biotechnology (pseudonym Biotech)	44
	4. Electrical materials	1
	5. Employee satisfaction	1
	6. Financial Information Services (UK) (pseudonym FIS)	2
	7. Financial services	7
	8. Financial services	1
	9. Financial services	1
	10. Financial services	1
	11. Financial services	1
	12. Financial services	1
	13. Financial services	3
	14. Financial services	3
	15. Government IS Organization	1
	16. Insurance	2
	17. Insurance	3
	18. Manufacturing (pseudonym US manufacturing)	3
	19. Manufacturing	2
	20. Manufacturing	2
	21. Mining	1
	22. Retailer (pseudonym Retail)	7
	23. Software company	2
	24. Telecommunications	1
	25. Transportation	1
Offshore suppliers, captive centers, joint ventures	1. US-owned IT/BPO rural sourcing supplier (CrossUSA)	3
	2. US-owned IT/BPO rural sourcing supplier (Rural Sourcing)	1
	3. US-owned captive center in India	5
	4. US-owned captive center in India	1
	5. US-owned captive center in India	7
	6. US-owned captive center in China (Oracle)	2
	7. US-owned captive center in China (pseudonym Financial Services)	2
	8. US-owned captive center in China (pseudonym Staff Augmentation)	2
	9. US-based staff augmentation firm	1
	10. US-based staff augmentation firm	1
	11. US/Indian joint venture in India	7
	12. US/Indian joint venture in India	1

Continued

Table 1.1 Continued

Company role in offshore outsourcing	Company description	Number of research participants
	13. US/Indian joint venture in India	1
	14. UK-owned captive center in India	1
	15. Indian-owned IT/BPO supplier	1
	16. Indian-owned IT/BPO supplier	2
	17. Indian-owned IT/BPO supplier	4
	18. Indian-owned IT/BPO supplier	2
	19. Indian-owned IT/BPO supplier	3
	20. Indian-owned IT/BPO supplier	2
	21. Indian-owned IT/BPO supplier	1
	22. Indian-owned IT/BPO supplier	11
	23. Indian-owned IT/BPO supplier	1
	24. Indian-owned IT/BPO supplier	16
	25. European-owned captive center in India	1
	26. European-owned captive center in India	1
	27. European/Indian joint venture in India	2
	28. Chinese–owned IT/BPO supplier (Neusoft)	11
	29. Chinese–owned IT/BPO supplier (DHC)	1
	30. Chinese-owned IT supplier (NewLand)	1
	31. Chinese-owned IT supplier (Netai Techno)	1
	32. Chinese-owned IT supplier (Crystal)	8
	33. Canadian-based IT/BPO supplier	11
Offshore advisors	1. Consulting firm	1
	2. Consulting firm	1
	3. Consulting firm	1
	4. Consulting firm	2
	5. Legal firm	1
	6. Legal firm	1
	7. Legal firm	1
	8. Legal firm	1
	9. Legal firm	1
	10. Legal firm	1
Chinese economic and development zone officials	1. Chief Executive Officer	1
	2. Deputy Director	1
	3. Deputy General Director	1
	4. Director of the Economic & Trade Bureau	1
	5. Director, Vice Chairman President	1
	6. IT and Multi – Media Department Manager	1
	7. Project Executive Foreign Investment Service Center	1
	8. Vice Director Legal Counsel	1
	9. Vice Director Senior Engineer	1
Total number of participants		232

The supplier organizations

Suppliers are well represented with 115 interviews. Among the supplier interviews, 50 were interviewed in person in India at supplier sites in Bangalore, Mumbai, and Hyderabad. Twenty-five participants were interviewed in India by telephone from the US by two of our doctoral students, Vidya Iyer and Prasad Rudramuniyaiah. In China, 28 supplier employees were interviewed in person. Twelve supplier participants worked in the United States. For example, the three employees from the first supplier listed in Table 1.1 are from a small US company that provides rural sourcing services to US clients. (The rural sourcing model is explored in the final chapter.) The two US-based staff augmentation firms actually recruit globally (mostly from India) to staff workers at US client sites.

The size of the supplier organizations in terms of annual revenues ranged from $800,000 for a Chinese owned supplier to $90 billion for a large US-based global supplier. The mean revenue among the suppliers was $7.8 billion and the median revenue was $980 million. The size of the supplier organizations in terms of employees ranged from 40 people to 200,000 people. The mean number of employees in the supplier firms was 25,010 people and the median number of employees was 2,800 people. Three of the large US IT/BPO suppliers have global presences in nearly 100 countries, with significant employee numbers in India, other parts of Asia, Western Europe, and South America. Three of the largest Indian suppliers earn more than $2 billion in revenues and are quickly becoming contenders among the top US-based global IT suppliers. We also have good representation among the Indian boutique suppliers that are competing based on vertical expertise.

The advisors and officials

Among the 10 advisory firms in our study, six are legal firms that provide legal services for offshore contracts, local laws, and arbitration. Four companies provide consulting services to help clients select offshore locations and engage offshore suppliers. The second author also interviewed nine Chinese economic and development officials in Dalian.

Categorizing the research participants into four high level categories – clients, suppliers, advisors, and officials – does not really paint the full picture of global IT sourcing. In reality, the stakeholder landscape is much more complex.

Clients and suppliers must manage many stakeholders

Most offshore outsourcing research distinguishes between two groups of stakeholders: clients and suppliers. In reality, this duality is too simplistic. Within client firms, for example, there are at least six different classes of stakeholders: senior management, IT management, business unit managers, IT staff, end users, and in-house specialists such as lawyers, auditors, and human resource specialists (see Figure 1.1). Various client stakeholders expect different things from global sourcing and outsourcing suppliers and more importantly – they may hold radically different perceptions as to its success. Senior management frequently expect and assess global sourcing based on total savings achieved. End users typically focus only on service excellence and high quality of deliverables – regardless of costs because they don't directly pay for IT. Client IT staff may focus on technical quality and speed of delivery. Client specialists may focus on controls (for auditors), contracts (for lawyers), and redundancy implications (for HR specialists). Satisfying all these stakeholders simultaneously is impossible. After 20 years of research, we can confidently say that 100% of client stakeholders will never be 100% satisfied with outsourcing suppliers. (Client stakeholders are never 100% satisfied with in-house IT services either.)

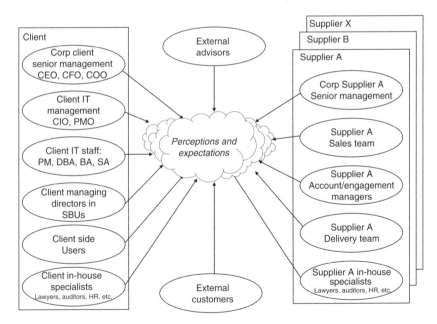

Figure 1.1 Global sourcing stakeholders

The supplier organizations are equally complex. Suppliers house a myriad of stakeholders, all expecting different things from client relationships. Senior supplier management typically focuses on profit margin and revenue growth. The sales team looks to sell big deals fast. The supplier delivery team wants interesting work. The supplier engagement managers are in the thorny position of satisfying all the supplier's stakeholders in addition to satisfying all the client-side stakeholders. In addition, supplier engagement managers compete with their peers for the supplier's best human and technical resources for their account.

To further complicate the stakeholder landscape, clients frequently engage multiple suppliers. One supplier may be working on an upgrade for the client's software that is currently hosted and maintained by another supplier. In our research, we found multiple suppliers coordinating work for a shared client, even though there was no contractual mechanism to formalize the inter-supplier relationship. Additional stakeholders may include the client's external customers who may have strong preferences against offshore outsourcing and external advisors hired by the client to help find suppliers and negotiate contracts.

The complex stakeholder landscape suggests that the success of offshore outsourcing will largely depend on managing the relationships among a diverse group of stakeholders. This book is unique in that we address offshore outsourcing from the perspective of many stakeholders (see Table 1.2). On the client slide, the majority of participants are IT managers in charge of global IT sourcing (including chief information officers, program management office directors, and directors of application development or IT services) and IT staff in charge of delivery (including project managers, data base administrators, technical architects, business analysts, and systems analysts). We were only able to interview four client side senior managers (CEO or CFO) because senior managers from client organizations typically delegate responsibility for global IT sourcing to their top IT managers.

On the supplier side, we interviewed 31 senior managers, most frequently the CEO. In contrast to the client side, senior supplier managers were anxious to participate in the research study to highlight their organization's capabilities. We also interviewed 61 supplier employees directly servicing US clients as either engagement managers or delivery team members. We were particularly interested in these stakeholder groups because they are largely neglected by research. Together, all these stakeholders represent the rich context and significant managerial challenges for creating a shared vision for global IT sourcing. How can so many diverse groups be ushered in the same direction? Few client organizations are successful at managing

Table 1.2 Stakeholder representation of research participants

Stakeholder category	Stakeholder group	Number of research participants
Client	Senior management (CEO, CFO, COO, VP)	4
	IT management (CIO, PMO, Directors)	31
	IT staff	67
	Users/business unit managers	3
	Specialists	2
Supplier	Senior management	31
	Sales and marketing	13
	Account/engagement managers	11
	Delivery team	50
Advisors	Lawyers	6
	Consultants	5
Officials	Economic and software park officials	9
Total number of participants		232

all the stakeholders the first time they engage offshore suppliers. In the next section, we introduce the idea of the offshore outsourcing learning curve.

The offshoring learning curve

In our 2006 paper published in *Sloan Management Review,* we described the typical client learning curve for offshoring IT work[9] (see Figure 1.2). During phase I, managers become aware of offshore through marketing hype ("you'll save 60% off your IT costs") or irrational propaganda ("software outsourcing will hurt America's supremacy"). Managers quickly learn about potential benefits, costs, and risks by talking to peers, consultants, and reading research. Most managers initially begin offshore sourcing with pilot projects to reduce costs on a few targeted projects (phase II). Phase II can be quite disappointing, as we found that failures were common. Chapter 2 provides an extensive case study on a biotechnology company's phase II experiences. Clients like this biotechnology company who went offshore solely for cost reasons found that quality of deliverables was often poor. The primary causes are the client's lack of organizational readiness and lack of in-house capabilities to make the most of the supplier's resources.

As learning accumulates, managers progress to phase III when they seek more benefits from moving IT work offshore besides cost savings. Here, clients pay more attention to ensuring that the supplier will be successful

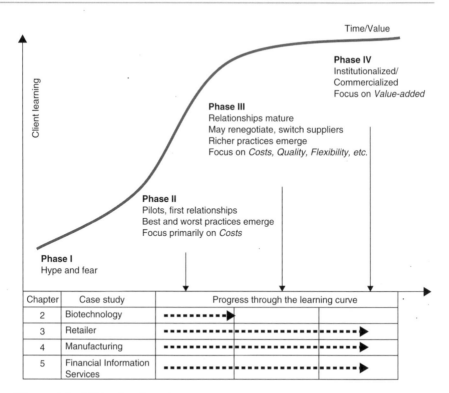

Figure 1.2 Offshoring learning curve

by investing more in social capital, knowledge transfer, and other measures discussed in this book. Clients have more realistic expectations about cost savings and better understand their own roles in ensuring success.

More mature adopters in phase IV have successfully integrated offshore suppliers into their global sourcing network. The global sourcing model is "institutionalized," meaning that offshore suppliers or captive centers are embedded and accepted in the organization. In Chapter 3, we highlight the experiences of a large US retailer (assigned the pseudonym "Retail") that has institutionalized offshore outsourcing during its ten year relationships with Indian suppliers. When a practice becomes institutionalized, it does not mean that the organization will forever continue with the practice. The possibility for managers to change course always exists. In practice, we see this in the form of backsourcing, where CIOs may decide to bring functions back in-house after many years of institutionalized outsourcing. In theory, Anthony Giddens[10] developed structuration theory that explains this phenomenon. He argues that although much of social interaction becomes routine (i.e. people tend to do the same things over and over again), at any time social routines can be changed by agents with the power, sanctions, and signification to do so.

More mature adopters in phase IV may also use offshore outsourcing to strategically enable corporate strategies, such as increasing business agility, infusing innovation through the development of new products, bringing products to market faster and cheaper, and even commercializing IT. In addition to Retail, we present two detailed cases of organizations in phase IV of the learning curve. In Chapter 4, we highlight the experiences of a US industrial equipment manufacturer (assigned the pseudonym "US Manufacturing") that uses offshore suppliers to help build innovative embedded software for its core products. In Chapter 5, we present the case of a financial information services firm (assigned the pseudonym "FIS") that dispersed finance work to six regional service centers (near-shoring), a new captive center in India (offshoring) and several outsourcing suppliers.

The entire learning curve takes some organizations years to conquer. The slow pace begins in phase II, where many companies we studied picked pilot projects that were too small and tested only a single supplier. False starts and switching suppliers kept US Manufacturing in phase II for three years. It wasn't until the company invested in social capital that they were able to realize significant value from offshore outsourcing.

By focusing on the learning from the US clients in the later phases of maturity, we can extract the roles of the client leadership in shepherding the stakeholders and in ensuring offshore expectations are met. We begin with the roles assigned to the CIO.

Sourcing roles of the client CIO

The CIO's role in sourcing varied significantly within our client firms depending on the size of the organization. In small organizations, CIOs assumed more roles and some were directly responsible for finding and engaging suppliers. In large organizations, the CIO delegated many of these tasks to a Program Management Office or to a team of IT leaders. In this section, we look at the roles of CIOs primarily from the perspective of large organizations. These roles represent the set of responsibilities shared by all CIOs, whether they are IT leaders from small or large organizations.

Most advisors state that the primary role of the CIO is to align the sourcing strategy with the IT and business strategies. But what exactly does this mean? In this section, we dissect this platitude into seven specific roles of the CIO:

1. Establish expected IT and business benefits.
2. Select the right approach to offshoring.
3. Enamor suppliers by being an attractive client.
4. Communicate the sourcing strategy to all stakeholders.

5. Provide enough resources to implement the sourcing strategy.
6. Build social capital with key supplier executives.
7. Seek independent assessment of sourcing strategy effectiveness.

1. Establish expected IT and business benefits

One of the CIO's main roles in offshore outsourcing is to establish the expected IT and business benefits. Expected benefits almost always include total cost savings, but may also include faster delivery speed, ability to focus in-house IT staff on more higher-value work, access to supplier resources and capabilities, and process improvement. We identified 12 benefits client firms expected from offshoring (see Figure 1.3). The benefits are interdependent and CIOs must consider the trade-offs. The typical tradeoffs are in terms of high quality, low costs, and rapid delivery. A supplier told us, "customers can have two of those, but not all three at once." Another common trade-off is between tight control over intellectual property versus using the supplier to enable innovation.

CIOs should place emphasis on the benefits that best match the overall IT and business strategies. CIOs typically aligned the offshore strategy

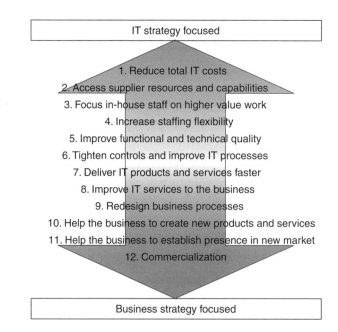

Figure 1.3 Reasons for offshoring IT work

with the IT strategy by focusing on the first four expected benefits – lower total IT costs, access supplier resources and capabilities, focus in-house staff on higher value work, and increase flexibility by ramping IT staff up and down to match fluctuating demand. Among our cases, some CIOs went further by aligning the offshore strategy with the business strategy. These CIOs wanted offshore outsourcing to help their business redesign business processes, create new products and services, or establish a presence in new market.

When considering an offshore destination for IT work, some CIOs intelligently asked, "Does the business have or want to have a significant presence in this country?" The CIO from one aerospace company selected Malaysia as their IT offshore destination because his company sells planes in that country. The Malaysian government requires that some of the manufacturing be done in Malaysia and the IT presence helped to meet that business requirement. Another CIO from a hardware company selected China because he knew his company wanted to sell computers there. One US CIO chose Canada because he wanted suppliers in close physical proximity to their end customers for rapid deployment. Other participants selected offshore locations where they have existing manufacturing or R&D facilities. The existing facilities served as a launch pad, with current employees serving as guides to the country, suppliers, and culture. Some CIOs used offshore outsourcing to help the business develop new products faster.

Identifying the number of expected benefits from offshore outsourcing and its role in the IT and business strategies will also help CIOs decide whether incremental or radical changes are needed to ensure success.

2. Select the right approach to offshoring

When considering offshore approaches, CIOs have many choices. To simplify the selection, we narrow the types of choices down to

- incremental or radical approaches, depending on the number of expected benefits;
- engagement models, depending on the type of work, client capabilities and supplier capabilities (see Figure 1.4).

Most CIOs in our research expected offshore outsourcing to produce the first four benefits listed in Figure 1.3 and subsequently sought incremental changes to achieve these expectations. Biotech and Retail provide

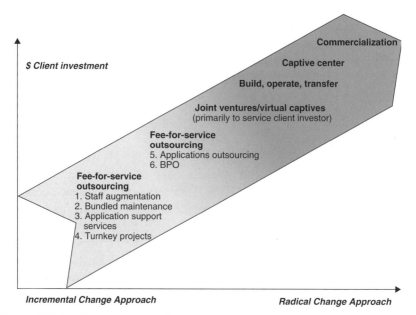

Figure 1.4 Offshoring approaches

two examples of incremental change approaches. A few senior executives in our study expected much more from a sourcing strategy. For example, the CFO from FIS sought benefits 1 through 10. The subsequent sourcing strategy required radical transformation of financial services within the firm. His team completely redesigned the services and delivery models world-wide. Incremental changes and radical transformation approaches are compared in Table 1.3.

In most of our client organizations, CIOs initiated offshore outsourcing on a small scale to "test the waters." CIOs charged a team of IT leaders to investigate whether the organization could leverage offshore suppliers to lower IT costs, access IT skills, and/or meet a temporary resource need. Organizations typically started offshore by engaging one or more offshore suppliers to work on small pilot projects. This approach is incremental, tactical, and low-risk.

The main value organizations derived from an incremental approach was an immense amount of learning about themselves. Most clients, like Biotech and US Manufacturing did not achieve their overall expected cost savings and complained about the quality of supplier deliverables. But the learning they accumulated with the pilot projects allowed both to reassess their offshore strategy. For Biotech, this meant expanding their IT work to a captive center in India, primarily to help their business organization

Table 1.3 Incremental versus radical approaches

	Incremental change	Radical transformation
Description	Client selectively engages offshore suppliers on a small scale	Client radically redesigns its services, sourcing strategy, and delivery models
Motto	"Test the waters" "Start small, stay small."	"Do it once, do it big, do it right"
Trade-offs	Client learns which internal capabilities are needed to achieve expected benefits from offshore outsourcing. However, incremental approaches often result in few benefits due to the inability to attract a committed supplier, lack of enough internal resources committed to success, and lack of scale to achieve total cost savings. But consequences of failure are minimal because so little is invested.	Potential to achieve better results than incremental approach because scale is large enough to be attractive to suppliers and scale is large enough to achieve significant total cost savings (and other benefits). However, senior management must commit significant resources to achieve the transformation. Consequences of a failure – if one occurs – will be much greater when compared to an incremental approach.
Client profile	• Client inexperienced with offshore outsourcing • Client with flat IT budgets • Client sought few benefits – mostly minor cost reductions and access to supplier resources	• Client experienced with offshore outsourcing or can leverage prior experience with domestic outsourcing • Client with mandate for significant cost reductions and service improvements • Client willing to invest resources needed to achieve results
Offshoring approach	• Fee-for-service: 1. Staff augmentation 2. Bundled maintenance 3. Application support services 4. Turnkey projects	• Fee-for service: 5. Applications outsourcing 6. BPO • Joint ventures/virtual captives • Build-Operate-Transfer • Captive centers • Commercialization • Mixture of above
Case studies in this book	Biotech (Chapter 2) Retail (Chapter 3) US Manufacturing during phase II in the learning curve (Chapter 4)	US Manufacturing during phases III and IV in the learning curve (Chapter 4) FIS (Chapter 5)

sell products to India. The incremental engagements with offshore suppliers were abandoned because senior IT leaders realized they did not have the internal capabilities or cultural compatibility to successfully engage offshore suppliers. For US Manufacturing, this meant an entirely different approach to offshoring – one that focused on building social capital and investing in knowledge transfer to ensure success.

Most client organizations use fee-for-service engagement models to enact an incremental approach. With fee-for-service offshoring outsourcing, the client signs a contract with an external service provider that bases some resources offshore. There are many ways to engage suppliers in fee-for-service relationships. Below we list six fee-for-service models and explore each in more detail in Chapter 3. The six fee-for-service models are sequenced by the amount of change required in the organization. Staff augmentation requires the least amount of organizational change, whereas BPO requires the most organizational change.

Staff augmentation engagements: offshore suppliers supplement client-led teams with supplier staff located on the client's site or offshore.

Bundled maintenance engagements: the offshore supplier works with the client's IT leads to handle small maintenance items and minor requests for existing applications.

Application support services engagements: the offshore supplier works directly with users to support existing applications.

Turnkey project engagements: the offshore supplier is responsible for the management and delivery of a predefined project.

Application outsourcing engagements: the offshore supplier is responsible for supporting IT applications associated with a business process.

Business process outsourcing (BPO) engagements: the offshore supplier is responsible for an entire end-to-end business process.

In Chapter 3, we present lessons that explain how IT managers can match the right fee-for-service engagement model to type of IT work, client capabilities and supplier capabilities. These lessons are high-level and targeted towards CIOs, Program Management Officers, and Applications Directors.

Across our client organizations, the main learning derived from an incremental approach is that the client must develop significant internal capabilities in order to achieve sourcing objectives. Initially, organizations often under-estimated the amount of internal resources needed to coordinate and support internal project managers, suppliers, and users. Much of this can be remedied with a robust PMO (see section on PMO roles in this chapter).

In general, the greater the expected benefits, the more radically the CIO must transform service delivery to meet those expectations. Among the cases highlighted in this book, by far the financial information services firm (FIS) had the most expected benefits and subsequently the most radical transformation approach. The CEO from that company wanted the CFO to cut financial costs by 33%, improve service, and increase controls. From 2001 to 2006, the finance leaders met those mandates by redesigning financial services, erecting seven service centers around the world, and outsourcing specialized financial services to third party suppliers. The benefits of radical transformation are that (a) more benefits can be realized (b) the scale is large enough to be attractive to suppliers, and (c) the scale is large enough to achieve total cost savings. However, consequences of a failure – if one occurs – will be much greater. Clients used several models to enact radical change approaches, including joint ventures, virtual captive centers, build-operate-transfer, captive centers, and commercialization.[11]

With joint ventures/virtual captive centers, the client and supplier both have investments in the offshore facilities. With joint ventures, clients and suppliers both invest in a new business entity. To the outside world, the joint venture is a separate business. However, most joint ventures we studied primarily service the client investor. Clients chose this model when they were willing to sacrifice some control in exchange for the supplier's local expertise. Among our client companies, several large companies partnered with smaller Indian firms. Clients liked this model because it required less investment and less risk than a captive center. The Indian suppliers liked this model because they could use the client's stature to organically grow their business.

With a virtual captive center, the company owns the physical operations, but the staff is employed by a third party supplier.[12] Presumably, the virtual captive center offers the best of both worlds – the client investor still maintains strategic control but the supplier is better equipped to attract, develop, and retain local IT talent.

With the build-operate-transfer (BOT) model, the supplier owns, builds, and operates the facility on behalf of the client, then transfers ownership to the client after completion. Clients use this model as an interim step on the road to owning a captive center. Rather than try to traverse the quagmire of local laws and customs on their own, the client hires a supplier with a local presence to build the captive center on their behalf. The supplier typically runs the operation until stability has been achieved, at which time ownership transfers to the client.

In 2003, JD Edwards signed a six-year BOT contract with Covansys. When PeopleSoft bought JD Edwards later that year, Peoplesoft renegotiated the deal and signed a three-year BOT contract with Covansys and Hexaware. The suppliers built PeopleSoft's India Services Center (ISC) and India Development Center (IDC), staffed the centers, and trained employees.

According to the CIO of a consulting firm, of his 75 US clients he helped to offshore outsource, none of them actually went through with the transfer phase of the BOT model. By then, his clients were comfortable with the supplier and did not want to take over the facilities. One participant quipped the reason he backed out of the transfer was, "I don't know who to call when the lights go out, and they do!"

With the captive center model, the client builds, owns, staffs, and operates its own offshore facilities. With captive centers, senior managers must be willing to invest their own resources to build human, intellectual, technical, and physical capital. Such investment is only warranted if senior managers make strong commitments to offshoring in terms of a large volume of work over a long period of time. Captive centers are also justified when control over the work is vital, such as when the work content is secretive or sensitive, or because customers demand it.

According to the CEO of NeoIT, an offshore consulting company, most IT suppliers who set up captive centers use the cost savings to reduce their overall rate for services. One example of a captive center is IBM Global Services. IBM actually created a captive center in India to reduce IT costs for one of its large clients, AT&T. At the time, AT&T had a seven-year contract with IBM worth nearly $1 billion. The AT&T CIO pushed IBM to create a captive center. Nearly 40% of AT&T's application development was subsequently done offshore through IBM's captive center, with AT&T claiming 30% cost savings.

Among our client companies, the financial information services firm (FIS) made the most extensive use of captive centers. In Chapter 5, we explain how this company erected seven captive centers on four continents to significantly reduce costs, improve service, and tighten controls.

With commercialization, companies create revenue-generating subsidiaries. In our previous book, we also highlighted two organizations – BAE Systems and Lloyds of London – that engaged suppliers to help commercialize their back offices.[13] Both of these client organizations engaged the UK supplier Xchanging to establish jointly-owned businesses. With BAE Systems, Xchanging created an enterprise called XHRS for human resource services and another enterprise called XPS for procurement services. For Lloyd's of London, Xchanging created enterprises for policy and claims administration.

Many companies switch models or use blended approaches. Some companies, such as FIS, use multiple models. That company combines captive centers and fee-for-service outsourcing in its global shared services network. Some organizations switch models after conquering the learning curve. One of our informants from a financial services company began with a fee-for-service model. But as volume of work increased to 3000 full time equivalents, the client is considering a captive center to reclaim the Indian supplier's 30% profit margin. According to the Vice President of Technologies for this company: "Once I have a very good feeling about how the Indian market is progressing, I plan to move to a captive center and recoup the margin my vendor is currently gaining."

In creating the sourcing strategy, the CIO must also consider whether their plans will be attractive to suppliers. In general, suppliers are attracted to experienced clients offering big, interesting deals.

3. Enamor suppliers by being an attractive client

When planning the role of external suppliers within the sourcing strategy, CIOs need to understand that their ability to attract a great partner largely depends on their "client attractiveness". In our research, CIOs who launch small pilot projects to test offshore outsourcing are frequently disappointed that suppliers did not commit their best resources to their account. We found that suppliers are attracted to clients with the following attributes:

- The client's current contract offers a real opportunity for future additional revenues and good profit margins with this client and other clients because of this deal.
- The client provides an opportunity for the supplier to enter into new markets.
- The client offers the supplier an opportunity for knowledge transfer to supplier.
- The client has prior relationships with suppliers that have been successful.
- The client understands and commits to providing key internal capabilities to ensure the supplier's success.
- The client is prestigious.

The size of the client's contract is really the key to a client's attractiveness. Although it takes time to build a good supplier relationship, suppliers will be more motivated to allocate their best resources to clients with large contracts. Like clients, suppliers incur large transaction costs to assemble bids, negotiate contracts, and manage client accounts. Suppliers can only afford to devote their best resources to clients with a large volume of current business or the very real possibility of a large volume of business in the future.

The US client organizations in our study claiming the most cost savings from offshore all have large contracts with their existing offshore suppliers. One telecommunications company, for example, has reached a high level of maturity with four offshore suppliers (three in India and one in the Philippines). Through these four suppliers, the client engages 1,000 people offshore, with a target growth rate to 2,000 people. The telecommunication company claims a net savings of 40%. It has a good idea of cost savings because the maintenance work is repeatable and they know what it costs to do the work in-house.

In addition to contract size, suppliers also want experienced clients. A supplier once told us, "the customer from hell is the naïve customer". Suppliers cannot be successful unless the client devotes enough internal resources to enable their success. Clients must also appreciate and help protect a supplier's margin if they hope to get the best resources and best services from that supplier.

Concerning client prestige, large offshore suppliers have a well established customer base, so becoming a prestige client for a large supplier may be difficult unless the client's new contract is worth tens of millions of dollars. However, small offshore suppliers may be quite eager to partner with a well-known client to help establish their reputation. One US insurance company, for example, finds that their small partners "go the extra mile" to service their needs. However, the CIO uses a "30% guideline" which states that the insurance company will never comprise more than 30% of the supplier's revenues. Otherwise, the CIO would feel too responsible if he wanted to terminate the relationship.

4. Communicate the sourcing strategy to all stakeholders

In our research, we found that some CIOs were reticent to share a sourcing strategy that introduced an offshore component until all the details had been planned. These CIOs reasoned that it was better to have most of the answers ready for the IT staff before making an official announcement. *Within our case studies, however, we found that IT staff were less likely to panic or sabotage an offshore outsourcing initiative if CIOs announced the offshore outsourcing initiative as soon as the organization was ready to search for suppliers*. This statement was true even for organizations in which the CIOs anticipated layoffs as a consequence of offshore outsourcing, but who were not yet sure which IT staff or how many IT staff would be affected. We summarize four cases to illustrate this lesson.

Delaying communication may cause the staff to panic and sabotage the offshore engagement. At one financial services company, the CIO and his top leadership team viewed offshore outsourcing as a potential way to decrease the immense application backlog caused by the refinancing boom. But the CIO chose to keep the pilot project low key rather than panic the IT staff while they were simply "testing the waters." One day, the domestic IT staff showed up for work to find 11 people from Indian working in cubicles. The domestic IT staff began to panic and question the future of their careers. The Indian workers were isolated and treated with suspicion, if not contempt. The IT staff found frequent reasons for complaining about the offshore outsourcing projects. Eventually, the CIO held a town hall meeting and told the staff that there would be no layoffs caused by offshore outsourcing. In fact, offshore outsourcing avoided the firing of internal IT staff by providing flexible staff augmentation that could be scaled back after the refinance boom.

Even when no lay-offs are planned as a consequence of offshore outsourcing, CIOs need to continually assuage fears. In contrast to the previous example, the CIO at Biotech was very open about the offshore pilots and told the internal IT staff that offshore outsourcing was about "doing more with a flat budget" and that no internal IT workers would be fired as a result of offshore outsourcing. Even with open communications, there was some backlash. When dealing with the internal IT staff on offshore outsourcing, one IT leader noted that it is important to separate the emotional issues from the real issues.

> Different people perceive offshore outsourcing in different ways. And I guarantee, we have the full spectrum. We were aware of that and wanted to be sure that it did not impact our workforce in a negative way. So we spent a great deal of time trying to understand all of the dynamics. Trying to keep the communications as transparent as possible without trying to needlessly scare people. So it's a tricky balance. (Global Leadership Team Member, biotechnology company)

The CIO from Retail found out that an initial announcement may not suffice. At this company, the CIO engaged their first Indian supplier to help with Y2K in 1997. At that time, offshore outsourcing was not in the public's consciousness. The IT staff did not perceive that the selection of an Indian supplier was a threat – the Indian supplier was just another preferred contractor. However, during the 2004 US presidential and congressional elections, the IT staff began to panic over their jobs. Their reaction stunned the CIO and other senior IT managers:

> I think the [IT staff's] reaction was, "we're losing American jobs and I'm going to lose mine." We pointed out that offshore outsourcing allows us to retain your job because it's lowering our prices. We have to find a better way to communicate that as we roll this out [the increased use of offshore outsourcing.] (Director of Contract Management, retailer)

In response to the question about the IT staff's concern in 2004, the CIO said: "When you start the conversation with 'we are eliminating zero jobs', you can have a pretty short conversation."

Even when lay-offs are planned, announce the sourcing strategy as soon as the organization begins searching offshore. In the previous three examples, CIOs had an easy message to sell because offshore outsourcing resulted in no planned layoffs. But some organizations, like the financial information services firm (FIS), used a sourcing strategy to dramatically reduce costs, partly by reducing internal headcount. The lesson, however, is still the same – announce the sourcing strategy as soon as the organization begins searching offshore.

At FIS, senior leaders from the finance organization announced the transformation program to the FIS staff as soon after they selected India as the location for their new captive center. The employees were told that the team did not know exactly who would be impacted yet, but that everyone would know within five months. Some employees would be included in the succession and some employees would be given severance packages. The employees appreciated the advanced notice. Some employees knew 18 months in advance that they would no longer have a job at FIS.

We call the situation at FIS as "asking staff to build their own guillotine." Among our case companies, that situation worked if redundant staff were given hefty bonuses to stay during the transition and if their redundancy packages were tied to the successful transition of work to new offshore employees.

5. Provide enough resources to implement the sourcing strategy

CIOs need to invest enough resources to make sure the sourcing strategy will be successful. The main resources needed are

- top internal talent to manage the offshore program;
- top project managers to lead project teams;

- outside consultants to help select destinations, investigate suppliers, and negotiate contracts;
- training for internal staff;
- training for supplier staff;
- on-site supplier managers (who cost more than supplier staff located offshore);
- sufficient funds for travel, infrastructure, etc.

Simply stated, it takes money to save money. At FIS, the CFO invested $13.5 million upfront in order to achieve the expected benefits. In contrast, one of the biggest causes of offshore outsourcing failure in our case companies was insufficient internal resources. We were shocked that so many PMOs, for example, were understaffed considering all the roles they were expected to fulfill. Insufficient resources were primarily found in companies using offshore outsourcing primarily to reduce total IT costs. CIOs were legitimately afraid to invest too many resources because they knew these additional costs would erode much of the expected savings. However, total cost savings cannot be generated unless the client commits enough of these internal resources. The solution is that the offshore outsourcing program has to be large enough to generate overall savings given the required investment in internal resources.

6. Build social capital with key supplier executives

While CIOs from large organizations are not involved directly with project work involving offshore suppliers, it is important that CIOs establish relationships with the supplier's senior management. The CIO's relationship with senior supplier executives increases the supplier's commitment to the client organization, provides a conduit to access the supplier's best resources, and establishes the clout to more quickly remedy problems.

The CIO at Retail meets with the supplier's leadership twice a year. Besides these planned interactions, the CIO also intervenes when crises loom. He spoke many times with the offshore supplier's CEO and operating officers about the nuclear tensions between India and Pakistan:

> I had their chief officers calling me at least monthly to update me on the political situation and their planned responses. They were positioning resources in Canada to be able to pick up operations and provide business continuity outside of India. We have tremendous respect for that part of their culture that kept us informed. (CIO, retailer)

CIOs and their direct reports also benefited from attending their supplier's key user meetings and appearing with suppliers at key sourcing conventions. For example, IT leaders from Retail attend the summits sponsored by one of their large Indian suppliers. The summits include the supplier's largest clients and the open discussion format allows the group to identify and solve problems. The head of the Retail's PMO said, "It was really good to hear the other [clients] complaining about the same things we are challenged by. It was very brave of [the supplier] to bring us all together and give us the opportunity to complain. It showed me they were not too big to look at themselves and try to improve."

7. Seek independent assessment of sourcing strategy effectiveness

CIOs should occasionally engage an independent third party to assess the effectiveness of sourcing strategy. Although it was common among our cases for CIOs to assign this task to internal teams or the PMO, we found that lower level IT employees are less likely to honestly report on sourcing issues. Our favorite quote comes from a Biotech informant: "You didn't want to tell them [senior management] the bad news too much. Because, this was their baby and you didn't want to say, 'You have a terribly ugly baby!'" (Software Architect, biotechnology company).

At this company, the PMO reported each month that offshore outsourcing was successful in meeting cost objectives, yet our own interviews with 44 participants found mixed results. We found that success varied widely across projects. Many team leads and project managers did not report significant issues to their superiors because the message was "offshore outsourcing had to succeed." While a CIO's strong commitment to success is a key enabler, the commitment cannot come at the price of lost learning. Independent assessments of a sourcing initiative will objectively gather learning across projects without compromising the IT staff's confidentiality.

Roles of the PMO

Our research found that a strong Program Management Office (PMO) significantly contributes to the success of offshore outsourcing. Unfortunately, most PMOs were initially understaffed. Consequently, project managers were often forced to assume many of these roles, which overwhelmed them and distracted them from their other duties. However, in mature organizations, PMOs were fully staffed and provided critical capabilities to ensure offshore success. Mature PMOs filled the following roles:

1. Evaluate offshore locations.
2. Assess supplier capabilities.
3. Help negotiate contracts.
4. Select engagement models.
5. Prepare the infrastructure.
6. Identify training needs for internal staff and supplier staff.
7. Design structural interfaces.
8. Design organizational processes.
9. Develop and monitor comprehensive metrics.
10. Authorize supplier invoices.
11. Resolve issues and conflicts.
12. Work with business units.
13. Diversify the supplier portfolio.
14. Monitor sourcing trends.
15. Gather and disseminate learning and best practices.

These roles are discussed below.

1. Evaluate offshore locations

We have already advised the CIO that sourcing destinations should be selected for business reasons as well as for cost reasons. Because many CIOs delegate the selection of offshore destinations to PMOs (or to a team of IT Leaders), the same advice applies. In our experience, however, most PMO leaders select offshore destinations based only on IT cost and IT risks. Using these IT criteria, most of our US client companies initially selected India for their first offshore destination, and for good reasons. Most industry analysts rate India *highly* on government support, labor pool, educational system, cost advantage, quality, and English proficiency. Furthermore, most industry analysts rate India *moderately high* on infrastructure and cultural compatibility. If "nobody ever got fired in the 1970s for buying IBM" then "no PMO was ever criticized for selecting India." Among our US clients, more analysis went into the selection of a second offshore location. Beyond India, our US clients have established secondary offshore destinations in the Philippines, China, Costa Rica, Malaysia, Canada, and other countries. A multi-country strategy is a sound way to mitigate risks. Start-up suppliers around the world are eager to partner with US clients.

Heads of PMOs are also advised to hire an intermediary consulting firm to serve as offshore guide to the country, suppliers, and culture. A good advisory firm will also help PMO leaders consider a wide range of sourcing locations, such as rural sourcing and nearshoring (see Chapter 8). The 2007 Black Book of Outsourcing[14] identified the top offshore advisory firms as Equaterra, Morgan Chambers, NeoIT, Everest, TPI, Pricewaterhouse Coopers, Ovum Orbys, Stradling Global Sourcing, and PA Consulting.

Some experts estimated that by 2005, sixty-four percent of offshore contracts were brokered by intermediaries.[15] Biotech certainly found value in hiring an intermediary: "I think it absolutely engaged us more quickly with respect to them informing the offshore suppliers of our situation and setting up the arrangements. We would have just had to spend a lot more of our own time with all of that. So I think it streamlined the initial process." – Global Leadership Team Member, biotechnology company

The intermediary consulting firms are also moving up the value chain by offering offshore project management training to US clients, training joint teams on cultural compatibility, creating transition plans, and developing project metrics. One note of caution, however. Some US clients hired intermediaries who were paid finders fees by suppliers or had family members working as top executives in supplier firms. These are serious conflict of interests. Thus, clients must ensure that intermediaries are independent of suppliers.

2. Assess supplier capabilities

Concerning offshore suppliers, there are many choices. Some clients move offshore via one of their domestic suppliers such as EDS, IBM, and Accenture. These established suppliers manage the offshore resources so the client doesn't have to navigate through legal, time zone, human resource, or cultural issues. Other clients prefer to select Tier 1 offshore suppliers such as Wipro or Infosys because of their maturity and stability. Other clients look for smaller niche suppliers with domain expertise and an eagerness to partner with a US client. Still others select suppliers like Globalign that help clients find and engage offshore resources via large staff augmentation firms like Manpower.

As the search narrows down to a few destinations, PMOs begin touring supplier facilities and meeting with the supplier's current clients. Here we offer the following advice: ***don't evaluate supplier resources; do evaluate supplier capabilities that build competencies***. Figure 1.5 illustrates the relationship between supplier resources, capabilities, and competencies. Most PMOs are only evaluating suppliers at the resource level. They are impressed with supplier facilities, educated workforce, and IT tools. One supplier told us, "if we can get a client to our headquarters, we can make the sale." A supplier's resources, however, are only valuable to a client if those resources are leveraged on the client's behalf in terms of client-facing capabilities. A supplier's CMM or CMMI capability does not suffice as evidence of the supplier's ability to transform resources into client-facing capabilities.

In our prior research, Feeny, Lacity, and Willcocks identified 12 supplier capabilities that benefit clients.[16] These are:

- ***Leadership Capability*** to identify, communicate, and deliver the balance of activities required to achieve present and future success for both client and supplier.
- ***Planning and Contracting Capability*** to develop and contract for business plans which deliver "win/win" results for client and supplier over time.
- ***Organization Design Capability*** to design the client interfaces to best achieve the business plan.

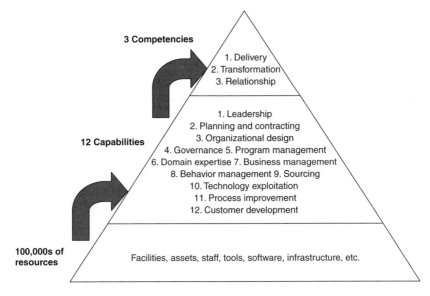

Figure 1.5 Supplier resources, capabilities, and competencies

- *Governance Capability* to define, agree, track, and assess the performance of service over time.
- *Program Management Capability* to prioritize, coordinate, ready the organization, and deliver across a series of inter-related change projects.
- *Domain Expertise Capability* to apply and retain sufficient professional knowledge of the target domain to meet user requirements.
- *Business Management Capability* to consistently deliver against both client service level agreements and the supplier's required business plans.
- *Behavior Management Capability* to motivate and manage people to deliver service with a "front office" culture.
- *Sourcing Capability* to access whatever resources are required to deliver service targets.
- *Technology Exploitation Capability* to swiftly and effectively deploy technology in support of critical service improvement targets.
- *Process Improvement Capability* to design and implement changes to the service process to meet improvement targets.
- *Customer Development Capability* to transition "users" of an internally provided service to "customers" who make informed choices about service level, functionality, and the costs they incur.

The 12 supplier capabilities establish the basis for three supplier competencies: the ability to create aligned incentives between client and supplier (relationship competency), the ability to deliver daily operations while still generating a good margin (delivery competency), and the ability to meaningfully transform the client's operations to decrease costs and improve service (transformation competency). We believe that PMOs can make much better decisions about supplier selection if they assess suppliers based on these 12 capabilities and 3 competencies.

3. Negotiate contracts

Most PMOs negotiate contracts with the assistance of internal lawyers and intermediary advisors. Hiring a legal expert for domestic outsourcing has been a standard best practice for 15 years. Many legal firms specialize in outsourcing, such as Pillsbury Winthrop, Shaw Pittman and Milbank Tweed Hadley & McCloy. The need for legal expertise with offshore sourcing is even more pronounced because clients must abide by different legal systems and more regulatory requirements.

In conjunction with our research, we have spoken with six different lawyers specializing in offshore outsourcing. These lawyers help clients with tax implications, protection of intellectual property, business continuity, regulatory compliance, visa formalities, dispute resolution, and governing law. Concerning dispute resolution, all the participants focused on the goal of reducing the risks of conflicts that could lead to litigation, and for good reason. Litigation in the Indian court system is frequently a fifteen-year process. Also, Indian courts do not enforce legal judgments or awards made in the US. In contrast, India will enforce arbitration, so that has become the standard clause for resolving client/supplier disputes. Concerning tax implications, one participant said he helped a client set up operations in Mauritius because it is a tax free zone. He also determined the amount of ownership in a joint venture required for favorable taxation and negotiated how parties would bear the costs of any tax law changes. Concerning the protection of intellectual property rights, legal experts help by writing further assurance clauses or by establishing a chain of title.

At a high level, PMOs need to understand the trade-offs between fixed-price and time and materials contracts. Different contracts incent suppliers differently. In the offshore context, US clients found that fixed-price contracts incented suppliers to staff projects with their most productive people to increase their margin. Suppliers clearly prefer fixed-price contracts because they are often associated with turnkey projects for large, interesting assignments. But the downside was that the suppliers sometimes produced sloppy work (despite the productive staff) to meet unrealistic deadlines. Most clients conclude that fixed-price contracts are most suited for projects with clear requirements so that the suppliers can submit realistic bids.

From the client perspective, time and materials contracts produced better quality work because the client retained control. However, time and materials contracts can incent suppliers to place new employees on the account because the client subsidizes the employee's learning curve. Also, supplier employees who are unproductive take more hours to complete tasks, again reflected in the client's bill. Some clients try to mitigate this risk by interviewing each supplier employee. This practice places the client in the business of managing the supplier's resources, which can increase transaction costs and create animosity between client and supplier. From the supplier perspective, time and materials contracts are not preferred because they are typically associated with staff augmentation models. Mature offshore suppliers do not want to compete in this space because work typically focuses on discrete programming tasks.

One US client company experimented with both types of contracts. Satisfied with neither, it opted for a modified time and materials contract. It created a stratified pricing structure in which it paid as much as $10 more per hour for superior supplier employees. The client understood that better people are more productive, thus reducing overall costs.

4. Select engagement models

While we argued that the CIO must select the right approach to offshore outsourcing, it was common that the head of the PMO was charged with selecting the engagement models, particularly when the company was pursuing an incremental approach (see Figure 1.4). The most common engagement models for an incremental approach entailed "fee-for-service" models. We have much more to say about these fee-for-service models in Chapter 3. The key learning from Chapter 3 is that an engagement model must fit not only the type of IT work, but must also match the client's capabilities and supplier's 12 capabilities.

5. Prepare the infrastructure

Many of the clients we studied underestimated the difficulty in integrating offshore supplier employees into the processes and workflows of their firms. Security concerns (access to systems and corporate data), human resource issues (modifying systems to use passport numbers instead of social security numbers) and the need to duplicate the development and testing environments must be addressed prior to project launch. The PMO needs to take the lead in creating and improving the processes necessary to ease the "on boarding" of offshore suppliers. Some clients realized this too late. According to the PMO Director of one client company:

> It really took us a long time to figure out how to make it [the on boarding process] run smoothly. Since the suppliers needed access to systems from various business units and IT sectors, we had to cross organizational boundaries and create new protocols and rights profiles. However, without these processes, the suppliers sit idle waiting for us to build a tunnel in the VPN. We should have had all these processes in place much earlier than we did.

6. Identify training needs for internal staff and supplier staff

PMOs must identify the training needs for internal staff and supplier staff. The purpose of training is knowledge transfer between both parties.

Internal staff must learn how to integrate offshore suppliers within their project teams and offshore suppliers must learn about the client's business processes, requirements, and work practices. Most US clients initially provided the internal staff with only rudimentary training on the supplier's culture and provided no formal training to suppliers. Such a low level of training is insufficient, and most US clients learn this lesson only after pilot projects falter. Training is a key enabler of offshore outsourcing success, as illustrated through many of our cases.

Give offshore suppliers domain specific training to protect quality and lower development costs. When US Manufacturing began to engage their Indian supplier, they initially provided little training to offshore suppliers. It wasn't until the initial offshore efforts failed that the client company recognized the need to fully train supplier employees. In their second attempt with offshore outsourcing, the manufacturing company decided to give the supplier's delivery team the same training that it provided to new internal employees. The content of this training included IT tools, methodologies, technologies, facility tours, and introductions to peripheral departments. The training dramatically increased the client's transaction costs. However, these upfront transaction costs were needed to protect quality and lower development costs in the long run to ensure the supplier was knowledgeable and productive. To protect the training investment, the PMO made the supplier ensure that trained supplier employees remained on the account for a certain period of time, or the supplier had to reimburse training costs.

Besides formal training, clients transfer domain knowledge to the supplier by having the suppliers' key liaisons, leads, and managers on-site. The knowledge transfer process between the client and these key on-site supplier leads can take weeks or even months. Furthermore, it is very difficult for these on-site supplier leads to manage their remote teams. So some clients, like one insurance company we studied, end up bringing over much of the supplier's delivery team. This way, the on-site supplier liaison could better coordinate interfaces among client users, client IT staff, and the supplier's delivery team. This practice can swell on-site/offshore ratios to be as high as 70% onshore and 30% offshore. Such ratios can seriously erode cost savings because onshore employees cost twice as much as offshore employees. So PMOs must balance the need for intensive knowledge transfer against the high costs of on-site employees.

7. Design organizational interfaces

How will the supplier employees interact with client stakeholders? Who talks to whom? Our research has uncovered three models of organizational

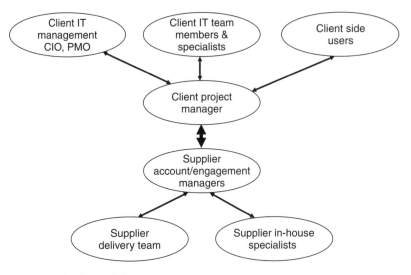

Figure 1.6 The funnel design

interfaces, each with its own set of benefits and costs. The funnel design, shown in Figure 1.6, is used by Retail and US Manufacturing. This design provides the greatest constriction of the communication pathways between the client and their supplier. Since communication from local business units and technical staff is funneled through the project managers and then to the on-site engagement manager, this model places a high degree of importance on the supplier's selection for an on-site engagement manager. This reliance on a specific individual does pose risk to both the parties. The retail company, for example, experienced one major failure with a large Indian firm because the engagement manager originally chosen to lead the engagement did not possess the skills or experience to work with a Fortune 100 company. Once the shortcomings were brought to the attention of the supplier, a more experienced engagement manager was put in place. However, time and confidence in the supplier were lost. Despite the risks associated with this model, the benefits include better control over the engagement, and a single point of contact to mitigate scope creep and the cultural, time zone and communication risks.

The network design (shown in Figure 1.7) offers much greater pathways of communication between the client and the supplier. The network design, used by Biotech on some projects, shows communication taking place between all stakeholders from both the client and supplier organizations. Particularly interesting is the direct link between local business units and the supplier. This linkage offered mixed results for Biotech. One

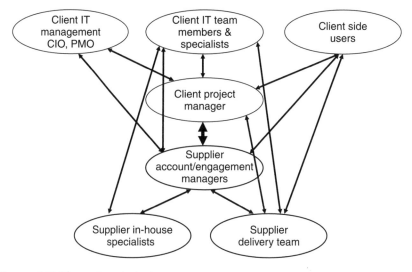

Figure 1.7 The network design

project that allowed a local business unit to communicate directly with the supplier to define requirements was successful. The local business unit in this case was very low on IT's priority list and users felt neglected. Once connected with the offshore delivery team, their needs were assessed, requirements gathered and the project proceeded with a greater focus on the user. This project came in on time and under budget and with very high customer satisfaction numbers for the offshore supplier.

One project nearly failed due to this linkage. The *post mortem* showed that when the local business unit (whose needs are often boundless) was allowed to communicate directly with the supplier (whose promises of delivery are often boundless), scope, feature and budget creep proceeded unchecked. While the project was completed, it was constantly delayed and finished well over budget.

The third model, which we call the mirror design, was initially documented by Kaiser and Hawk[17] (see Figure 1.8) and more recently assessed by Oshri et al.[18] Kaiser and Hawk reported on an eight-year relationship between a US financial insurance company and an India-based supplier that evolved from outsourcing to co-sourcing. Co-sourcing describes a close supplier/client relationship in which the supplier augments or even replaces the client's IT competencies. The supplier even serves as team lead for some types of work. To effectively manage the supplier's increased responsibility, the two partners realized they needed multiple levels of formalized communication. They designed the Dual Project Management

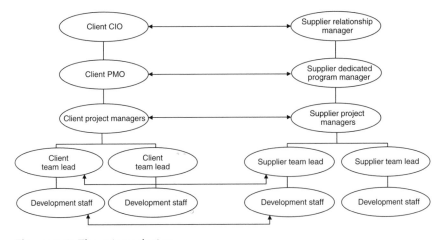

Figure 1.8 The mirror design

Source: Adapted from Kaiser and Hawk (2004).

Hierarchy, or the mirror design. This model has a significant onshore supplier presence, including the supplier's systems analysts on the development staff. This increases costs compared to the previous two models, but is warranted by the higher value work provided by the supplier.

Oshri et al. (2007) documented a similar mirrored design between ABN AMRO and Tata Consultancy Services (TCS). ABN AMRO is a Dutch-based company that signed a $1.2 billion contract with five suppliers, including TCS. The global scale of this deal required an organizational design that allowed high-level control of the relationship, as well as knowledge transfer at the local level. The mirrored organizational design was found to be highly effective in coordinating the relationship at both the global and local levels.

8. Design organizational processes

Whereas the structural interfaces focus on "who talks to whom," the procedural interfaces focus on "what is passed when." What do clients pass to suppliers in terms of statements of work and detailed requirements, and what do suppliers pass to clients in terms of deliverables and status reports? Here enters the issues surrounding the Capability Maturity Model (CMM) and Capability Maturity Model Integrated (CMMI).[19] While the Indian suppliers we studied were all certified at CMM level 4 or 5, the US clients were usually lower. At higher levels of certification, an immense amount of documentation is required. US project managers had never before been through such a rigorous process to define requirements.

At Biotech, for example, requirements definition is an informal process when done onshore. Project managers speak frequently with users who are usually located on campus headquarters. The user feedback cycle is quick. In contrast, project managers working on the offshore pilots had to engage in many formal and planned communications with suppliers and users to create the required documents. One client said, "the overhead costs of documenting some of the projects exceeded the value of the deliverables."

So what can be done to more effectively coordinate work with the supplier's CMM/CMMI processes? The following practices were used by participants.

Elevate your own organization's CMM/CMMI level to close the process gap between you and your supplier. Research has shown that higher levels of CMM are associated with higher product quality, but also increases the development effort.[20] Participants suggested that the best way to extract value from the supplier's CMM/CMMI processes was to become CMM/CMMI certified themselves:

> A real problem we had was our CMM level 1.5 guys talking to the vendor's level 5 guys. So together, we have worked out a plan with our vendor to help bring our CMM levels up. When we do, it will be a benefit to both of us; our specifications will be better and so they can use them more efficiently. (Director of Application Development, transportation company)

The outstanding issue is the level of certification required to effectively work with suppliers. The Vice President at a financial services company believes that clients only need to approach level 2 to extract value. The Officer of IT Services at another financial services company believes client organizations need at least a level 3. Still other client organizations believe higher certification levels (at least CMM/CMMI 4) are required to interact with suppliers.[21]

Bring in a CMM/CMMI expert with no domain expertise to flush out ambiguities in requirements. US clients often complain that the requirements process is long and requires much expensive iteration. This is usually because the US client doesn't understand how the supplier will interpret the requirements. Some US clients, for example, were surprised that supplier team members did not understand the concept of a mortgage. One US client was surprised that the suppliers did not allow female name fields in the software to be altered unless recently married. In another example, the Indian supplier left-justified numeric data fields, causing the frustrated PMO director to lament: "Is this how ridiculously detailed my requirements are supposed to be?" One CEO of an Indian supplier sought a unique solution to minimize the misinterpretation of requirements definitions. He brings in a CMM level 5 expert to the client site who purposefully has no domain knowledge. This enables him to identify ambiguities in the requirements documents that the offshore delivery team will likely have, thus reducing the number of iterations.

Negotiate "Flexible CMM/CMMI." The project manager at one financial services company noted, "You ask for one button to be moved and the supplier has to first do a twenty page impact analysis – we are paying for all this documentation we don't need." He is negotiating for exactly which documents his company will and will not pay. This will enable him to only use the CMM/CMMI processes he perceives adds significant value. While this practice is unique, a customized interface with each client could serve to increase the supplier's costs, which may eventually result in higher prices.

Some Indian suppliers are accepting, rather than fighting this practice, by actively marketing the idea of "Flexible CMM" or "Flexible CMMI." The managing director of a tier 2 Indian supplier recognized the frustration and reluctance of US clients to wade through the necessary steps for the supplier to maintain CMM certification. He says:

> My clients are telling me, "You do what you have to do to pass your audits, but I can't afford all of this documentation!" So we have developed a flexible CMM model which maintains the processes necessary for high quality but keeps the customer facing documentation and overhead to a minimum. Our customers have reacted favorably and our internal process are still CMM 5.

9. Develop and monitor comprehensive metrics

All participants identified the need for metrics that consider costs, quality, timeliness, and risks, but few participants were fully satisfied with current assessment measures. US Manufacturing had the most comprehensive set of metrics. The PMO tracks in-house, domestic and offshore suppliers' costs, quality, and productivity using a standardized activity measure. The data is captured by an in-house dashboard and analyzed monthly by management to monitor real development costs and trends. They learned that real savings from offshore do not occur until after they have invested significant upfront training of every offshore developer and team leader.

They also share this data with suppliers so that all parties understand the total cost trends.

In contrast to US Manufacturing, most PMOs had very poor metrics to assess total cost savings. The most common cost savings metric was calculated by multiplying the costs of the offshore hours and comparing this number with what it would have cost the client had domestic contractors been assigned the work. The number, however, does not consider transaction costs, productivity, or quality. Some US clients used comparative cost measures that did include transaction costs and overhead costs. One telecommunication company, for example, calculates net savings as equal to Employee Loaded Rate - Vendor Steady State - Transition Costs – Overhead. But again, this measure does not factor in productivity or quality.

Beyond trying to calculate total cost savings, PMO managers tracked performance using cost per function point,[22] error rates, percentage of work products delivered on-time, and other metrics found in Table 1.4. Because no metric is perfect, PMOs need a balanced scorecard approach that provides an overall indication of the value of the offshore relationships in terms of cost, quality, productivity, and cooperation. Of course the politics of measurement cannot be ignored. For example, one PMO manager said, "When I go ask our internal IT department to give me an estimate on how long it would take them to do this piece of work they say 'X' but my [offshore] supplier says Y, who do I believe?"

Table 1.4 Metrics used by client participants

Metrics used by clients	Description of Metric
Total cost savings	Nearly every PMO manager struggled with good measures to calculate total cost savings. The most common cost savings metric was calculated by multiplying the costs of the offshore hours and comparing this number with what it would have cost the client had domestic contractors been assigned the work.
Cost per function point	Function points are a measure of an IT project's *size*. Once the size of an application is determined in terms of total number of function points, productivity metrics are calculated by dividing the total function points by total cost of the project or by number of hours worked to complete the project. Clients with good function points metrics can then compare the productivity of projects done onshore with projects done offshore.
Error rates	Error rates measure the number of errors per unit of work, typically implemented as number of errors per 1000 function points. Error rates are calculated during the testing phase as well as after systems are implemented.

Continued

Table 1.4 Continued

Metrics used by clients	Description of Metric
Percentage of work products delivered on time	This metric tracks the supplier's ability to meet agreed upon deadlines and is designed to assess the supplier's delivery competency. However, clients must also keep in mind that they might be the source of bottlenecks that cause suppliers to deliver late. Some clients implemented daily meetings to ensure that supplier work was not halted because the supplier was waiting for the client to respond to a query.
Cooperation satisfaction score	This perceptual measure captures how well the supplier cooperates with the client to address conflicts, bottlenecks, and emerging issues in the relationship.
Percentage of unfavorable turnover	This metric tracks the supplier's unplanned turnover.
Percentage of supplier business	This metric considers how much of the supplier's revenues come from the client organization. One US client PMO wanted this number to be high, believing that a high percentage would motivate better service from the supplier. Another US client PMO wanted this number to be low because he doesn't want to be obligated for the supplier's failure if he later chooses to terminate the relationship.
Percentage of supplier of choice	This metric tracks the dollars spent on preferred suppliers compared to dollars spent on non-preferred suppliers. This metric was used by a PMO who was trying to whittle the company's use of over 60 suppliers down to a handful of preferred suppliers.
Utilization rates	This metric considers the number of hours a pre-paid supplier employee works per week. Utilization rates are used when clients retain a certain number of the supplier employees each month for a fixed fee. One US client pays an offshore supplier a retainer for five supplier employees and seeks to utilize at least 90% of the time for which they paid. This same company also tracks "recoverable utilization" which is the percentage of offshore supplier costs that can be directly charged to an external customer account.
Quality of code	These subjective metrics of code quality are typically assessed by the client's quality assurance team using five or seven point Likert scales.
On-site/offshore ratios	This ratio tracks the location (and thus costs) of supplier employees. Some companies have ratio targets, aiming to keep at least 70% of the supplier employees offshore. The ratios, however, need to vary based on type of work. During requirements definition, the ratios may need to be quite high – with over 50% of supplier employees on-site.
Employee-to-supplier work ratio	This comparative efficiency metric assesses the relative productivity of in-house employees versus offshore employees. In most cases, in-house employees could produce more work (as measured in function points) than offshore suppliers in a given time period, but the offshore employees were significantly less expensive.

10. Authorize supplier invoices

Within most of our US client organizations, supplier invoices were sent directly to the PMO. The PMO typically involved the project managers to verify the invoices (such as hours worked on a project) and authorized the accounts payable staff to make the payment. In some cases, this represents a significant investment of time. Matching invoices from multiple suppliers (each with different calculations and formats) with internal progress reports can be daunting. PMOs should establish specific processes and procedures for how time is accounted, which activities are billable and share these processes with the suppliers to facilitate reimbursement.

11. Resolve issues and conflicts

While project managers resolve many of the issues and conflicts that arise during a project, PMOs need to intervene on issues pertaining to poor supplier engagement managers, uncooperative business users, or panicky internal staff. In our research, conflicts usually involved poor performing suppliers or invoice discrepancies. Project managers felt that it was the PMO's responsibility to investigate and resolve these issues. For example, when Biotech terminated a contract with a small vendor, the PMO was responsible for disengaging the supplier and reassigning other suppliers' employees to the unfinished projects. Similarly, PMOs investigated and addressed suppliers' claims that certain invoices were unpaid or that project managers' calculations were incorrect.

12. Work with business units

PMOs often had to sell business units on the idea of using offshore suppliers. One tricky issue was charge back. If business units were charged back the same rates whether offshore suppliers were used or not, PMOs had to persuade business users to allow their projects to be sent offshore. From the business users' perspective, the additional overhead of dealing with offshore suppliers was not worthwhile. In contrast, business users were more willing to allow offshore suppliers to work on their projects when chargeback rates were lowered. The PMO from one financial services firm allows business units a choice for application development. The business units can source IT from three preferred offshore suppliers or from several domestic suppliers. Rates are lower with the offshore suppliers, but risks are lower with the domestic suppliers. The CIO and head of the PMO believes the business unit managers should be the ones assessing the trade-offs.

13. Diversify the supplier portfolio

Concerning the *number of suppliers*, most clients found that at least two offshore suppliers were needed to motivate continued supplier performance. In contrast, reliance on a single supplier presents significant operational and strategic risks including loss of market pressure on rates and a high concentration of intellectual property in one supplier. While maintaining engagements with multiple suppliers does entail additional transaction costs, the use of multiple suppliers successfully mitigates many risks associated with outsourcing.[23]

US Manufacturing uses multi-sourcing to mitigate some of the risks associated with offshore outsourcing. It has active engagements with two large Indian suppliers and one small, boutique supplier which specializes in embedded software development. The three suppliers compete for additional work:

> We don't want to manage a whole bunch of suppliers. However we need the market pressure to make sure we are getting good prices. By letting the two large suppliers and the small one bid on projects, and having the preferred list, we let them [the suppliers] know that we are interested in enlarging the engagement but we are also watchful of the costs. (Director of Software Center of Excellence, manufacturing company)

A truly global network of IT suppliers treats domestic and offshore suppliers as legitimate competitors. Clients with this view have integrated Program Management Offices (PMO), rather than separate PMOs for domestic and offshore suppliers. Clients with an integrated PMO request quotes from all suppliers, rather than pre-selecting certain types of work for certain types of suppliers. One consequence can be significant price reductions from domestic suppliers. When Retail introduced offshore suppliers, one consequence was that it pressured their domestic suppliers to cut rates by 10% to 50%:

> We were paying about $100 for commodity type coding (with domestic suppliers). The domestic suppliers saw the writing on the wall. We put out a bid to the approved list of domestic contractors and the current director of the PMO made it very clear that we were not going to pay

those kind of prices anymore. Our domestic prices dropped from about $100 per hour to $80 and some of the rates even dropped into the $50 range for some services. (Director of Contract Management, retailer)

14. Monitor sourcing trends

PMOs are responsible for monitoring sourcing trends in the external market place, and determining how those trends might affect their own organization. Sourcing trends are tracked by the top advisor firms and clients are well-advised to become members of their advisory services. Clients may test the capabilities of some these advisory firms by signing up for their free webinars (which we have found to be quite excellent) and white papers. Many excellent reports are available on the web (see the references in Chapter 8 for reports by Everest Group, Evalueserve, International Association of Outsourcing Professionals (IAOP), and The Black Book of Outsourcing.) Attending the key sourcing conferences is also an excellent way to keep abreast of sourcing trends. The Sourcing Interest Group and International Association of Outsourcing Professionals offer excellent conferences at least once a year. Attending the supplier's annual users group meeting allows clients of the same supplier to interact and share practices relevant to a specific supplier. Many local organizations also provide PMOs opportunities to discuss offshore outsourcing issues with peers, including local chapters of the IAOP, the Society for Information Management, and offshore users groups.

15. Gather and disseminate learning and best practices

This role requires the PMO to gather and disseminate learning about best practices from both internal and external sources. To gather learning from internal sources, PMOs sponsored meetings or brown-bag lunches with project managers leading teams with offshore suppliers. PMO leaders had to stress that they wanted project managers to be frank, but also had to gear discussions towards best practices to prevent meetings from deteriorating into complaint sessions. In some organizations, project managers were not frank because they feared being viewed as uncooperative, thus we have also advised CIOs to seek independent assessments of offshoring success in addition to the PMO's role.

Externally, the same sources described in the previous role can help PMO managers identify best practices to ensure offshoring success. In addition, academic research is particularly valuable here. Academic research independently assesses sourcing practices. Any members of the Society of Information Management may access excellent academic articles written for senior IT managers on sourcing (and many other IT management topics) in *MIS Quarterly Executive* at www.misqe.org. Published academic studies that examined practices to help ensure outsourcing success are listed in Table 1.5.[24] There are also several special issues forthcoming in top IS journals that should be available in early 2008,[25] as well as a collection of current academic research forthcoming from the *Third International Conference on Outsourcing of Information Systems*.[26]

Table 1.5 Academic research on offshore outsourcing of IT work

Research publication	Empirical base	Findings
Bruno et al. (2004)	Secondary sources and six case studies to compare the software industries in Algeria, Egypt, Morocco, and Tunisia.	Partnerships between multi-national firms and indigenous firms are important success factors in developing countries.
Carmel and Agarwal (2002)	13 case studies of client firms sending IT work offshore.	Most clients follow a progressive stage model of offshore outsourcing.
Carmel, E., and Tjia, P. (2005)	Primary and secondary sources	This book, published by Cambridge University Press, addresses offshore fundamentals, managerial competency, and stakeholder perspectives.
Carmel (2006)	Case study on the Indian supplier, Infosys	Practices to manage time zone differences.
Choudhury and Sabherwal (2003)	Five case studies, including three cases that entailed offshore outsourcing of IT work to India and Columbia.	Outsourced projects frequently began with simple controls that required additional controls to improve performance.
Davis et al. (2006)	Viewpoint	History, prospects, and challenges of IT offshoring
Dibbern (2004)	Extensive review of the academic IT sourcing literature based on 84 studies published between 1991 and 2000.	*Why* firms outsource (mostly to reduce costs, access resources, focus internal resources on more strategic work), *what* firms outsource (mostly a portion of their overall IT portfolio), *how* firms outsource (mostly by formal processes), and IT outsourcing *outcomes* as measured by realization of expectations, satisfaction, and performance.

Continued

Table 1.5   Continued

Research publication	Empirical base	Findings
Drezner (2004)	Viewpoint	Argues the benefits of off-shore outsourcing to counter the political backlash.
Dutta and Roy (2005)	Simulation	Causal foundation for growth in offshore outsourcing of IT work.
Ein-Dor et al. (2004)	Secondary sources to compare the software industries in Israel, Finland, Singapore, and New Zealand.	Developed and tested a model of eight independent variables that affect IT industry success within a country.
Farrell, D. (2006)	Surveys conducted by McKinsey	Best practices for selecting offshore destinations.
Gopal et al. (2003)	Case study of an Indian Supplier. Used data on 93 projects to identify the determinants of contract choice.	Requirements uncertainty, project team size, and resource shortage explain contract choice, which in turn explains project success.
Kaiser and Hawk (2004)	Case study of a financial services company outsourcing IT work to an Indian supplier.	Documents how the relationship progressed over eight years from a small pilot to strategic co-sourcing.
King (2004)	Viewpoint	Argues that overall, offshore outsourcing benefits IT.
Krishna et al. (2004)	Unspecified number of case studies of clients offshore outsourcing IT work to Indian suppliers.	Best practices based on choice of projects, managing the relationship, staffing, and training.
Matloff (2005)	Viewpoint	Argues that exporting IT jobs and importing IT workers harms US IT workers, US firms and the broader economy.
Matsumoto (2005)	Case study of a global bank that set up a global support center in Singapore.	Staged process of moving work offshore. Competitive advantage of Singapore.
McFarlan (2005)	Editorial Preface	Identifies five emerging issues in global IT sourcing.
Nair and Prasad (2004)	Secondary sources to use a SWOT analysis of Kerala (a state in India).	Kerala is well placed to compete based on infrastructure, language proficiency, IT, and costs. But other weaknesses must be addressed.
Oshri et al. (2007)	Interviews with 150 people; in-depth case study of Tata Consultancy Services	The authors identified eight practices for managing dispersed expertise.

Continued

Table 1.5 Continued

Research publication	Empirical base	Findings
Oza and Hall (2005)	Interviews with 18 Indian software firms.	Main difficulties with offshore outsourcing of IT work are cultural differences, expectation mismatch, language differences, loss of control, job loss and transition.
Pfannenstein and Tsai (2004)	Secondary sources to provide an overview of the status of offshore IT outsourcing.	Summarized the statistics, benefits, costs, and risks of offshore IT outsourcing.
Rottman and Lacity (2006)	Interviews with 159 participants in 21 client organizations, 10 supplier organizations, and nine advisory organizations.	Practices for managing offshore outsourcing of IT work.
Sabherwal (1999)	Studied 18 IT projects, of which 16 projects the supplier was located in a different country than the client.	Found a relationship among governance structure (contract), trust, and performance.
Sakthivel (2007)	Unable to determine	Identified 18 risks and risk control factors for offshore development.
Zatolyuk and Allgood (2004)	Secondary sources used to examine the software industry in the Ukraine.	Found that the Ukraine has significant advantage to compete in global ITO market.

Roles of the client project managers

Whereas offshore strategies are set by senior IT leaders and organizational support is provided by PMOs, it is the project managers who are most impacted by offshore outsourcing. (We use the term "project manager" to simplify the landscape, but recognize these roles may be performed by people holding titles such as team lead or director of applications development, maintenance, or support.) How do project managers' roles change as a consequence of offshore engagements? At a high level, the main role of a project manager is the same: to deliver high quality applications and services on time and on budget. In reality, their ability to fulfill this role was significantly affected by the offshore engagements. Overall, our research found that US project managers micro-managed their offshore supplier teams to a much greater degree than they managed their domestic contractor teams. The increased oversight was needed to mitigate higher risks, to gradually build trust with new supplier employees, and to coordinate delivery teams who were more remote and culturally diverse.

Our research uncovered 20 effects of offshore suppliers on the project manager's ability to deliver projects on time, on budget, and with promised functionality and quality. These effects are listed below and more fully discussed in Chapter 3.

1. Project managers had to fill many of the roles that should have been performed by the PMO.
2. Project managers needed a mentor the first time they managed a project with offshore resources.
3. Project managers needed to thoroughly verify offshore supplier's work estimates, which tended to be optimistic.
4. Project managers experienced higher transaction costs which threatened their ability to deliver projects on budget.
5. Project managers experienced project delays which threatened their ability to deliver projects on time.
6. Project managers had to do more knowledge transfer upfront.
7. Project manager were often forced to short-cut the knowledge transfer process because of deadlines set by senior IT managers.
8. Project managers had to ensure that knowledge transfer was successful by testing the supplier employee's knowledge.
9. Project managers had to ensure that the supplier followed pre-agreed knowledge renewal practices.
10. Project managers had to ensure that supplier's knowledge about the new applications or technologies was transferred to the client.
11. Project managers had to gain knowledge about new applications or technologies independent of suppliers to insure that the supplier's information and bids were valid.
12. Project managers had to provide greater detail in requirement definitions.
13. Project managers had to integrate the supplier's CMM/CMMI processes into their own project management processes.
14. Project managers had to ensure the supplier's employees were fully trained as promised by suppliers.
15. Project managers had to motivate the supplier to share bad news.
16. Project managers needed to set more frequent milestones.
17. Project managers needed more frequent and more detailed status reports.
18. Project managers needed more frequent working meetings to prevent client-caused bottlenecks.
19. Project managers accompanied offshore suppliers to all client-facing meetings.
20. Project managers had to make offshore suppliers feel welcome and comfortable.

While this list seems daunting, we also note that project managers said that offshore suppliers helped their projects by providing access to scarce skills, staffing projects quickly, and speeding development when time zone differences were coordinated. Project managers also reported that offshore supplier employees were bright and eager to please. In mature organizations, project managers had enough support from their PMOs to mitigate many of the negative effects, and had enough experience and history with their offshore suppliers to effectively work together.

Guide to the chapters

The remainder of this book more fully explores the concepts introduced in this chapter. The complex stakeholder landscape, learning curve phases and various approaches to offshoring are more fully explored in chapters to come. The point of each chapter is to extract detailed best, worst, and emerging practices for achieving maximum benefit from global IT sourcing.

Chapter 2 addresses phase II learning by exploring the experiences the biotechnology company had with offshoring 21 IT projects to six suppliers in India. Offshore outsourcing is primarily explained from the perspective of three client stakeholders: senior management, IT management, and IT staff. Senior managers and the official documents from the PMO report that offshore outsourcing was successful in reducing the company's IT costs. But interviews with knowledgeable participants actually managing the projects suggest that many projects were not successful in meeting cost, quality, and productivity objectives. A highlight of this chapter is an analysis of seven project characteristics that differentiated successful from unsuccessful projects. These project characteristics are type of IT work, size of supplier firm, location of supplier employees (on-site/offshore), dollar value of the contract, size of the project, timing of the project, and client unit managing the project.

Chapter 3 follows the retail company from phase II through IV on the learning curve. Back in 1997 when Retail engaged their first Indian supplier to help with Y2K, Retail's IT managers did not perceive the selection of an Indian supplier as a radical new model called "offshoring" – the Indian supplier was just another preferred contractor. This company exemplifies phase IV in terms of institutionalizing the engagement of offshore suppliers within their organization. The chapter presents lessons on the six engagement models used in fee-for-service outsourcing. The lessons are high-level and targeted towards CIOs, Program Management Officers, and

Applications Directors. The chapter also investigates in detail 20 changes to the project manager's role when offshore suppliers are engaged.

Chapter 4 describes US Manufacturing's journey from phase II through IV on the learning curve. Phase II was an utter failure because the company only focused on costs and neglected to build the proper connections to the offshore suppliers. But the company learned that to get all they wanted from suppliers in terms of costs, quality, flexibility, control, and innovation they needed to invest in "social capital." Social capital is simply the idea that knowledge and resources are exchanged, work gets done, and value is created through social relationships. Our research at this company found 11 specific practices for building social capital. These practices show managers how to invest the *right amount* of social capital to ensure that they get overall value from offshore outsourcing in terms of quality and speed without completely eroding cost savings.

Chapter 5 addresses all the client stakeholders involved in the creation of global shared services, including senior management, functional management, business unit managers and users, the functional staff that was retained, the new functional staff hired offshore, the functional staff made redundant by offshore, and the outsourcing partners. This company dramatically cut costs by dispersing work to six regional service centers (near-shoring), a new captive center in India (offshoring) and through outsourcing partnerships. This company is an excellent example of using a blended, radical transformation approach to extract value from global sourcing. The chapter identifies nine detailed practices on the creation of global shared services.

Chapter 6 compares and contrasts the relative advantages of Indian and Chinese suppliers to compete in the global ITO/BPO market. Findings are based on face-to-face interviews with ITO/BPO suppliers and captive center managers located in these countries and on secondary data. In terms of the current market size, India is clearly the leader with ITO exports exceeding $17 billion in 2005 compared to China's $2 billion. Furthermore, India mainly exports ITO/BPO services to English-speaking firms in the US and UK, whereas China exports ITO/BPO services mostly to Japanese firms. Despite the difference in size and customer base, many Western companies are interested in China as a secondary destination beyond India. China has much to offer in terms of a good infrastructure, large workforce, and low wages. However language, cultural, and intellectual property barriers are significant. Western companies currently erecting captive centers or importing IT services from Chinese suppliers are primarily doing so for business reasons, such as establishing a presence in the China to better sell products and services there, rather than for IT cost reasons alone.

Chapter 7 focuses exclusively on the Indian IT employees doing work for US clients. Hearing their voices is quite awakening. One reason suggested for the high turnover among offshore supplier staff is that they do not relish routine coding or maintenance work – the bulk of what many clients send offshore. Much like their US counterparts, Indian staff want client-facing, design, and development work based on new technology platforms. Five practices are discussed in this chapter to increase job satisfaction and reduce turnover among Indian IT professionals.

Chapter 8 presents thirteen emerging trends as evident from our case studies, government reports, and industry analysts. The trends indicate growth in all global ITO/BPO markets as well as niche markets such as rural sourcing, nearshoring, knowledge process outsourcing, and freelance outsourcing. Furthermore, countries from all six continents will actively participate in these markets as both clients and providers.

Notes

1. Such IT work includes development, testing, and delivery of new software applications as well as remote support, upgrades, maintenance, and monitoring of existing software applications and services.
2. We define "offshore outsourcing" as outsourcing work to a supplier located on a different continent than the client. We define "near-shoring" as outsourcing work to a supplier located in an adjacent country or to a supplier located on the same continent as the client. We define "offshoring" as moving work from one client location to a client location on a different continent.
3. *CIO Magazine* reported in 2003 that savings may not be realized because the transaction costs (vendor selection, transitioning work, layoffs and retention, lost productivity, additional processes, and managing the contract) of offshore outsourcing can be as high as eight times the cost of the offshore labor.
4. Beal, B., "Survey Shows Satisfaction with Offshore Outsourcing," 10 February 2004, available on: http://searchcio.techtarget.com/original Content/0,289142,sid19_gci949702,00.html
5. DiamondCluster, *2005 Global IT Outsourcing Study*, available on: http://www.diamondcluster.com/Ideas/Viewpoint/PDF/DiamondCluster 2005OutsourcingStudy.pdf
6. Aron, R. and Singh, J., "Getting Offshoring Right," *Harvard Business Review*, Vol. 8, No. 12, December 2005, pp. 135–43.

7. Carter, T., "Cheaper's Not Always Better," *Dr. Dobb's Journal*, February 2006, available on: http://www.ddj.com/184415486

8. Hatch, P., *Offshore 2005 Research*, Ventoro, Ver. 1.2.5, 22 January 2005.

9. Rottman, J., and Lacity, M., "Proven Practices for Effectively Offshoring IT Work," *Sloan Management Review*, Vol. 47, No. 3, Spring 2006, pp. 56–63.

10. Giddens, A., The Constitution of Society: Outline of the Theory of Structuration, University of California Press, 1986.

11. See also Ross, J. and Beath, C., "Sustainable IT Outsourcing Success: Let Enterprise Architecture Be Your Guide," *MIS Quarterly Executive*, Vol. 5, No. 4, December 2006, pp. 181–92.

12. There are a number of recent articles addressing the trend of virtual captive centers. See: Allen, P., "Late to the Game of Offshoring? Take a Look at Virtual Captive Operations," 5 January 2007, available on: http://considerthesourceblog.typepad.com/consider_the_source/2007/01/late_to_the_gam.html, Foster, C., and Funk, J., "The Offshore Solutions Spectrum: Getting the Best Fit," *Journal of Sourcing Leadership*, Vol. 3, No. 1, July 2006, and *The Sourcing Leadership Exchange*, Technology Partners International white paper, Spring 2006.

13. Willcocks, L., and Lacity, M., *Global Sourcing of Business and IT Services*, Palgrave, 2006.

14. The Black Book of Outsourcing: State of the Outsourcing Industry, 2007 Results of Service Provider Buyers, Users, and Analysts, by the Brown-Wilson Group, Inc.

15. Field, T., "The Man In The Middle," *CIO Magazine*, April, 2002.

16. Feeny, D., Lacity, M., and Willcocks, L., "Taking the Measure of Outsourcing Providers," *Sloan Management Review*, Vol. 46, No. 3, Spring 2005, pp. 41–8.

17. Kaiser, K., and Hawk, S. "Evolution of Offshore Software Development: From Outsourcing to Cosourcing," *MIS Quarterly Executive*, Vol. 3, No. 2, June 2004, pp. 69–81.

18. Oshri, I., Kotlarsky, J., and Willcocks, L., "Managing Dispersed Expertise in IT Offshore Outsourcing: Lessons from Tata Consultancy Services," *MIS Quarterly Executive*, Vol. 6, No. 2, June 2007, pp. 53–65.

19. CMM was developed by the Software Engineering Institute (SEI) at Carnegie Mellon University in Pittsburgh between 1987 and 1997. CMMI was developed by members of industry, government, and the SEI to improve usability of maturity models by integrating many different models into one framework. The SEI no longer supports CMM,

but since appraisals are only done once, many organizations still use and market their CMM rating.

20. Harter, D., Krishnan, M., and Slaughter, S., "Effects of Process Maturity on Quality, Cycle Time, and Effort in Software Product Development," *Management Science*, Vol. 46, No. 4, April 2000, pp. 451–66.

21. For detailed cases on implementing CMM within an organization, see Jalote, P., *CMM in Practice*, Addison Wesley, 2000, and Adler, P., McGarry, F., Irion Talbot, W., and Binney, D., "Enabling Process Discipline: Lessons from the Journey to CMM Level 5," *MIS Quarterly Executive*, Vol. 4, No. 1, 2005, pp. 215–27.

22. To a businessperson, the concept of a function point may be quite confusing. A function point is supposed to capture a business function that has value to the user. In reality, function points are calculated by examining the number of functions provided by an application's outputs (such as predefined reports), inquiries (such as ad hoc reports), inputs (such as data entry screens), data files (users don't see these directly), and interfaces to other applications (such as passing a data file). There are typically many function points associated with each (for example, one physical report will have many function points), thus the number of function points is much larger than merely counting the number of outputs, inquiries, inputs, files, and interfaces.

23. Lacity, M., and Willcocks, L., *Global IT Outsourcing*, Wiley, Chichester, 2001.

24. Bruno, G., Esposito, G., Iandoli, L., and Raffa, M., "The ICT Service Industry in North Africa and Role of Partnerships in Morocco," *Journal of Global Information Technology Management*, Vol. 7, No. 3, 2004, pp. 5–26.

25. The special issue of *MIS Quarterly* on Offshoring of IT Work is edited by Dr. William King and Dr. Reza Torkzadeh. The special issue of the *Journal of Information Technology* on Global Sourcing of Services, Knowledge and Innovation is edited by Dr. Julia Kotlarsky and Dr. Ilan Oshri.

26. The conference proceedings will be edited by Dr. Rudy Hirschheim, Dr. Armin Heinzl, and Dr. Jens Dibbern and published by Springer-Verlag in 2008.

References

Adler, P., McGarry, F., Irion Talbot, W., and Binney, D., "Enabling Process Discipline: Lessons from the Journey to CMM Level 5," *MIS Quarterly Executive*, Vol. 4, No. 1, 2005, pp. 215–27.

Allen, P., "Late to the Game of Offshoring? Take a Look at Virtual Captive Operations," 5 January 2007, available on: http://considerthesourceblog. typepad.com/consider_the_source/2007/01/late_to_the_gam.html

Aron, R., and Singh, J.,"Getting Offshoring Right," *Harvard Business Review*, Vol. 8, No. 12, December 2005, pp. 135–43.

Beal, B., "Survey Shows Satisfaction with Offshore Outsourcing," 10 February 2004, available on: http://searchcio.techtarget.com/originalContent/ 0,289142,sid19_gci949702,00.html

Bruno, G., Esposito, G., Iandoli, L., and Raffa, M., "The ICT Service Industry in North Africa and Role of Partnerships in Morocco," *Journal of Global Information Technology Management*, Vol. 7, No. 3, 2004, pp. 5–26.

Carmel, E., and Agarwal, R., "The Maturation of Offshore Sourcing of Information Technology Work," *MIS Quarterly Executive*, Vol. 1, No. 2, June 2002, pp. 65–77.

Carmel, E., and Tjia, P., *Offshoring Information Technology: Sourcing and Outsourcing to a Global Workforce*, Cambridge University Press, 2005.

Carmel, E., "Building Your Information Systems from the Other Side of the World: How Infosys Manages Time Zone Differences," *MIS Quarterly Executive*, Vol. 5, No. 1, March 2006, pp. 43–53.

Carter, T., "Cheaper's Not Always Better," *Dr. Dobb's Journal*, February 2006, available on: http://www.ddj.com/184415486

Choudhury, V., and Sabherwal, R., "Portfolios of Control in Outsourced Software Development Projects," *Information Systems Research*, Vol. 14, No. 3, September 2003, pp. 291–314.

Davis, G., Ein-Dor, P., King, W., and Torkzadeh, R., "IT Offshoring: History, Prospects, and Challenges," *Journal of the Association for Information Systems*, Vol. 7, No. 11, November 2006, pp. 770–95.

DiamondCluster, *2005 Global IT Outsourcing Study*, available on: http://www.diamondcluster.com/Ideas/Viewpoint/PDF/Diamond Cluster2005OutsourcingStudy.pdf

Dibbern, J., Goles, T., Hirschheim, R., and Bandula J., "Information Systems Outsourcing: A Survey and Analysis of the Literature," *Database for Advances in Information Systems*, Vol. 34, No. 4, Fall 2004, pp. 6–102.

Drezner, D., "The Outsourcing Bogeyman," *Foreign Affairs*, Vol. 83, No. 4, May/June 2004, p. 22.

Dutta, A., and Roy, R., "Offshore Outsourcing: A Dynamic Causal Model of Counteracting Forces," *Journal of Management Information Systems*, Vol. 22, No. 2, Fall 2005, pp. 15–36.

Ein-Dor, P., "IT Industry Development and the Knowledge Economy: A Four Country Study," *Journal of Global Information Management*, Vol. 12, No. 4, October/December 2004, pp. 249.

Farrell, D., "Smarter Offshoring," *Harvard Business Review*, June2006, pp. 85–92.

Feeny, D., Lacity, M., and Willcocks, L., "Taking the Measure of Outsourcing Providers," *Sloan Management Review*, Vol. 46, No. 3, Spring 2005, pp. 41–8.

Field, T., "The Man In The Middle," *CIO Magazine*, April, 2002.

Foster, C., and Funk, J., "The Offshore Solutions Spectrum: Getting the Best Fit," *Journal of Sourcing Leadership*, Vol. 3, No. 1, July 2006.

Giddens, A., *The Constitution of Society: Outline of the Theory of Structuration*, University of California Press, 1986.

Gopal, A., Sivaramakrishnan, K., Krishnan, M., and Mukhopadhyay, T., "Contracts in Offshore Software Development: An Empirical Analysis," *Management Science*, Vol. 49, No. 12, December 2003, pp. 1671–83.

Harter, D., Krishnan, M., and Slaughter, S., "Effects of Process Maturity on Quality, Cycle Time, and Effort in Software Product Development," *Management Science*, Vol. 46, No. 4, April 2000, pp. 451–66.

Hatch, P., *Offshore 2005 Research*, Ventoro, Ver. 1.2.5, 22 January 2005.

Jalote, P., *CMM in Practice*, Addison Wesley, 2000.

Kaiser, K., and Hawk, S., "Evolution of Offshore Software Development: From Outsourcing to Cosourcing," *MIS Quarterly Executive*, Vol. 3, No. 2, June 2004, pp. 69–81.

Krishna, S., Sahay, S., and Walsham, G., "Managing Cross-Cultural Issues in Global Software Outsourcing," *Communications of the ACM*, Vol. 47, No. 4, April 2004, pp. 62–6.

Lacity, M., and Willcocks, L., *Global IT Outsourcing*, Wiley, Chichester, 2001.

Matloff, N., "Globalization and the American IT Worker," *Communications of the ACM*, Vol. 47, No. 11, November 2004, pp. 27–30.

Matsumoto, H., "Global Business Process/IS Outsourcing to Singapore in the Multinational Investment Banking Industry," *Journal of Information Technology Case and Application Research*, Vol. 7, No. 3, 2005, pp. 4–24.

McFarlan, F.W., "Globalization of IT-Enabled Services: An Irreversible Trend," *Journal of Information Technology Case and Application Research*, Vol. 7, No. 3, 2005, pp. 1–3.

Nair, K., and Prasad, P., "Offshore Outsourcing: A SWOT Analysis of a State in India," *Information Systems Management*, Vol. 21, No. 3, Summer 2004, pp. 34–40.

Oshri, I., Kotlarsky, J., and Willcocks, L., "Managing Dispersed Expertise in IT Offshore Outsourcing: Lessons from Tata Consultancy Services," *MIS Quarterly Executive*, Vol. 6, No. 2, June 2007, pp. 53–65.

Oza, N., and Hall, T., "Difficulties in Managing Offshore Software Outsourcing Relationships: An Empirical Analysis of 18 High Maturity Indian Software Companies," *Journal of Information Technology Case and Application Research,* Vol. 7, No. 3, 2005, pp. 25–41.

Pfannenstein, L., and Tsai, R., "Offshore Outsourcing: Current and Future Effects on American IT Industry," *Information Systems Management*, Vol. 21, No. 4, Fall 2004, pp. 72–80.

Ross, J. and Beath, C., "Sustainable IT Outsourcing Success: Let Enterprise Architecture Be Your Guide," *MIS Quarterly Executive*, Vol. 5, No. 4, December 2006, pp. 181–92.

Rottman, J., and Lacity, M. (2006), "Proven Practices for Effectively Offshoring IT Work," *Sloan Management Review*, Vol. 47, No. 3, Spring 2006, pp. 56–63.

Sabherwal, R., "The Role of Trust in Outsourced Relationships," *Communications of the ACM*, Vol. 42, No. 2, February 1999, pp. 80–6.

Sakthivel, S., "Managing Risk in Offshore Systems Development," *Communications of the ACM*, Vol. 50, No. 4, April 2007, pp. 69–75.

The Sourcing Leadership Exchange, Technology Partners International white paper, Spring 2006.

Willcocks, L., and Lacity, M., *Global Sourcing of Business and IT Services*, Palgrave, 2006.

Zatolyuk, S., and Allgood, B., "Evaluating a Country for Offshore Outsourcing: Software Development Providers in the Ukraine," *Information Systems Management*, Vol. 21, No. 3, Summer 2004, pp. 28–33.

CHAPTER 2

A client's experiences with its initial offshore outsourcing program

Joseph Rottman and Mary Lacity

Introduction

This chapter presents a case study of a Fortune 500 biotechnology company (hereafter called Biotech)[1]. In our learning curve (Figure 1.2), the Biotech case maps to Phase II – pilot projects driven by the promise of cost savings. This chapter presents a highly realistic picture of the client's experiences with offshoring of IT work for the first time and how best and worst practices quickly emerge from experience. In telling this story, we hope that other clients may apply Biotech's lessons to accelerate their own path on the learning curve.

Biotech employs approximately 15,000 employees spread across 400 locations in more than 40 countries. Our research, based on 44 interviews and over 2,000 documents, focuses on the IT group at US headquarters. This group comprises about 600 IT workers, of which 400 are Biotech employees and 200 are domestic contractors. Biotech engaged six Indian offshore suppliers on 21 IT projects during 2003 through 2005. The official documents from the Program Management Office (PMO) report that offshore outsourcing was successful in reducing Biotech's IT costs. But interviews with knowledgeable participants suggest that many projects were not successful in meeting cost, quality, and productivity objectives. Like practitioner reports discussed in Chapter 1, many Biotech participants struggled with high transaction costs associated with the management of offshore workers on many of their projects.

The chapter proceeds with a description of Biotech's journey offshore. We then explain Biotech's mixed results with offshore outsourcing at two levels of analysis. At the organizational level of analysis, we found evidence that Biotech's offshore strategy to simply replace domestic contractors with cheaper, offshore suppliers was a poor fit with Biotech's social and cultural contexts. Specifically, we found that:

1. Strong social networks between Biotech IT employees and domestic contractors could not easily be replicated with offshore suppliers.
2. Biotech's "sneaker-net" culture among business users, IT employees and domestic contractors could not easily be replicated with offshore suppliers.
3. Biotech's IT managers had more difficulty assessing relevant skills and experiences for offshore suppliers than domestic contractors.
4. Biotech's project management processes and expectations were often incompatible with offshore suppliers.

At the project level of analysis, we found that Biotech participants:

1. Rated projects that engaged *one, large offshore supplier* higher than projects that engaged one small offshore supplier or multiple suppliers.
2. Rated projects with *some offshore-supplier employees on-site* higher than projects with all supplier employees offshore.
3. Rated projects with *greater-valued contracts* higher than projects with lesser-valued contracts.
4. Rated *larger-sized projects* higher than smaller-sized projects.
5. Rated projects from specific *organizational units* higher than other organizational units.
6. Participants rated both *development and maintenance/support projects* equally.
7. Participants rated *recent projects* higher than older projects.

We conclude the chapter with four overall lessons for clients and suppliers. First, an offshore strategy must either fit with the client's norms and practices, or the client may have to change norms and practices to achieve offshore success. Second, clients and suppliers must invest in social capital to facilitate knowledge transfer. One of the best mechanisms for building social capital is to bring more supplier employees on-site. Third, clients may achieve greater success with bigger commitments to suppliers. Offshore outsourcing has higher transaction costs than other sourcing models, so larger projects and larger contracts are needed to achieve total cost savings. In addition, larger commitments to suppliers increase the likelihood that the suppliers will pay significant attention and devote its best resources to clients. Finally, clients need robust measures to monitor and manage offshore outsourcing programs. One of the main messages from the Biotech case is that poor measures signal the wrong messages.

Biotech's journey offshore

As stated above, Biotech is a Fortune 500 company and a leading provider of biotechnology-based products. According to 10-K (annual) reports, Biotech experienced flat revenues yet increasingly positive net income from 1999–2001. According to the CIO, in 2001, senior management was beginning to feel the financial pains of a major litigation, increased competition, and rising costs of inputs. Predicting losses for 2002, senior management sought to cut the budgets of overhead departments.[2] For 2002, the CIO's IT budget was reduced by 5 percent. "Doing more with less" became the CIO's major challenge for 2002.

Senior IT leads explore offshore outsourcing as a means to reduce IT costs. In Spring 2002, the CIO tasked the senior IT leadership team, comprised of 12 senior IT managers (called IT leads), to develop a strategy to cope with the tighter IT budget. One of their proposals was to possibly move some IT work offshore. The CIO and IT leads reasoned that every hour of work done offshore could potentially save the company $40.

The CIO and IT leads intend to replace domestic contractors with cheaper offshore IT workers. The participants were in agreement pertaining to the reasoning behind the projected cost savings. Most of Biotech's IT workforce resides in the corporate IT department on the headquarters campus. The corporate IT department comprises about 600 people, including 200 domestic contractors. The domestic contractors earn hourly wages of about $65. If domestic contractors could be replaced with offshore workers who typically earn $25 per hour, then the CIO and IT leads reasoned they could save at least $40 per hour. Thus, their number one objective was to reduce IT costs, primarily by replacing some of the domestic contractors with cheaper offshore equivalents. (There was no evidence that the CIO or IT leads intended to use offshore to replace any Biotech IT employees.) According to the CIO:

> One was simply looking at how much work do we give India? And if you make the assumption that we would be doing that work anyway, it's pretty easy to calculate the cost if you [would] have done it

in the US versus doing it in India. It becomes a pretty straightforward calculation.

IT leads visit offshore clients in the US and suppliers in India. In summer of 2002, three IT leads (all of whom we interviewed) pursued their offshore investigation by visiting offshore clients in the US. Convinced by the cost savings they saw in other client organizations, they hired an offshore consultant to serve as a guide to India and to Indian suppliers. They said they selected India as the offshore venue because Biotech already had research and development (R&D) facilities in Bangalore, India. In that facility, they reasoned, Biotech had full-time IT employees who could potentially play a significant role in managing offshore outsourcing.

In August of 2002, two IT leads made the trip to India. They found many different approaches to offshore outsourcing (captive centers, joint ventures, fee-for-service), but the bottom line was "It was quite an advantage from the cost perspective." (IT lead)

Upon returning from India, the IT leads began to rally senior-management support for offshore outsourcing. The CIO approved and created a new Program Management Office for offshore projects. The role of the PMO was to transfer knowledge about offshore contracting, negotiations, and management:

> The idea was that we could each do individual efforts but if there was a [Program] Management Office, it would make the effort a little bit easier for everybody who wanted to do it. So, if somebody wanted to pursue an offshore project, they didn't have to learn everything from scratch. There's a lot of overhead in terms of contractual work and negotiations that has to be accomplished. So, by putting that in the Program Management Office, everyone can do the project and feel unconstrained by those issues. (IT lead)

The CIO mandates offshore outsourcing. Because offshore outsourcing would likely meet with resistance from the internal IT staff, the CIO implemented the strategy as a mandate:

> As I looked at rolling this out, I knew we needed a critical mass of projects and people involved, and offshoring was not a very popular topic. There was some fear of losing jobs and of losing contractors who are tightly integrated into our design teams. So, if I just waited for volunteers, I might not have reached that mass. So we used a rather heavy hand. I don't know another way to do it. (CIO)

New projects would require that at least 15 percent of the budget be outsourced offshore. In total, the CIO budgeted $6.2 million for offshore during 2003–5.

The head of the PMO and IT leads select suppliers. The offshore consultant helped the IT leads and head of the PMO identify potential suppliers. After due diligence, the IT leads and PMO head narrowed the list of potential suppliers through interviews and supplier presentations. The IT leads and PMO head were interested in engaging suppliers with significant science domain knowledge, as well as willingness to participate in small projects during the start-up stage. Two large suppliers decided not to participate due to the small scale of the initial projects. Ultimately, Biotech engaged six Indian suppliers. Two suppliers were large, earning more than $1 billion in revenues in 2005. Four suppliers were small, the largest of which earned less than $150 million in 2005.

Biotech launches 21 projects offshore in 2003–2005. To kick off the offshore initiative, the CIO and the IT leads held a town-hall meeting for all IT employees. During this meeting, the offshore strategy and the role of the PMO were introduced. IT employees were told that no employee would lose their job as a consequence of offshore outsourcing.

The offshore consultant, in cooperation with the PMO, delivered several cultural-awareness training sessions to educate the IT staff on the challenges of managing Indian suppliers. All initial staff members involved in offshore outsourcing (at all levels) attended. To illustrate the purpose of these sessions, the following excerpt from the document "Introduction to Offshore" is provided below:

> The experience of doing a project offshore is new to [Biotech]. Offshore projects, while presenting important opportunities for cost reduction, also present significant differences to project managers, team members and clients. The purpose of this section is to describe the best practices and resources available to help [Biotech] people become accustomed to working on offshore projects.

These sessions covered Indian economy, culture, music, and educational institutions. Particular attention was paid to the differences between US and Indian cultural norms. The PMO created and distributed an "Illustrated Guide to Offshore" to IT employees.

IT leads started bringing projects to the PMO in early 2003. The PMO was tasked with coordinating project selection, project management, tactical duties (human resource-related tasks for the on-boarding of supplier resources, facilitating system account creation, interfacing with Biotech IT security for login IDs, etc.), and tracking all statements of works (SOWs), invoices, and timesheets. During 2003 and 2004, the PMO and IT leads met to discuss successes and failures in the offshore initiative and to assess supplier performance. Two small suppliers were identified as poor performers and when the engagements expired, contracts were not renewed.

In all, 14 projects were launched in 2003, six projects in 2004, and one project in 2005. The number of offshore-supplier workers peaked in October 2004 at 68 and, as of June 2005, Biotech engaged 35 offshore workers. As of summer 2005, a total of $4.1 million dollars had been paid to offshore suppliers.

The official word from the PMO: offshore outsourcing is realizing projected cost savings. During the 2003–5 timeframe, the PMO was in charge of reporting on the project status of offshore projects. The PMO created monthly and yearly reports on the total costs of offshore outsourcing. Every document reports total cost savings. For example, the document titled "2004 IT Offshore Accomplishments," states that as of 23 July 2004, Biotech saved $560,000 with offshore outsourcing. According to the head of the PMO and the Offshore Project Coordinator, the number is based on multiplying the costs of the offshore hours and comparing this number with what it would have cost had they used domestic contractors. The number does not consider transaction costs, productivity, or quality. Thus, month after month, the PMO documents report that offshore outsourcing is successful in meeting Biotech's cost-savings targets.

The burning question: is offshore outsourcing really worthwhile? The head of the PMO questioned whether these cost savings were realistic. During our first interview with him, he said:

> It is clear that we saved money on a per hour basis, there is no way to argue about that, but did [the offshore supplier] do it as fast as we would do it? The other big complaint came from the project managers: "Managing offshore projects is really hard." If I had to count up how hard this is, then we lost money. That is clearly anecdotal since they don't keep track of how much they spend on domestic project in terms of project management.

Based on our initial five interviews, we understood the PMO's suspicion about the actual outcomes of offshore outsourcing. In addition to the head of the PMO, one other IT lead expressed skepticism about the official story that offshore outsourcing was saving Biotech money: "I wish we had better project and budget metrics. We really don't know how to translate the 'hourly savings' into a real number. I am not sure at the end of the day what our savings would be."

However, two other IT leads seemed to think offshore outsourcing, in general, was successful. The first quote by an IT lead claimed that overall economic benefits were met:

> I think the one comment I'll make is, all of our startups were difficult. I don't think there's one startup that happened in that March to July 2003 timeframe that didn't hit some startup issues. But the conversation that I had with leadership here at [Biotech], was that none of these projects missed any of their deliverables. They all delivered on the date. They all delivered at the economic level we expected. And when I say, pretty much on the dates, we probably had one or two that missed a little bit, but I wouldn't call those significant. (IT Lead)

The following quote captures what one IT lead thought about the anecdotal complaints from project managers:

> If Biotech's project managers work overtime with offshore because they have to come in early or stay late to take a call or have a conference with India, then they mentally count it differently than if they were just working overtime on some domestic project. That is one complaint we hear often, "My work day is extended because of offshoring."(IT Lead)

The CIO concludes:

> Our offshore experiences have certainly been mixed. I am working with the IT leads now to do a kind of "good, bad and ugly" analysis to see where we are and what worked and how we can utilize the offshore model. I think that some of the setbacks were due to the suppliers' shortcomings and some of them were due to how we do business at [Biotech]. We need to understand which were which and go from there.

Thus, there were different opinions as to whether Biotech actually met their offshore objective to reduce IT costs. To move beyond random anecdotes, the head of the PMO wanted to capture the opinions of all the IT employees involved in offshore outsourcing. We assessed their opinions at a project level so that we could find attributes to help explain differences in project outcomes. The next sections explain the project outcome indicator we used, the attributes we measured, and the overall project-level findings.

Particpants' project ratings

Traditionally, practitioners define project success[3] as a project being delivered on time, on budget, with promised functionality.[4] At Biotech, there were no formal metrics to uniformly assess project success across the 21 projects, other than to compare offshore expenses with what those hours would have cost if Biotech had used domestic contractors. We created a project indicator of success based on subjective evaluations of the people who were knowledgeable about the project.

Subjective evaluations are the most common form of IT project evaluation for projects of less than one year's duration. For example, researchers found that most small and medium-sized IT projects (less than one year to complete) are subjectively evaluated by people involved in the project in a technical, business, or managerial capacity. In comparison, they also found that most large projects (more than one year to complete) are evaluated using hard numbers, such as return on investment, payback period, and net present value.[5] This difference in evaluation methods is likely due to the fact that small projects are expensed, whereas large projects must pass through the capital budgeting process.

We interviewed 44 participants (see Table 2.1) who were intimately involved on a project at various levels (IT leads, program leads, team leads, project leads, and architects) to assess the overall success of a project. We asked participants: "Considering the degree to which project objectives were met, budgets and schedules were met, and the quality of the delivered product, what letter grade would you assign the project?"

For each specific project discussed by a participant, the participant assigned a standard US letter grade (A, B, C, D, or F). We used the standard US grading system because it is a common frame of reference for the US participants. Based on the interviews, it was clear that all participants could clearly articulate and defend a letter grade.

Among the 21 projects for which participants graded the project outcome, 17 projects had at least two participants independently assign a grade. For four projects, one participant assigned a grade. To calculate the average grade for each project, we converted letter grades reported by participants to numbers. We assigned A = 4, A–/B+ = 3.5, B = 3, B–/C+ = 2.5, C = 2, C–/D+ = 1.5, D = 1, D– = 0.5, and F = 0. In Table 2.2, we show the 21 projects (labeled A through U), the number of participants that

Table 2.1 Biotech participants and titles

Title of participant	Number of participants with this title
Application architect	1
Architecture lead	1
CIO	2
Client systems team lead	1
Commercial IT lead	1
DBA project lead	1
DBA team lead	2
Development coordinator	1
Engagement manager	1
IT lead	4
IT team lead	7
Manager data management team	1
Manager IT	1
Offshore project coordinator	1
Program lead	2
Program services lead	1
Project lead	2
Project manager	3
Senior project manager	1
Software architect	1
Team lead HR services	1
Team lead IT HR	1
Team lead SAP	1
Team lead SATT	1
Team lead tech services	1
Technical architect	1
Technical lead	2
Web administrator	1
Total	**44**

Table 2.2 Participants' ratings of project outcomes

Project	Number of participants who assigned a grade	Letter grades assigned by participants	Average projectrating using A = 4, A–/B+ = 3.5, B = 3, B–/C+ = 2.5, C = 2, C–/D+ = 1.5, D = 1, D–/F+ = 0.5, and F = 0	Standard deviation of average project rating
A	3	C+, D, F	1.17	1.26
B	1	C–	1.50	n/a
C	3	D+, D, A–	2.00	1.32
D	5	F, F, F, F,F	0.00	0.00
E	3	F, C, B	1.67	1.53
F	4	C, B, B, D	2.25	0.96
G	5	A, A, A, B, B	3.60	0.55
H	4	F, F, F, D	0.25	0.50
I	1	D	1.00	n/a
J	2	B, C–	2.25	1.06
K	2	F, D,	0.50	0.71
L	3	A, A, C	3.33	1.15
M	4	C, D, C–, B	1.88	0.85
N	4	C, F, F, F	0.50	1.00
O	3	B+ , B+ ,B+	3.50	0.00
P	3	B, C+, D+	2.33	0.76
Q	9	D, C, D, D, B, B, F, B, B	1.89	1.17
R	2	C+, D	1.75	1.06
S	1	C–	1.50	n/a
T	1	D	1.00	n/a
U	3	C–, B, B	2.50	0.87
	Overall		**1.73 (mean)**	**1.02**
			1.75 (median)	

graded the project, the letter grades assigned, the average project rating after converting letters to numbers, and the standard deviation. The overall mean project rating was 1.73 and the median was 1.75 (indicating a grade of between a C and a C–).

In some instances, participants had a shared view of project outcome as evidenced by the similar grades for a project. For example, all five participants independently graded Project D as an "F." Project D entailed Database Administration (DBA) support tasks. The project was managed in the US and delivered by Biotech's captive center in Bangalore. The project deliverables were late and frequently wrong. According to one

DBA team lead: "The project was bloody awful! I had business users demanding, 'Don't send it to Bangalore – they will just screw it up and we will have to redo all the work and it will take five times as long!'"

In other instances, participants had different perceptions of project outcome. Project C provides an example. Project C entailed the visual mapping of DNA to help scientists manage the lineage of traits. Project C was graded by three participants: an IT team lead (graded the project a D), a software architect (graded the project a D+), and a project lead (graded the project an A–). One explanation for the divergent views may be that participants viewed different outputs. The IT team lead and software architect viewed the project outputs directly from the supplier. They defended their grades as follows:

> [The offshore supplier] would send me code that would not compile! I would have to fix the code, submit it to the code repository and then run it. That is the code that feeds the status: the vendor's bad code that we fixed. (Software Architect)
>
> When we would actually get the beginnings of code [from the supplier], I would have to look at it and I remember thinking, "This is a bunch of crap!" I would have to create the class and sequence diagrams, send them back to the supplier and then re-code before submitting it. For [Project C] it would have been easier to write the code myself. (IT Team Lead)

In contrast, the project lead viewed the outputs only after the IT team lead and software architect had fixed the supplier's errors. This may explain his higher grade: "I never talked with the supplier's developers, just the project lead for the offshore team ... I think it went OK, some issues with code, but in general, I think it went well" (project lead).

It is quite clear from our interviews that the projects sourced offshore were not as uniformly successful as the official PMO reports. Whereas the PMO reports focused only on the cost part of the services, the participants focused on cost, quality, and speed. The participants' assessments are much richer and less uniformly enthusiastic than the PMO reports. What was really going on at Biotech? To answer this question, we conducted two levels of analysis. At the organizational level, we found evidence that Biotech's offshore strategy to simply replace domestic contractors with cheaper, offshore suppliers was a poor fit with Biotech's social and cultural contexts. At the project level of analysis, we found that different project attributes explained differences in project outcomes.

Organizational-level analysis: Offshore outsourcing was a poor fit

From the case-description section, it is clear that the official word in PMO documents was that offshore outsourcing was meeting Biotech's objective to reduce IT costs. Based on the project ratings from knowledgeable participants, results were obviously mixed, and generally less positive than the "official word." This section focuses on the broader contextual issues to explain why offshore sourcing of IT work resulted in mixed results at Biotech.

Initially, the CIO and IT leads' strategy was to replace, person-for-person, domestic contractors with offshore IT workers. Four findings suggest why this strategy was a poor fit with Biotech's social and cultural contexts.

1. Strong social networks between Biotech IT employees and domestic contractors could not easily be replicated with offshore suppliers. Although prior research suggests significant differences between contractors and permanent employees,[6] this was not evident at Biotech. At Biotech, we learned that domestic IT contractors are treated like Biotech IT employees. They are housed in the same types of cubicles with permanent workers, wear the same identification badges, attend the same meetings, and are tightly integrated into project teams. One reason for the lack of distinction is that Biotech often uses domestic-contractor positions as a precursor to full-time positions. Indeed, among the 44 people we interviewed, ten were previously domestic contractors before becoming full-time Biotech employees. The following quotation describes the close integration of domestic contractors and Biotech employees:

> Our culture is totally different from a contract-resource point of view. I came from some other companies. I was shocked when I came into [Biotech] to see how the contractors were actually integrated into the scene. I mean, I couldn't tell [who was a contractor and who was a full-time employee]. Same meetings; you have as many responsibilities as some of the senior managers have here. Some [contractors] have been around sometimes for over a decade. This is a totally different paradigm. (IT Lead)

In contrast, the Indian offshore IT workers were obviously treated differently. Despite efforts to integrate the offshore workers into the teams, internal Biotech employees never felt a sense of connection with them. According to an IT team lead, "We even tried bringing over some people from India for team building, and it worked when they were here, but when they went back, the team aspect fell apart." In addition to the social disconnection, there were technical barriers as well. Due to security concerns and bandwidth constraints, offshore workers were not allowed to access production data or Biotech's internal systems, such as the code repository. This hampered development and created obstacles for the offshore workers.

2. Biotech's "sneaker-net" culture among business users, IT employees, and domestic contractors could not easily be replicated with offshore suppliers. At Biotech, we learned that requirements analysis is an informal process. Because IT workers reside on the same campus as business users, Biotech's IT employees and domestic contractors typically walk over to meet business users to seek or clarify functional requirements. Thus, the process was called "sneaker-net" by some participants. Like the social networks that facilitate knowledge transfer between IT employees and domestic contractors, there are also social networks that facilitate knowledge transfer among IT employees, domestic contractors, and business users. According to the CIO, "Here at [Biotech], we have always worked very closely with our contractors and our business sponsors. Tight collaboration is part of our DNA. That makes this offshoring pretty tough."

Furthermore, the CIO said that requirements are not only informally *gathered*; requirements are also informally *documented*. He said requirements are typically "documented" on white boards or in personal notebooks. A web developer corroborated the CIO's statement:

> A lot of times in our environment, the developers will be involved in requirements, meaning taking their own notes and gathering that understanding. And that's not something that happened with offshore. We had to retranslate what he had to paper and then translate it to them, and it doesn't work very well. I think, in a development environment, it's important that the developers be part of requirements gathering, so that they can understand what it is and why it is.

Biotech's "sneaker-net" culture did not fit well with offshore. Indian-based IT workers did not have access to users to establish the social networks needed to facilitate knowledge transfer. A project manager in R&D said: "We had no way to get requirements from the user and get them to the offshore team. We could have easily done this project onshore because we know how to go back and forth with the user, but the offshore team just couldn't do it."

In hindsight, an IT lead acknowledged that Biotech had not thought through the knowledge-transfer process: "We didn't have anything in place that was really allowing us to transfer the knowledge. There was, like, a huge leak."

3. Biotech's IT managers had more difficulty assessing relevant skills and experiences for offshore suppliers than for domestic contractors. Biotech IT managers interview domestic contractors in person and contact previous employers to verify résumé claims. In contrast, Biotech IT managers interviewed offshore workers by phone and relied on the supplier managers to verify qualifications. According to several participants, this process resulted in a poor skills match. For example, according to a development coordinator:

> Our domestic ABAP[7] contractors would have three to five years of ABAP experience and six to ten years of other IT experience. The offshore contractors would come to us as "experienced," but that meant they had two to three years of IT/ABAP experience, total. They didn't understand IT projects – let alone the ABAP processes.

One IT team lead, stated, "We never knew if what was on the résumé would actually be what the guy would actually be able to do. The interview process was hit and miss." Finally, a software architect echoed the frustration with inexperienced supplier employees:

> The supplier would send us a guy with "five years' experience." But when we worked with him we would realize he really had only one true year of experience. He had done the exact same tasks at five different engagements. So he only had one real year of experience five times.

4. Biotech's project management processes and expectations were often incompatible with offshore suppliers. Despite the cultural-awareness training, many participants were unprepared for the cultural differences between US IT workers and Indian IT workers. In the US, domestic contractors are trusted to speak up when deadlines slip or they do not understand requirements or processes. An application architect describes the trust he has in his domestic contractor to communicate with him:

> And I make it clear to my contractors, if you don't understand something, you're in my office, every day. I mean, I got one contractor who is reasonable, $54 bucks an hour, really reasonable guy. He basically comes in my cube, probably, 15 times a day, and that's what we have

to do. We've got a couple other guys that are very similar to him and, basically, come in all the time for clarification.

In contrast, we heard from many participants that the offshore IT workers could not be relied upon to report that the project was behind schedule or that they did not understand the requirements. The following four quotes serve as evidence about not reporting project delays:

> When the project was going so far off course, they never really told us that they were behind on deadlines. They always said everything was going well. (Offshore project coordinator)
>
> Well, probably the biggest awareness that was raised was their tendency to not want to deliver bad news. (Technical lead)
>
> An iteration was due on Monday. On Friday the guy [Indian project manager] says "It's fine. A little bit of a stretch, but it is fine." And on Tuesday he's asking for another two weeks! So they missed it by 100 percent. They didn't feel like they could tell us if they were going to miss it. This seems to be the modus operandi, dig and dig and spade and spade to get anybody to tell you that things are wrong. Because they just simply won't. They will tell you it is great. (Head of the PMO)

One IT lead summed it up by saying, "The place could be on fire and they would say, 'Oh it's great, a little warm, but it is great!'" The following quote addresses the offshore supplier's reticence to express incomprehension: "You can sometimes be talking with someone and across the table they'll be shaking their head as if they understand and agree with everything you're saying. You find out later that they didn't understand what you were talking about" (IT lead).

> During an offshore outsourcing class the second author attended, Biotech's offshore consultant talked about the cultural challenges at Biotech. According to him, Biotech's Indian suppliers view time more fluidly than Westerners. He said, "If an Indian IT worker knows how to complete a task, even though he knows it will be late, then he would view it as unnecessary to contact the customer. He is the expert and the customer should trust that he is professionally completing the task".

Project-level analysis

For Biotech, bigger was better Besides assessing participants' views on project outcomes, we assessed which attributes differentiated highly rated projects from poorly rated projects. We coded the documents and transcribed interviews into data categories and mapped these categories against the project rating. The data categories were selected based on prior research as well as data categories that emerged from the interviews. We examined the following data categories:

1. Size and number of offshore supplier(s) engaged on the project
2. Supplier engagement model used on the project as indicated by the physical location of offshore-supplier managers and developers
3. Contract value in terms of dollars paid to the supplier on a project
4. Project size in terms of duration in number of days
5. Organizational unit within IT managing the project
6. Project type (either development of new applications or maintenance/ support of existing applications)
7. Year the project was started
8. Contract type (fixed price or time and materials)

Because project ratings are numeric, there are several ways to divide the data into categories of "success." We divided the data into two. We categorized individual projects that rated above the mean project rating of 1.73 as the "more successful projects" and projects that rated below the project mean as the "less successful projects." Given the sample contains 21 projects, dividing the data into two categories by mean seemed the most reasonable criterion. (We note that the mean and median are nearly identical and selecting the median would not change results.) Our analysis yields the eight project-level findings.

1. Overall, participants rated projects that engaged one large offshore supplier higher than projects that engaged one small offshore supplier or multiple suppliers. Prior research has found that outsourcing to a single supplier, particularly under circumstances of high asset specificity, is riskier than using multiple suppliers.[8] However, multi-sourcing creates higher transaction costs than outsourcing to a single supplier.[9] Prior research has used the client as the unit of analysis.[10] Thus, these studies addressed the question, "Did/should the *client* engage more than one supplier?" At the client level, Biotech multi-sourced by engaging six offshore suppliers. But we viewed this research as an opportunity to ask the question at a project level: "Does the number of suppliers on a *project* matter?"

In addition to single versus multi-sourcing, we also examined the size of the supplier (large versus small). Practitioners and researchers have noted that size of suppliers affects their capabilities,[11] which, we reason, would affect a project's outcome. On the one hand, large suppliers would likely have better sourcing capabilities, economies of scale, and economies of scope to help them deliver successful projects.[12] On the other hand, small suppliers may pay more attention to the client because the client represents a larger portion of their revenues.[13] We did not conjecture whether large or small suppliers would have higher success rates, but instead viewed this research as an opportunity to investigate the effect of supplier size on project outcome.

Among the 21 projects, Biotech engaged one small Indian supplier on 12 projects, one large Indian supplier on five projects, and multiple suppliers on three projects. In addition, one project used Biotech's captive center in Bangalore. When mapping suppliers to project outcomes in Table 2.3, the two most definitive findings based on this analysis are:

1. Participants rated four out of five projects (80 percent) that engaged one *large* supplier above the mean project rating.
2. Participants only rated five of the 12 projects (42 percent) that engaged one *small* supplier above the mean project rating.

The participants provide insights to these findings. According to the participants, a major advantage of the larger suppliers was that they had greater access to experienced IT personnel. An IT lead with over 25 years with Biotech said:

> [The small vendors] would take forever to find resources with the skills and levels of experience we need. The small vendors did not seem to be able to attract and retain good people. That really hurt our

Table 2.3 Project rating vs. size and number of offshore suppliers

	Project rating		
Offshore supplier size	Number of more successful projects	Number of less successful projects	Percentage of more successful projects
One large supplier (greater than $1 billion in annual revenue)	4	1	80%
Multi-sourced	2	1	67%
One small supplier (less than $150 million annual revenue)	5	7	42%
Captive center	0	1	0%

projects – it took longer to ramp up and if there was unplanned turnover – we were dead. The larger vendors seemed to have a much deeper bench. Cycling on and off a project was much smoother with the larger vendors and we did not have to spend as much time explaining technologies or methodologies to them. Turnover seemed much less of an issue with the larger vendors.

One program lead expressed dissatisfaction with the smaller suppliers. In his experiences, the smaller suppliers lacked the experience to accurately bid and manage projects. He said:

> [The small supplier] just didn't get it. We estimated internally (using offshore rates) that a project we had pegged for offshore should cost about $80,000 and take about six to nine months. The supplier's bid was $40,000 and they estimated it would take four months. I wanted an accurate estimate of the effort and time it would take, more so than just trying to get the lowest dollar I could on the project. So I told the supplier they were significantly off in their bid and asked them to resubmit. The second bid came in at $60,000 with a timeframe of six months. By this time, we were already running behind schedule and needing to pursue offshore, so we accepted the bid. The supplier ended up spending an additional six months and we ended up fixing a lot of the code and doing the testing ourselves.

Table 2.3 also shows that participants rated two of the three multi-sourced projects above the mean project rating. Because only three projects were multi-sourced, we must be very cautious in deriving conclusions based on this data. However, the team lead SAP provided insight into the efficacy of using multiple suppliers on a project:

> You have to understand what the supplier wants and what the supplier brings to the table and how your project fits in. For example, [a large supplier] should bring in process expertise and great talent, but they aren't interested in my $5,000 little project. However, small suppliers are often hungry for business and can bring in specific skills. So, when we gave large, generic chunks of projects to the large vendors and smaller, more specific chunks to the small vendor, it worked pretty well.

2. Overall, participants rated projects with some offshore supplier employees on-site higher than projects with all supplier employees offshore. We defined the supplier-engagement model as the physical location of offshore-supplier managers and developers. Biotech used three supplier-engagement models to organize the 21 projects. The cheapest model in terms of hourly wages entailed having all the offshore-supplier employees (managers and developers) in India. This model was used on 12 projects. The most expensive model had some offshore-supplier managers and developers on-site. This model was used on five projects. The middle model had some offshore developers on-site, but no offshore supplier manager on-site. This model was used on four projects.

We cross-tabulated the supplier-engagement model with project rating. Table 2.4 shows that participants rated seven of the nine projects (78 percent) that had some supplier managers and/or developers on-site higher than the mean project rating. In contrast, participants rated four of the twelve projects (33 percent) that located all the supplier employees offshore higher than the mean project rating.

According to multiple participants, project managers at Biotech were under extreme pressure to keep projects costs low. Because any offshore supplier employee on-site is paid onshore rates (about $65 per hour versus about $25 per hour offshore), project managers were pressured to keep as much of the supplier headcount offshore as possible. However, some participants said that quality suffered when all of a supplier's employees were offshore because they did not understand Biotech's requirements and could not easily communicate with Biotech's IT staff and business users. Several participants concluded that an on-site engagement manager (OEM) and some on-site developers were needed to better understand and communicate requirements and thus ensure quality. According to a program lead:

> If this project was to be staffed by domestic contractors, we would have just added two new contractors. However, since we were new

Table 2.4 Project rating vs. supplier engagement model

Offshore supplier-engagement model	Project rating		
	Number of more successful projects	Number of less successful projects	Percentage of more successful projects
Some supplier managers and developers on-site	4	1	80%
Some supplier developers on-site but no supplier managers on-site	3	1	75%
No supplier managers or developers on-site	4	8	33%

to offshore, we priced in an OEM to interface between the business sponsors and the two offshore developers. We realized that all project cost savings were lost, but the OEM helped us improve our processes, interviewed and managed the developers and was responsible for status updates.

Project Q is another example in which participants viewed an on-site engagement manager as critical to success. Project Q required new development of Biotech's SAP systems. According to the team lead HR Services:

> SAP is a rather business-critical system around here, so we understand the risk. SAP is running our core business functions and it's doing it globally. So we already had the mentality of protecting our environment. And even though the OEM is expensive, they are worth it. They interface between our analysts and the offshore developers and save a lot of time and rework. They help to protect our environment.

3. Overall, participants rated projects with greater-valued contracts higher than projects with lesser-valued contracts. Practitioners have frequently told us that the more strategic a client account, the more attention the supplier will pay to the account. The two most important determinants of a supplier's perception of a strategic account are current revenues generated from the account and the potential for future revenues generated from the account.[14] We wondered: Does value of the contract matter?

We used actual dollars spent as the indicator of contract value because Biotech closely tracked these figures for each project. Using dollars spent, the contract values ranged between $4,300 and $1,363,098, with a mean contract value of $193,000 and a median contract value of $64,473.

For this analysis, we cross-tabulated contract value with project rating. Because the mean contract value ($193,000) is substantially different than the median contract value ($64,473), we analyzed both. Table 2.5 and Table 2.6 show the results.

Table 2.5 is based on the *mean* spend as dividing line between greater- and lesser-valued contracts. It shows that participants rated 71 percent of the greater-valued contracts above the mean project rating, compared to 43 percent of the lesser-valued contracts. Table 2.6 is based on the *median* spend as dividing line between greater- and lesser-valued contracts. It shows that participants rated 70 percent of the greater-valued contracts above the mean project rating, compared to 30 percent of the lesser-valued contracts. Thus, contract value mattered.

Table 2.5 Project rating vs. contract value using mean

Contract value	Project rating		
	Number of more successful projects	Number of less successful projects	Percentage of more successful projects
Greater value (greater than $193,000 mean spent)	5	2	71%
Lesser value (less than the $193,000 mean spent)	6	8	43%

Table 2.6 Project rating vs. contract value using median

Contract value	Project rating		
	Number of more successful projects	Number of less successful projects	Percentage of more successful projects
Greater value (greater than $64,473 median spent)	7	3	70%
Lesser value (less than the $64,473 median spent)	3	7	30%

4. Overall, participants rated larger-sized projects higher than smaller-sized projects. For over 25 years, IT researchers have recognized the relationship between project size, risk, and outcome.[15] In general, prior research has found that larger-sized projects are riskier and have lower success rates than smaller-sized projects.[16] For example, Carroll (2005)[17] found that small projects (less than six months) had a success rate of 50 percent, medium-sized projects (six to nine months) had a 40 percent success rate, and none of the projects in the sample (n = 22) over nine months were successful. Aladwani (2002),[18] in a study of 42 IT projects, found that project size negatively affects project planning, which negatively impacts project success. Practitioners and researchers suggest that large projects should be transformed into smaller projects through phased functionality, prototyping, or pilot testing to reduce risk and increase success.[19]

We wanted to determine the extent to which project size sheds light on Biotech's project outcomes. There are a number of ways to measure project size (lines of code, function points, duration in days or months, dollars spent, and man hours). We used duration of the project in days because Biotech's PMO closely tracked this number. (Biotech did not track total costs of the project, only the costs directly invoiced by the offshore suppliers.) Using duration, the project sizes ranged from 11 days long to 1,030 days long. The average project was 350 days long and the median project was 272 days long.

For this analysis, we cross-tabulated project size with project rating. We initially used three rules to categorize projects as "larger" versus "smaller." The rules were (1) Gudea's (2005)[20] cut-off of over/under one year in duration, (2) over/under the mean duration of 350 days, and (3) over/under the median duration of 272 days. However, rules (1) and (2) are coincidentally equivalent with our data. Table 2.7 and Table 2.8 show the results.

Table 2.7 is based on the *mean* and *one-year cut-off* as dividing line between longer (larger) and shorter (smaller) projects. It shows that participants rated 63 percent of the larger-sized projects above the mean project rating, compared to 46 percent of the smaller-sized projects. Table 2.8 is based on the *median* duration as dividing line between larger- and smaller-sized projects. It shows that participants rated 70 percent of the larger-sized projects above the mean project rating, compared to 30 percent of the smaller-sized projects.

Table 2.7 Project rating vs. project size using mean

	Project rating		
Project duration	Number of more successful projects	Number of less successful projects	Percentage of more successful projects
Longer (longer than one year)	5	3	63%
Shorter (less than one year)	6	7	46%

Table 2.8 Project rating vs. project size using median

	Project rating		
Project duration	Number of more successful projects	Number of less successful projects	Percentage of more successful projects
Longer (longer than 272 days)	7	3	70%
Shorter (less than 272 days)	3	7	30%

Some of the participants claimed that smaller-sized projects could not meet financial objectives because the transaction costs of dealing with the offshore suppliers swallowed the projected cost savings. Below are some of the quotes supporting this interpretation:

> On the smaller projects, the overhead costs of documenting some of the projects exceeded the value of the deliverables. (IT Lead)
>
> I think we used a shotgun approach with all these little projects. I think they were too small and too scattered to consolidate any savings or even any learning. You had people all over [Biotech] doing little projects and we could not capture any savings or any metrics. (Web Administrator)
>
> A lot of our projects were too small. We had one, maybe one and a half, resources working offshore and the overhead was killing us trying to keep track of what was going on offshore. (Program Lead)

Conversely, one IT team lead explained that larger projects allowed Biotech to recover overhead by benefiting from mounting experience:

> The larger projects I did seemed to work a little better. It took quite some time to figure things out, and with the smaller projects, they would end at that point. With the larger ones, we could use the learning and relationships we built for longer periods of time and improve as we went along.

5. Overall, some organizational units had higher participant-rated projects than other organizational units. During the interviews, it became apparent that some groups seemed to be experiencing more success with offshore outsourcing than others. As Figure 2.1 shows, six units report directly to the CIO. Five of these units engaged offshore suppliers for at least one project: Enterprise Architecture, ERP, R&D, Marketing, and Web.

Participants from five of the six units that report directly to the CIO managed at least one offshore project. Table 2.9 cross-tabulates these five units against project rating. Projects managed by the Web and ERP units all scored above the mean project rating. The most interesting finding, however, is that the R&D unit did the most offshore projects, yet participants rated only 30 percent of projects above the mean project rating.

The level of domain-specific knowledge required by these different units may explain the results. Some participants noted that projects within the R&D area required the supplier to have very specific scientific knowledge,

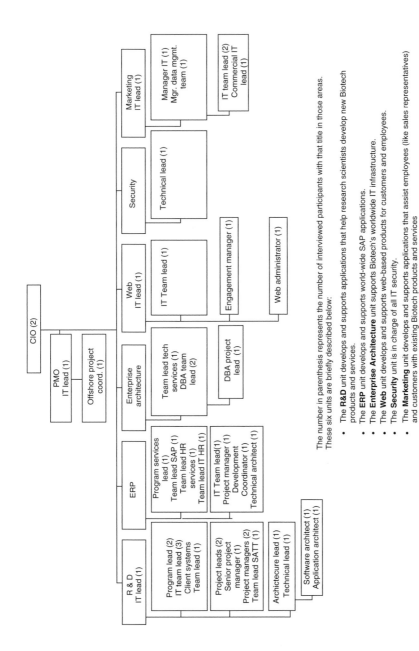

The number in parenthesis represents the number of interviewed participants with that title in those areas. These six units are briefly described below:

- The **R&D** unit develops and supports applications that help research scientists develop new Biotech products and services.
- The **ERP** unit develops and supports world-wide SAP applications.
- The **Enterprise Architecture** unit supports Biotech's worldwide IT infrastructure.
- The **Web** unit develops and supports web-based products for customers and employees.
- The **Security** unit is in charge of all IT security.
- The **Marketing** unit develops and supports applications that assist employees (like sales representatives) and customers with existing Biotech products and services

Figure 2.1 Organizational chart of Biotech's corporate IT department

Table 2.9 Project rating vs. organizational unit

Organizational unit within Biotech	Project rating		
	Number of more successful projects	Number of less successful projects	Percentage of more success-ful projects
Web	3	0	100%
ERP	2	0	100%
Marketing	3	2	60%
R&D	3	7	30%
Enterprise architecture	0	1	0%

whereas the Web and ERP units required more common knowledge. According to an IT lead in the R&D area:

> What makes some of this [offshore outsourcing] hard is that we are making up the questions at the same time we are asking the supplier to come up with answers. We are inventing new products with highly scientific processes and foundations. In our area, we are really "out there" in regards to the kinds of things we are creating

Conversely, all of the projects in the less scientifically intense areas of Web and ERP were rated above the mean. A team lead SAP explained:

> A lot of what we do in our area is more generic than in the [R&D] area. The bulk of our work is change requests to our SAP systems. The suppliers are well equipped in the SAP tools like ABAP. Once we accurately explain the specifications and modifications needed to fulfill the change request, the ABAP part is fairly straightforward.

6. Contrary to expectations, participants rated both development and maintenance/support projects equally. Prior IT outsourcing research has examined the types of IT work that clients outsource:[21] applications development and maintenance, systems operations, telecommunications, end-user support, and systems planning and management. In a survey of 188 IT executives, Popper and Zenger (1998)[22] found that type of IT work affected outcomes. Specifically, outsourcing of systems operations and telecommunications led to increased client satisfaction. They also found that outsourcing applications development and maintenance, end-user support, and systems management did not lead to increased client satisfaction. The researchers hypothesized a negative relationship between technological uncertainty and outsourcing satisfaction based on transaction cost economics (TCE). Based on all this research, we conjectured that the new software development projects would entail more uncertainty, and would thus contribute to lower project ratings, as predicted by TCE.[23]

For this analysis, we cross-tabulated project type with project rating (see Table 2.10). Based on prior research, we speculated that new development projects would have more risk and thus lower project ratings than projects involving maintenance or support of existing systems. However, evidence did not support this speculation. Overall, participants rated both development (53 percent) and maintenance/support (50 percent) above the mean project rating nearly equally. According to an interview with a software architect, it was evident that the type of project did not matter because all the work was new to the suppliers. He said:

> It really didn't matter the types of work we gave to the supplier. Even for what we considered to be routine, like maintenance, they had to learn the system, the tools and how we worked. Even though it was old to us, it was like new development to the supplier. For example, we have a Lotus Notes database to maintain, it was very difficult to find Notes experts. They had to learn the system from scratch.

7. Overall, participants rated recent projects higher than older projects. Based on prior research, we thought that earlier projects would have lower ratings than later projects. For example, researchers[24] found that more recent contracts had higher frequencies of success than older contracts. They attributed this finding to learning-curve effects. Three research studies on offshore outsourcing also found learning-curve effects.[25] All three studies found that clients use offshore outsourcing more strategically over time.

Table 2.10 Project rating vs. project type

	Project rating		
Project type	Number of more successful projects	Number of less successful projects	Percentage of more successful projects
New software development	8	7	53%
Support and/or maintenance of existing software	3	3	50%

Table 2.11 Project rating vs. project start year

	Project rating		
Project start year	Number of more successful projects	Number of less successful projects	Percentage of more successful projects
During 2003	6	8	43
During 2004 or 2005	5	2	71

For this analysis, we compared the project ratings for earlier projects, which were launched in 2003, against projects that were launched after 2003. Table 2.11 shows that participants rated 43 percent of the earlier projects above the mean project rating, compared to 71 percent of the later projects, indicating that organizational learning did occur.

Some participants stated that as projects and engagements matured, the quality of deliverables improved. For example, a team lead SAP in the ERP area said,

> It took us quite some time to figure out how different working with an offshore supplier was. We are very used to working with domestic contractors in a staff-augmentation model. Offshore is different. But, as time went on and the supplier helped to improve our documentation and requirements-definition processes, the change requests went more smoothly and our internal SAP consultants were better able to utilize the offshore resources. I am seeing much more bang for my buck now when compared to the beginning.

8. Contract type did not have enough variability to assess impact on project outcome. Researchers have found/argued that contract type is an important success factor in IT outsourcing. Contracts have been generally categorized as "classical," "neoclassical," and "relational."[26] In the context of IT outsourcing, contracts have been categorized as "standard contracts," "detailed contracts," "loose contracts," "mixed contracts," "buy-in contracts," or "partnerships"[27] or "fixed price" versus "time and materials,"[28] or "stage-by-stage" versus "two-stage."[29] Lacity and Willcocks (1998)[30] found that detailed contracts had the highest frequency of success. Lee, Miranda, and Kim (2004)[31] found that outsourcing was more successful when contract type was matched with IT strategy. Gopal *et al.* (2003)[32] specifically studied contracts with an Indian offshore provider. They found that contract choice significantly determined project profit. Lichtenstein (2004)[33] found that customers accept too much risk in contracts, compared to prescriptions from economic theories. Richmond and Seidmann (1993)[34] developed a mathematical model that argues that a two-staged contracting process leads to higher business value than stage-by-stage contracting. We wondered, "How does contract type affect project outcomes?"

At Biotech, however, we learned that there was no variability in contract type. Among the 21 projects studied at Biotech, 20 were time-and-materials contracts not to exceed a specified maximum amount. One project was managed through a captive center. Thus, we could not assess the affect of contract type on project outcome.

Thus far, we have explained Biotech's experiences with offshore outsourcing at the organizational and project levels. The next section points to learning from Biotech that may be valuable to other practitioners.

Lessons for clients and suppliers

The Biotech case offers four insights for clients and suppliers.

1. An offshore strategy must either fit with the client's organization's norms and practices, or the client may have to change norms and practices to achieve offshore success. Offshore suppliers often rely heavily on Capability Maturity Model (CMM) or Capability Maturity Model Integrated (CMMI) processes to ensure that business requirements are properly documented.[35] However, if their clients are operating at CMM/CMMI levels of two or below, the relationship may struggle with the issues experienced at Biotech. Suppliers may have to help clients improve their CMM/CMMI processes, or be flexible by finding ways to fit into the client's requirements analysis processes.

At Biotech, the "sneaker-net" culture and close social networks between business users, IT employees, and domestic contractors were a poor fit with offshore outsourcing. Within some project teams, Biotech participants changed the practices. Some Biotech project managers abandoned the "sneaker-net" process in favor of formal documentation of business, technical, and procedural requirements. Participants pursuing this option generally agreed that it facilitated knowledge transfer. According to a technical architect: "They [the offshore supplier] improved our internal processes. They all have been documenting procedures and processes. Now, we've got it so proceduralized that we've anticipated 90 percent of the questions."

But participants also complained that it significantly increased their project overhead. As previously noted, one IT lead said: "On the smaller projects, the overhead costs of documenting some of the projects exceeded the value of the deliverables." A software architect in R&D said: "We severely underestimated the amount of time and work it took to get the offshore team to understand first the needs of the users, then the tools we were using and then finally the capabilities we were shooting for."

2. Invest in social capital to facilitate knowledge transfer. Although Lesson 1 indicates the importance of process, a corollary to that lesson is that the people who perform the processes matter. Nahapiet and Ghosal (1998)[36] argue that social capital (such as social networks) helps to create intellectual capital (such as understanding user requirements). They also posit that organizations have an advantage over markets in creating and sharing of intellectual capital. Thus, maybe domestic contractors at Biotech performed better than offshore IT workers because domestic contractors are essentially insiders. We have one anecdote that suggests that offshore IT workers can essentially become "insiders" over time. A quote from an Indian project lead who has been a full-time Biotech employee for four years sums up the need for a greater understanding of the social networks in knowledge transfer:

> Communication was a real issue – even for me and I am from Mumbai. I found it hard during the conference calls to understand what they were saying, especially during the interviews and code reviews. And when we would send emails back and forth, I thought, "What are they trying to say, I don't understand where they are coming from." It would take two or three extra emails, just to make sure we were talking about the same things.

One good way to build social capital is to let the project team members meet face-to-face. It is much easier to switch to lower-cost media such as teleconferences and email after meeting people face-to-face. Some project managers at Biotech bore the cost of bringing the Indian developers onshore to meet Biotech employees face-to-face: "Once you get good at specking out what you need face-to-face, then an awful lot of the work happens by email and it's just follow-up questions, and lots of that happens by email" (global leadership team member).

The downside, of course, is the increased expense associated with face-to-face meetings. We do note, however, one IT team lead stated that meeting face-to-face solidified the team at first, but that "the team aspect fell apart" after the Indian workers returned to India. This suggests that social capital requires an ongoing investment to sustain benefits.

One of the best mechanisms for building sustainable social capital is to invest in on-site engagement managers. Biotech experienced significant challenges in transferring knowledge to the suppliers. The best solution to this challenge was to keep some supplier managers and developers on-site to build social networks. Unlike the "face-to-face" meetings suggested above, on-site engagement managers entail a long-term investment in social capital. Among the 21 projects, Biotech brought offshore supplier employees on-site for nine projects, of which seven scored above the mean project rating. Again, the benefit of this practice is that it facilitates knowledge transfer from user to offshore IT worker. Participants said it was worth the extra cost. In describing the on-site engagement manager used in the marketing unit at Biotech, a team lead said:

> He is talented, he knows his technology, is a good systems analyst and has good relationships with the team offshore. He's the one right now making a very cohesive environment. I think if we did not have a link there, we would be hurting. We have never had a situation where we've missed our deadlines for deliverables.

The drawback of this practice is that it increases costs.

Offshore suppliers must also protect knowledge after it is transferred. Because of increasing employee turnover rates,[37] Indian suppliers in particular must have good knowledge-management processes. Some participants at Biotech said that supplier turnover was a problem because when supplier employees left, they took the hard-earned, client-specific knowledge with them. An IT lead said:

> And the other thing, too, is their turnover rates. So those five-year guys on the offshore team, they're already looking to move. They're looking to move to a technical lead or architect or programming. And the opportunity is there. So, personally for them, it's a great opportunity, they could move at five years. And, so we can't even keep them on the offshore team.

Suppliers must find innovative ways to capture tacit knowledge by using, for example, video repositories, interactive training modules, mentoring, and shadowing to groom replacements.[38] In Chapter 4, we identify other practices to build social capital.

3. Clients may achieve greater success with bigger commitments. At Biotech, we found that the larger projects in terms of number of days and contract value had higher frequencies of success. We believe that this finding is attributable to (1) transaction costs and (2) supplier attention. Concerning transaction costs, offshore outsourcing has higher transaction costs associated with coordination, management, communication, and travel compared with insourcing or domestic outsourcing. In order to achieve total cost savings, the volume of work has to be large enough to compensate for the additional transaction costs. Of course, large commitments to offshore suppliers must be made cautiously, but the lesson may be that client managers should not expect significant cost savings while they are still conducting pilot projects and getting to know their offshore suppliers. It is only after progressing along the learning curve that service can be improved in terms of cost savings, quality, and speed.

Concerning supplier attention, it is no surprise that suppliers are motivated to allocate their top resources to their most prestigious clients. Prestigious clients commit large volumes of work over a long period time. Thus, the larger-sized projects and contracts at Biotech may have commanded more attention from their suppliers than smaller-sized projects and contracts.

4. Clients need robust measures to monitor and manage offshore outsourcing programs. Biotech's simple formula for calculating cost savings (cost of hours offshore versus what the hours would have cost onshore) disseminated the message that offshore outsourcing was successful. The PMO's official word that offshore was "successful" put pressure on participants to support senior management's "successful" agenda. As one software architect said, "You didn't want to tell them [senior management] the bad news too much. Because, this was their baby and you didn't want to say, 'You have a terribly ugly baby!'" Metrics that capture productivity, quality, process improvement, supplier compatibility, and organizational learning are needed to carefully manage offshore outsourcing. (See Chapter 1 for more on metrics.)

Epilogue

Like most first-time adopters with offshore outsourcing, Biotech is rethinking its strategy. Biotech is planning to migrate the strategic intent of offshore from "IS improvement" to "business impact."[39] According to the CIO, the plan is to reduce offshore outsourcing and increase the strategic role of the captive center (offshoring). This may seem illogical given that the project done at the captive center (Project D) was the lowest-rated project. However, the CIO now believes that he can best serve Biotech by helping his company sell Biotech products to the Indian market. He states:

> A set of IT Leads and I are heading to Bangalore soon and we plan to put a lot of energy into getting the captive center up to our internal standards. I know the captive center has a black eye with our internal users, but I see our development center there as a lever for increasing our exposure to the Indian markets. If we can get it running smoothly and then expand our headcount and visibility in India, that will help us to market and sell our products in a very large and growing market. I think showing the Indian government that we have a commitment to a large development center will go a long way to improving our relationship with India as an important customer to us.

As previously mentioned, three research studies on offshore outsourcing also found that clients use offshore outsourcing more strategically over time.[40] Both Carmel and Agarwal (2002)[41] and Rottman and Lacity (2006)[42] found that client organizations initially engage in offshore outsourcing to reduce costs, and then later use offshore outsourcing more strategically to increase revenues, access new markets, and to create agile sourcing networks.

Notes

1. We used a pseudonym because participants were guaranteed anonymity of their identities and the identity of their company.
2. Indeed, Biotech suffered an 8 percent drop in sales in 2002 and experienced net losses. Since 2003, both revenues and profits have increased.
3. Academics frequently use system use, system adoption, and system diffusion as indicators of success see Jeyaraj, A., Rottman, J., and Lacity, M., "A Review of the Predictors, Linkages, and Biases in IT Innovation Adoption Research," *Journal of Information Technology*, Vol. 21, No. 1, 2006, pp. 1–23. But these measures are more appropriate to assess from users. See Nelson, R., "Project Retrospectives: Evaluating Success, Failure and Everything in Between," *MIS Quarterly Executive*, Volume 4, No. 3, September 2005, pp. 361–72. Because our participants were project managers and team members, they were in a good position to assess budgets, deadlines, and quality of the product.
4. Nelson, "Project Retrospectives"; Standish Group International, CHAOS Chronicles V3.0, 2003. Available on: http://www.standishgroup.com/chaos/toc.php

5. Gudea, S., "IT Project Valuation Survey," posted on the Project Management Institute Website (2005), http://www.pmi.org/prod/groups/public/documents/info/pp_soringudea.pdf

6. Ang, S., and Slaughter, S., "Work Outcomes and Job Design for Contract Versus Permanent Information Systems Professionals on Software Development Teams," *MIS Quarterly*, Vol. 25, No. 3, September 2001, pp. 321–50.

7. ABAP (Advanced Business Application Programming) is the programming language for SAP, a leader in enterprise resourcing planning software.

8. Aubert, B., Dussault, S., Patry, M., and Rivard, S., "Managing Risk in IT Outsourcing," *Proceedings of the 32nd Annual Hawaii International Conference on System Sciences*, 1999, pp. 685–91; Currie W., and Willcocks, L., "Analyzing Four Types of IT Sourcing Decisions in the Context of Scale, Client/Supplier Interdependency, and Risk Mitigation," *Information Systems Journal*, Vol. 8, No. 2, April 1998, pp. 119–44; Gallivan, M., and Oh, W., "Analyzing IT Outsourcing Relationships as Alliances among Multiple Clients and Customers," *Proceedings of the 32 Annual Hawaii International Conference on Systems Sciences*, 1999, pp. 1–15; Williamson, O., "Comparative Economic Organization: The Analysis of Discrete Structural Alternatives," *Administrative Science Quarterly*, Vol. 36, No. 2, June, 1991, pp. 269–96.

9. Lacity, M., and Willcocks, L., Global Information Technology Outsourcing: Search for Business Advantage, Wiley, Chichester, 2001.

10. Chaudhury, A., Nam, K., and Rao, H., "Management of Information Systems Outsourcing: A Bidding Perspective," *Journal of Management Information Systems*, Vol. 2, No. 2, Fall 1995, pp. 131–59; Cross, J., "IT Outsourcing at British Petroleum," *Harvard Business Review*, Vol. 73, No. 3, May–June 1995, pp. 94–102; Gallivan and Oh, "Analyzing IT Outsourcing Relationships as Alliances among Multiple Clients and Customers."

11. Levina, N., and Ross, J., "From the Vendor's Perspective: Exploring the Value Proposition in Information Technology Outsourcing," *MIS Quarterly*, Vol. 27, No. 3, September 2003, pp. 331–64; Martorelli, W., Moore, S., McCarthy, J., and Brown, A., "Indian Offshore Suppliers: The Second Tier," Forrester Research Report, 14 July 2004, available at: http://www.forrester.com/Research/Document/Excerpt/0,7211,34847,00.html; Moore, S., Martorelli, W., and Brown, A., "Indian Offshore Suppliers: The Market Leaders., 8 April 2004, Forrester Research

Report, available at: http://www.forrester.com/Research/Document/Excerpt/0,7211,34181,00.html

12. Feeny, D., Lacity, M., and Willcocks, L., "Taking the Measure of Outsourcing Providers," *Sloan Management Review*, Vol. 46, No. 3, Spring 2005, pp. 41–8; Levina and Ross "From the Vendor's Perspective: Exploring the Value Proposition in Information Technology Outsourcing."

13. Feeny et al. (2005).

14. Feeny, D., "Managing IT Suppliers," presentation to UK Cabinet Office representatives, Said Business School, Oxford University, 28 February 2006.

15. Gopal, A., Sivaramakrishnan, K., Krishnan, M., and Mukhopadhyay, T., "Contracts in Offshore Software Development: An Empirical Analysis," *Management Science*, Vol. 49, No. 12, December 2003, pp. 1671–83; Keil, M., Rai, A., Mann, J., and Zhang, G., "Why Software Projects Escalate: The Importance of Project Management Constructs," *IEEE Transactions on Engineering Management*, Vol. 50, No. 3, 2003, pp. 251–61; Keil, M., and Montealegre, R., "Cutting Your Losses: Extricating Your Organization When A Big Project Goes Awry," *Sloan Management Review*, Vol. 41, No. 3, Spring 2000, pp. 55–68; McFarlan, F. W., "Portfolio Approach to Information Systems," *Harvard Business Review*, Vol. 59, No. 5, September–October 1981, pp. 142–50; Wallace, L., Keil, M., and Rai, A., "How Software Project Risk Affects Project Performance: An Investigation of the Dimensions of Risk and an Exploratory Model," *Decision Sciences*, Vol. 35, No. 2, Spring 2004, pp. 289–322.

16. Jones, C., *Assessment and Control of Software Risks*, Prentice-Hall, Englewood Cliffs, NJ, 1994.

17. Carroll, J., "The John Carroll Research Survey Results," Project Management Institute, 2005, available on: http://www.pmi.org/Prod2/groups/public/documents/info/pp_carroll.pdf

18. Aladwani, A., "IT Project Uncertainty, Planning, and Success," *Information Technology & People*, Vol. 15, No. 3, 2002, pp. 210–37.

19. Jones, *Assessment and Control of Software Risks*; Standish Group International, CHAOS Chronicles V3.0; Willcocks, L., Feeny, D., and Islei, G. (eds), *Managing IT as a Strategic Resource*, McGraw Hill, London, 1997.

20. Gudea, "IT Project Valuation Survey."

21. Ang, S. and Straub, D., "Production and Transaction Economies and Information Systems Outsourcing – A Study of the US Banking Industry," *MIS Quarterly*, Vol. 22, No. 4, 1998, pp. 535–52; Grover, V.,

Cheon, M., and Teng, J., "The Effect of Service Quality and Partnership on the Outsourcing of Information Systems Functions," *Journal of Management Information Systems*, Vol. 12, No. 4, Spring 1996, pp. 89–119.

22. Poppo, L. and Zenger, T., "Testing Alternative Theories of the Firm: Transaction Cost, Knowledge-based, and Measurement Explanations for Make-or-buy Decisions in Information Services," *Strategic Management Journal*, Vol. 19, 1998, pp. 853–77.

23. Williamson, "Comparative Economic Organization."

24. Lacity, M., and Willcocks, L., "An Empirical Investigation of Information Technology Sourcing Practices: Lessons from Experience," *MIS Quarterly*, September, Vol. 22, No. 3, September 1998, pp. 363–408.

25. Carmel, E. and Agarwal, R., "The Maturation of Offshore Sourcing of Information Technology Work," *MIS Quarterly Executive*, Vol. 1, No. 2, June 2002, pp. 65–77; Kaiser, K., and Hawk, S., "Evolution of Offshore Software Development: From Outsourcing to Co-Sourcing," *MIS Quarterly Executive*, Vol. 3, No. 2, June 2004, pp. 69–81; Rottman, J., and Lacity, M., "Proven Practices for Effectively Offshoring IT Work," *Sloan Management Review*, Vol. 47, No. 3, Spring 2006, pp. 56–63.

26. O. Williamson, "Transaction Cost Economics: The Governance of Contractual Relations," *Journal of Law and Economics*, Vol. 22, No. 2, October 1979, pp. 233–61.

27. Lacity and Willcocks, "An Empirical Investigation of Information Technology Sourcing Practices"; Lee, J., Miranda, S., and Kim, Y., "IT Outsourcing Strategies: Universalistic, Contingency, and Configurational Explanations of Success," *Information Systems Research*, Vol. 15, No. 2, June 2004, pp. 110–31.

28. Gopal *et al.*, "Contracts in Offshore Software Development"; Lichtenstein, Y., "Puzzles in Software Development Contracting," *Communications of the ACM*, Vol. 47, 2, February 2004, pp. 61–5.

29. Richmond, W., and Seidmann, A., "Software Development Outsourcing Contract: Structure and Business Value," *Journal of Management Information Systems*, Vol. 10, No. 1, Summer 1993, pp. 57–72.

30. Lacity and Willcocks, "An Empirical Investigation of Information Technology Sourcing Practices."

31. Lee, Miranda, and Kim, "IT Outsourcing Strategies."

32. Gopal *et al.*, "Contracts in Offshore Software Development."

33. Lichtenstein, "Puzzles in Software Development Contracting."

34. Richmond and Seidman, "Software Development Outsourcing Contract."

35. Adler, P., McGarry, F., Talbot, W., and Binney, D., "Enabling Process Discipline: Lessons from the Journey to CMM Level 5," *MIS Quarterly Executive*, Vol. 4, No. 1, March 2005, pp. 215–27.

36. Nahapiet, J., and Ghosal, S., "Social Capital, Intellectual Capital, and the Organizational Advantage," *Academy of Management Review*, Vol. 23, No. 2, 1998, pp. 242–65.

37. McCue, A., "Outsourcing Flops Blamed on Tunnel Vision," Silicon. com, published on ZDNet News: 22 June 2005, available on: http://news. zdnet.com/2100-9589_22-5757832.html; Srivastava, S., "Could Rising Wages Diminish India's Outsourcing Edge?" News Report, Siliconeer, 21 January 2005, available on: http://news.pacificnews.org/news/view_ article.html?article_id=167d1c86c1d28e7607c942fd9891938e

38. Rottman, J., "Successfully Outsourcing Embedded Software Development," *IEEE Computer*, Vol. 39, No. 1, January 2006, pp. 55–61.

39. DiRomualdo, A., and Gurbaxzni, V., "Strategic Intent for IT Outsourcing," *Sloan Management Review*, Vol. 39, No. 4, Summer 1998, pp. 67–80.

40. Carmel and Agarwal, "The Maturation of Offshore Sourcing of Information Technology Work"; Kaiser and Hawk, "Evolution of Offshore Software Development"; Rottman and Lacity, "Proven Practices for Effectively Offshoring IT Work."

41. *Ibid.*

42. Rottman and Lacity, "Proven Practices for Effectively Offshoring IT Work."

References

Adler, P., McGarry, F., Talbot, W., and Binney, D., "Enabling Process Discipline: Lessons from the Journey to CMM Level 5," *MIS Quarterly Executive*, Vol. 4, No. 1, March 2005, pp. 215–27.

Aladwani, A., "IT Project Uncertainty, Planning, and Success," *Information Technology & People*, Vol. 15, No. 3, 2002, pp. 210–37.

Ang, S., and Slaughter, S., "Work Outcomes and Job Design for Contract Versus Permanent Information Systems Professionals on Software Development Teams," *MIS Quarterly*, Vol. 25, No. 3, September 2001, pp. 321–50.

Ang, S., and Straub, D., "Production and Transaction Economies and Information Systems Outsourcing – A Study of the US Banking Industry," *MIS Quarterly*, Vol. 22, No. 4, 1998, pp. 535–52.

Aubert, B., Dussault, S., Patry, M., and Rivard, S., "Managing Risk in IT Outsourcing," *Proceedings of the 32nd Annual Hawaii International Conference on System Sciences*, 1999, pp. 685–91.

Carmel, E., and Agarwal, R., "The Maturation of Offshore Sourcing of Information Technology Work," *MIS Quarterly Executive*, Vol. 1, No. 2, June 2002, pp. 65–77.

Carroll, J., "The John Carroll Research Survey Results," Project Management Institute, 2005, available on: http://www.pmi.org/Prod2/groups/public/documents/info/pp_carroll.pdf

Chaudhury, A., Nam, K., and Rao, H., "Management of Information Systems Outsourcing: A Bidding Perspective," *Journal of Management Information Systems*, Vol. 2, No. 2, Fall 1995, pp. 131–59.

Cross, J., "IT Outsourcing at British Petroleum," *Harvard Business Review*, Vol. 73, No. 3, May–June 1995, pp. 94–102.

Currie, W., and Willcocks, L., "Analyzing Four Types of IT Sourcing Decisions in the Context of Scale, Client/Supplier Interdependency, and Risk Mitigation," *Information Systems Journal*, Vol. 8, No. 2, April 1998, pp. 119–44.

DiRomualdo, A., and Gurbaxzni, V., "Strategic Intent for IT Outsourcing," *Sloan Management Review*, Vol. 39, No. 4, Summer 1998, pp. 67–80.

Feeny, D., "Managing IT Suppliers," presentation to UK Cabinet Office representatives, Said Business School, Oxford University, 28 February 2006.

Feeny, D., Lacity, M., and Willcocks, L., "Taking the Measure of Outsourcing Providers," *Sloan Management Review*, Vol. 46, No. 3, Spring 2005, pp. 41–8.

Gallivan, M., and Oh, W., "Analyzing IT Outsourcing Relationships as Alliances among Multiple Clients and Customers," *Proceedings of the 32 Annual Hawaii International Conference on Systems Sciences*, 1999, pp. 1–15.

Gopal, A., Sivaramakrishnan, K., Krishnan, M., and Mukhopadhyay, T., "Contracts in Offshore Software Development: An Empirical Analysis," *Management Science*, Vol. 49, No. 12, December 2003, pp. 1671–83.

Grover, V., Cheon, M., and Teng, J., "The Effect of Service Quality and Partnership on the Outsourcing of Information Systems Functions," *Journal of Management Information Systems*, Vol. 12, No. 4, Spring 1996, pp. 89–119.

Gudea, S., "IT Project Valuation Survey," posted on the Project Management Institute Website (2005), http://www.pmi.org/prod/groups/public/documents/info/pp_soringudea.pdf

Jeyaraj, A., Rottman, J., and Lacity, M., "A Review of the Predictors, Linkages, and Biases in IT Innovation Adoption Research," *Journal of Information Technology*, Vol. 21, No. 1, 2006, pp. 1–23.

Jones, C., *Assessment and Control of Software Risks*, Prentice-Hall, Englewood Cliffs, NJ, 1994.

Kaiser, K., and Hawk, S., "Evolution of Offshore Software Development: From Outsourcing to Co-Sourcing," *MIS Quarterly Executive*, Vol. 3, No. 2, June 2004, pp. 69–81.

Keil, M., and Montealegre, R., "Cutting Your Losses: Extricating Your Organization When A Big Project Goes Awry," *Sloan Management Review*, Vol. 41, No. 3, Spring 2000, pp. 55–68.

Keil, M., Rai, A., Mann, J., and Zhang, G., "Why Software Projects Escalate: The Importance of Project Management Constructs," *IEEE Transactions on Engineering Management*, Vol. 50, No. 3, 2003, pp. 251–61.

Lacity, M., and Willcocks, L., "An Empirical Investigation of Information Technology Sourcing Practices: Lessons from Experience," *MIS Quarterly*, September, Vol. 22, No. 3, September 1998, pp. 363–408.

Lacity, M., and Willcocks, L., *Global Information Technology Outsourcing: Search for Business Advantage*, Wiley, Chichester, 2001.

Lee, J., Miranda, S., and Kim, Y., "IT Outsourcing Strategies: Universalistic, Contingency, and Configurational Explanations of Success," *Information Systems Research*, Vol. 15, No. 2, June 2004, pp. 110–31.

Levina, N., and Ross, J., "From the Vendor's Perspective: Exploring the Value Proposition in Information Technology Outsourcing," *MIS Quarterly*, Vol. 27, No. 3, September 2003, pp. 331–64.

Lichtenstein, Y., "Puzzles in Software Development Contracting," *Communications of the ACM*, Vol. 47, No. 2, February 2004, pp. 61–5.

Martorelli, W., Moore, S., McCarthy, J., and Brown, A., "Indian Offshore Suppliers: The Second Tier," Forrester Research Report, 14 July 2004, available at: http://www.forrester.com/Research/Document/Excerpt/0,7211,34847,00.html

McCue, A., "Outsourcing Flops Blamed on Tunnel Vision," Silicon.com, published on ZDNet News: 22 June 2005, available on: http://news.zdnet.com/2100-9589_22-5757832.html

McFarlan, F.W., "Portfolio Approach to Information Systems," *Harvard Business Review*, Vol. 59, No. 5, September–October 1981, pp. 142–50.

Moore, S., Martorelli, W., and Brown, A., "Indian Offshore Suppliers: The Market Leaders," 8 April 2004, Forrester Research Report, available at: http://www.forrester.com/Research/Document/Excerpt/0,7211,34181,00.html

Nahapiet, J., and Ghosal, S., "Social Capital, Intellectual Capital, and the Organizational Advantage," *Academy of Management Review*, Vol. 23, No. 2, 1998, pp. 242–65.

Nelson, R., "Project Retrospectives: Evaluating Success, Failure and Everything in Between," *MIS Quarterly Executive*, Volume 4, No. 3, September 2005, pp. 361–72.

Poppo, L., and Zenger, T., "Testing Alternative Theories of the Firm: Transaction Cost, Knowledge-based, and Measurement Explanations for Make-or-buy Decisions in Information Services," *Strategic Management Journal*, Vol. 19, 1998, pp. 853–77.

Richmond, W., and Seidmann, A., "Software Development Outsourcing Contract: Structure and Business Value," *Journal of Management Information Systems*, Vol. 10, No. 1, Summer 1993, pp. 57–72.

Rottman, J., "Successfully Outsourcing Embedded Software Development," *IEEE Computer*, Vol. 39, No. 1, January 2006, pp. 55–61.

Rottman, J., and Lacity, M., "Proven Practices for Effectively Offshoring IT Work," *Sloan Management Review*, Vol. 47, No. 3, Spring 2006, pp. 56–63.

Srivastava, S., "Could Rising Wages Diminish India's Outsourcing Edge?" News Report, Siliconeer, 21 January 2005, available on: http://news.pacificnews.org/news/view_article.html?article_id=167d1c86c1d28e76 07c942fd9891938e

Standish Group International, CHAOS Chronicles V3.0, 2003. Available on: http://www.standishgroup.com/chaos/toc.php

Wallace, L., Keil, M., and Rai, A., "How Software Project Risk Affects Project Performance: An Investigation of the Dimensions of Risk and an Exploratory Model," *Decision Sciences*, Vol. 35, No. 2, Spring 2004, pp. 289–322.

Willcocks, L., Feeny, D., and Islei, G. (eds), *Managing IT as a Strategic Resource*, McGraw Hill, London, 1997.

Williamson, O., "Transaction Cost Economics: The Governance of Contractual Relations," *Journal of Law and Economics*, Vol. 22, No. 2, October 1979, pp. 233–61.

Williamson, O., "Comparative Economic Organization: The Analysis of Discrete Structural Alternatives," *Administrative Science Quarterly*, Vol. 36, No. 2, June, 1991, pp. 269–96.

CHAPTER 3

A client's offshore outsourcing program becomes institutionalized

Mary Lacity and Joseph Rottman

Introduction

In Chapter 1, we presented the four phases of the offshore learning curve. We noted that the most mature customers in Phase IV typically pursue one of two strategies for offshore. Either, (1) offshore outsourcing becomes institutionalized or (2) offshore outsourcing actively contributes to corporate strategy. In this chapter, we present a Fortune 500 retail company that has been offshore outsourcing since 1997. Retail's ten years of offshore outsourcing has become "institutionalized," meaning that global sourcing is deeply embedded and accepted in the organization. Clients who primarily want to use offshore suppliers to lower costs, to do more work with a flat IT budget, and to keep internal headcount steady by using offshore suppliers to manage fluctuations in demand for services will benefit from reading this chapter.

This chapter explains the lessons learned during Retail's entire journey through the learning curve. Back in 1997 when Retail engaged their first Indian supplier to help with Y2K, Retail's IT managers did not perceive the selection of an Indian supplier as a radical new model called "offshoring" – the Indian supplier was just another preferred contractor (Phase II). Retail continued to use this supplier as its only Indian supplier for six years. By all accounts the relationship was successful in terms of lowering IT costs and producing high-quality work (Phase III). By 2002, however, Retail's CIO thought it prudent to use multiple offshore suppliers and engaged two more Indian suppliers and one Filipino supplier (Phase IV). Currently, Retail spends about $4 million per year on offshore outsourcing, which represents about 2 percent of their $200 million annual IS budget.

Throughout the course of their ten-year history, Retail learned many lessons about managing offshore suppliers. This chapter highlights lessons learned from Retail (and other client companies) pertaining to two broad areas:

1. The selection and use of six fee-for-service engagement models. As noted in Chapter 1, with fee-for-service offshoring outsourcing, the customer signs a contract with an external service provider that bases some resources offshore. In this chapter we present six engagement models for enacting the fee-for-service approach. Lessons focus on matching the right engagement model to the type of IT work, client capabilities and supplier capabilities. These lessons are high level and targeted towards CIOs, program management officers, and applications directors.

2. The changes to the project manager's role when offshore suppliers are engaged. This section presents lessons from the trenches. Whereas offshore strategies are set by senior IT leaders, it is the project managers who are most impacted by offshore outsourcing. How do project managers' roles change? What new processes and practices do project managers need to learn? A senior development director best captures the overall message from this section: "Where it is managed very closely, it works very well. Where it is not managed closely, we suffer."

Research base

The research base for the Retail case study included interviews with the CIO, three of his direct reports responsible for major application areas, application development managers, and the head of the Program Management Office. We also had access to many documents, including statements of work, status reports, organizational charts, and the reports from the offshore outsourcing task force. The people interviewed for this case uncovered many challenges with offshore outsourcing. However, it is important to keep in mind that their overall view of offshore outsourcing was still quite positive. We asked interviewees to rate the overall supplier performance on their two largest projects, and the average scores were quite high – 6.25 on a 7 point scale where a 7 indicated "extremely high" and a 1 indicated "extremely low." Overall quality scores averaged 5.75. Overall average cost savings were reported to be between 20 percent and 30 percent. Because of its success, Retail has gradually increased the use of offshore outsourcing every year.

We begin with a brief background on Retail's business and IT department to set the context for Retail's decision to engage offshore suppliers.

1997–2002: Retail sole sources to an Indian supplier

Retail is a Fortune 500 US-based retailer with over 1,000 retail stores in North America. Retail also sells products through Internet-based and paper-based catalogues. The company employs over 100,000 people. During the past ten years, financial performance has been strong, with the exception of one year of financial losses.

The IT department, with over 1,000 IT employees, is centralized and resides on Retail's sprawling corporate campus. The CIO reports directly to the CEO. The IT department is organized to mirror the two major business units (retail stores and catalogue sales) and to provide supporting IT services. The CIO has four direct reports in charge of (1) retail store systems, (2) catalogue and Internet systems, (3) corporate systems (infrastructure and support), and (4) a CTO in charge of technologies. Three of the CIO's direct reports participated in this research study and all three use offshore outsourcing within their areas.

The IT department has a very strong culture of hiring for life. Most IT employees are hired directly out of college and spend their entire careers at this company. Indeed, the people we interviewed had been with Retail for between 16 and 29 years, with the exception of one applications development manager who was hired for her offshoring expertise in 2003. Overall, turnover is low and morale is high within the IT department. This strong culture is one reason why offshore outsourcing did not threaten the internal staff, except as noted below during the 2004 anti-offshoring election propaganda.

To keep the number of internal IT employees stable, Retail's IT department has always used domestic contractors to meet temporary resource needs or to supplement in-house skill sets. On average, about 10 percent of Retail's IT department has been staffed by domestic contractors. These domestic contractors work on-site, side-by-side with internal IT employees. Retail hires the contractors through domestic contracting firms. In 1997, Retail had relationships with 35 such firms, although some of these firms only sourced one or two contractors to Retail. Their largest domestic contracting firm sourced 40 contractors.

Offshoring begins in 1997 for Y2K

As with many large US companies, Retail began looking offshore in preparation for Y2K. With 6 million lines of COBOL code to make Y2K compliant, the director of IS services at the time knew that additional manpower was needed to tackle the problem. He did not want to hire new IT employees to meet the temporary surge in demand caused by Y2K. Domestic contractors were in short supply and expensive because many companies were facing the same short-term need. In 1997, the director of IS services considered the possibility of an Indian-based supplier to help with Y2K. At that time, there were few Indian suppliers that were able to handle the large volume of work. He found one Indian supplier with enough manpower to do the work. (As of 2007, this Indian supplier has grown to be among the top five Indian suppliers.) He simply treated the Indian supplier as he did domestic contracting firms, by adding the Indian supplier to Retail's list of preferred suppliers. ***Thus, back in 1997, Retail did not really perceive the selection of an Indian supplier as a radical new model called "offshoring" – the Indian supplier was just another preferred contracting firm.***

The introduction of the Indian supplier did not cause a panic among the Retail's IT staff. Certainly no one feared losing their job because of Retail's "hire for life" culture. Indeed, the staff was relieved to have the help. Retail's project managers did not worry much about the fact that the Y2K supplier was based in India. According to a senior development director, who was a project manager at the time, project managers whose applications needed Y2K fixes were told to direct Y2K work to the Indian supplier. Just as some domestic contractors specialized in certain types of IT work, the Indian supplier specialized in Y2K.

Nearly every person interviewed for this case recalled that Retail had very positive experiences with the Indian supplier on the Y2K project. Everyone said that the supplier was extremely cooperative and competent. Retail was certainly a prestigious customer for the Indian supplier seeking to grow their business. As will be shown, this "high-status" account certainly explains some of the extraordinary levels of commitment the Indian supplier made to Retail on subsequent projects.

The Indian supplier is given a technology upgrade project in 1999

Before the Y2K project was complete, another project surfaced that needed immediate attention. Retail desperately needed a version upgrade to the mainframe CICS systems. No new business functionality was required, but it required considerable technical work to complete the upgrade. At first, Retail tried to use a fourth-generation language to expedite the upgrade, but that tool was wrought with significant technical problems. The director of IS then engaged the Indian supplier (called Supplier A) to tackle the CICS upgrade.

The CICS project was priced differently from Y2K, and indeed differently than from any of Retail's projects with domestic contracting firms. Previously, Retail had only used the time and material, staff-augmentation pricing model. The CICS project was priced as a turnkey system. Retail was pleased with this pricing model:

> We really picked [Supplier A] due to their ability to do a turnkey on it. If we had done it domestically, at that point in time, at least in my area, we weren't in any relationship with a domestic provider where they would have provided a turnkey solution. Since this was strictly a version upgrade, we wanted to keep it cheap. But our main concern was: can we do it quick and can we do it without much interruption to anything? And, so we capitalized on some of those [Indian-supplier employees] who were here for Y2K. So, they had some familiarity with us and our procedures. And, they just kind of dovetailed that in with this migration and really made it a pretty seamless operation from our side and certainly the costs worked out very acceptably. (Senior Development Director)

Supplier A used 12 full-time people for three months to complete the project. The supplier managed the project using a 1:4 on-site/offshore ratio. According to the senior development officer, the CICS project was a huge success in terms of cost, quality, and speed.

The Indian supplier is given many more projects from 2000–3

Based on the early successes with Y2K and the CICS upgrade, Retail began to give Supplier A more projects. We discuss three projects to illustrate the range of the Indian supplier's capabilities. Whereas Y2K and CICS projects were technical and based on the supplier's existing technical expertise, newer projects required either new domain expertise or very new technical skills. These projects all encountered initial problems, but all parties learned from their mistakes, solved the immediate problems, and instituted practices to minimize such problems in the future.

1. The charge-on-receipt project. Retail changed its business process for paying clothing manufacturers. The old process required clothing manufacturers to send Retail an invoice for clothes delivered to Retail. Retail then matched the invoice against the receipt and purchase orders. As any accountant knows, the matching of purchase orders to receipts to invoices is a highly complicated process because of the many-to-many relationships. One purchase order has many line items requiring delivery to multiple sites, thus generating multiple receipts and multiple invoices. The new business process was simpler because Retail would send payment to preferred clothing manufacturers upon receipt of materials by matching receipts to a pre-priced purchase order. The new business process obviously required significant changes to the accounts payable and general ledger systems.

The project cost $500,000. The project had a very aggressive deadline of four months. This project was at first managed leaner than previous projects. Instead of the 1:4 on-site/offshore ratio, Supplier A used a 1:6 on-site/offshore ratio. Specifically, Supplier A had two engagement managers on-site and 12 developers offshore. Retail allocated only one internal project manager to interact with the Indian supplier's two on-site engagement managers.

Retail's IT project manager and Supplier A's two engagement managers attended all the customer-facing meetings. Because the Indian engagement managers seemed to understand what the requirements were, Retail's IT project manager did not write up detailed functional specifications. He merely asked, "Do you understand what is needed?" and the Indian engagement managers said, "Yes."

One main problem surfaced during development. Retail's internal project manager could not review all the work coming from offshore fast enough. One person we interviewed described the situation as having one glove to catch 12 balls, simultaneously thrown. Retail's project manager only checked a sample of the work. Because the samples were acceptable, he assumed the entire population of work was acceptable. There were some minor problems during testing, but the supplier quickly fixed them. The project was completed within four months.

When the software was installed, significant problems with the code quickly surfaced. Some business logic was wrong, some month-end processes were wrong, and some technical bugs emerged. Retail's IT managers had to freeze the application. The three parties involved – accounting, IT, and Supplier A – cooperated to fix the application within three months.

In a *post mortem* on the project, three important lessons were learned. First, Retail needed to devote more internal people to review the work coming from offshore. Second, Retail's IT managers learned that trust is not a substitute for sound software development practices. In fact, ***the high level*** *of trust among the parties was actually detrimental to quality control because trust was used as a substitute for rigorous documentation of requirements.* As one participant said:

> We had tremendous rapport between all three parties – the accounting center and us and [Supplier A]. We just said: if we're comfortable that we think we got it, we probably got it. And if we don't have it, we're all here to make it right. So, we just didn't realize how far off we were on that. (Senior Development Director)

Third, Retail learned to ask more specific questions to test the Indian supplier's understanding. There are cultural differences when it comes to communication. Superficial questions such as "Do you understand?" prompt superficial responses. To Supplier A, a "yes" to that question meant, "Yes, I hear what you are saying to me" not "Yes, I understand the user's requirements."

The parties agreed to adhere to better software development processes in the future rather than to rely on trust. *Where trust appropriately comes into an outsourcing relationship is the commitment to repair mistakes and resolve issues.* The Indian supplier showed a real commitment to Retail by not charging Retail for the three months'-worth of fixes. Even though the supplier obviously lost money on this project, they thought it was more important to invest in the relationship and to maintain their reputation.

Even though the charge-on-receipt project was fraught with problems initially, one positive consequence was that the accounting center managers got to know the Indian engagement managers and were impressed that Supplier A fixed the errors at their own expense. The accounting center was willing to give the project described below to Supplier A.

2. Bundles of discretionary maintenance for accounting. Retail's accounting center is staffed in a different state than the IT department. The accounting center's staff of 700 accountants were constantly frustrated with IT's inability to rapidly meet unique requests for reports or minor adaptations to accounting systems. The senior development director said these requests were low priority because they were under the category of "wants" rather than "needs." IT's work backlog was too large to quickly respond to the "wants."

In 2002, the senior development director came up with an idea. What if he, in cooperation with the accounting center, bundled three months'-worth of discretionary maintenance requests and gave those to the Indian supplier? All three parties – accounting, IT, and the Indian supplier – agreed.

Every three months, Supplier A gets a new bundle. Because the requests require significant domain knowledge, the parties agreed to an on-site/offshore ratio of 1:2. Supplier A was given an ongoing contract for three full-time employees. One Retail IT project manager works with the one Indian engagement manager, who then directs the two offshore employees. Supplier A had excellent technical skills for the accounting center's DB2, COBOL, and Visual Basic applications. Supplier A soon developed the accounting expertise to meet requirements. The only issue that surfaced on this project was that the accounting center did not allocate enough time for accountants to do acceptance testing. Once again, Retail was not ready to "catch" what the supplier was "throwing" from offshore. The accounting center remedied that problem by assigning more time for accountants to review Supplier A's work.

Overall, Retail's senior development director called this ongoing project a huge success. First, Supplier A costs less than if he hired domestic contractors to do this work. Second, the technical quality is high, as verified by Retail's IT project manager. Third, surveys to the accounting center indicate that deliverables are more stable and more timely. The most interesting outcome, however, is that the accounting center's requests have gotten more sophisticated, and each time Supplier A adapts. The senior development director used the metaphor, "They used to request a ten-speed bicycle, now they ask for a Harley!"

3. Data warehouse transformation. Retail's IT department was moving from one database technology platform (hardware and software) to IBM's Active Data Warehouse. Retail thought that the project could be completed within seven months using 25 people. The senior development officer asked Supplier A to bid on the project. Although the Indian supplier did not have experience with IBM's Active Data Warehouse, both the senior development officer and the Indian engagement manager thought they could rely on the Supplier A's CMM 5 processes and "can-do" attitude. The bid was accepted.

One issue that surfaced during development was that the mainframe was only available in India during the night. This would require nearly all of Indian's offshore team to switch to a night shift. Rather than complain to Retail, the Indian supplier changed from day shift to night shift within 48 hours! This really impressed the senior development officer: "That endeared them to me. They didn't make a big fuss. They didn't say, 'Hey – do you know what it takes for me to bring in a night shift?' No questions, no nothing" (Senior Development Officer).

Despite the efforts of both parties, the project was delivered nine months later than initially anticipated. There were two reasons for the delay. First,

Retail's initial estimates were too low – it really required about 35 full-time people for seven months. Second, like any new technology, there were technical issues with the platform. Overall, Retail thought the Indian supplier quickly learned the new technology: "The stuff that [the Indian supplier] was lacking, they more than made up for. They came around the technical learning curve fast" (Senior Development Officer).

The Indian supplier moves up the value chain

One consequence of the long-term relationships with Supplier A was that the supplier has moved up the value chain. Retail now uses Supplier A for work more advanced than coding, testing, and maintenance. Database administration (DBA) is one small example. Initially, Retail never considered an offshore DBA. But as Supplier A's employees began to learn Retail's environment and began to build a good record of performance, Retail starting giving them DBA work. Although somewhat cheaper than a US-based DBA, the offshore rate was still $85 per hour. But the main reason for selecting Supplier A's DBAs was quality of work. Assortment planning is another notable example of giving Supplier A more value-added work.

The assortment planning project. Retail had a major shift in strategy for determining the type and volume of products to stock in retail stores. For all of Retail's history, product selection was decentralized at the store level. Each store manager would look at Retail's product offerings and decide which products, colors, sizes, and numbers they wanted in their stores. In about 2000, Retail's senior leaders decided to centralize assortment. Retail needed a centralized assortment IT system to enable the change in business strategy. Initially, Retail tried to purchase a system from a small US firm that offered a Java-based forecasting tool for assortment, but the system lacked a front-end interface to feed the forecasts. The small firm promised to build the front end, but after two years, it was clear they would never finish. Retail bought the application and the source code the small firm had completed so far. Retail's internal IT staff had exceptional COBOL and Visual Basic skills, but they did not have the critical mass of Java expertise. However, Supplier A did. Retail engaged Supplier A to help build one of their critical business applications.

Retail managed the project internally but used 52 of Supplier A's staff. Because this application required significant domain expertise, Retail paid for 12 supplier employees to remain on-site. Supplier A's employees on-site included a program manager, two project managers (one for assortment, one for allocation), a quality-assurance person to further test code coming from offshore, a person dedicated to performance fine-tuning, and seven people who did initial research, directed offshore teams, and provided other boundary-spanning activities. Forty coders were offshore.

The project had weekly milestones. Retail's project managers were very pleased with the Supplier A's on-site team. "We have good metrics to show that the onshore people are actually catching any mistakes [from offshore]" (Senior Development Director).

Overall, the senior development director rated the project very highly. However, one negative consequence of the project was that Retail's internal team did not learn enough about the application to support it in production. Supplier A was given the maintenance contract. A development director said, "If something happens to Supplier A, God forbid, we'd be at a complete standstill."

From sole sourcing to multi-sourcing: 2003–6

From 1997 until 2002, Retail's good relationship with the Indian supplier continued. Retail expanded the relationship on a project-by-project basis by appending more statements of work to the master service-level agreement. However, in late 2002, the CIO and his management team sought to diversify their offshore supplier portfolio:

> At a strategic level, I am convinced that we have to have multiple suppliers. We try to avoid, religiously, architectures or any environments that are going to cause us to be solely reliant upon a single supplier. (CIO)
>
> Don't get me wrong. I've been extremely happy with [Supplier A]. Every project they have done has been basically on time and on budget and their quality is good. I just think we need to use competition to keep the vendors honest and keep rates competitive. (Director of Corporate Systems)

The PMO director, along with senior IT leaders, began looking for more offshore partners. They initially had a list of ten potential suppliers. Eventually this list was whittled down to two additional Indian suppliers (called Supplier B and C). Well aware of the intense competition for IT talent in India, Retail's IT leaders also broadened their search to alternative destinations. They examined nearshore options in Canada and Mexico, as well as rural sourcing within the US. They also considered alternate Asian destinations, including the Philippines and China. They finally selected a small Filipino supplier to test the capabilities of that country. The director of Corporate Systems said that Retail selected the Philippines because of the cultural similarities, "They're almost a US colony." In addition, he believed the IT workers in the Philippines are in abundant supply and have nearly equivalent technical skills when compared to India.

Retail's experiences with the new suppliers are explained below.

Supplier B over-promises and under-delivers

Retail's IT leaders thought that it might be best to launch a new relationship with Supplier B by assigning them projects based on the supplier's expertise in IT technology and call centers. Retail engaged Supplier B for two projects.

Retail hired Supplier B to convert a legacy system to a new technical platform. Supplier B said the conversion would be no trouble, and both sides agreed to a set deadline. According to the director of Corporate Systems, Supplier B failed on all points – the programs were late and the quality was poor. The deliverables failed acceptance testing. Retail ended up forcing Supplier B to put many more employees on the account – at Supplier B's expense – to successfully complete the project: "We made them fix it on their dime, which they did, but it was painful" (Director of Corporate Systems).

A second project required Supplier B to serve as the first-line response to a merchandising application hotline. The support was disastrous. Whenever a user called the hotline, all Supplier B did was page Retail's Tier 2 support person: "So we paid for an extra hop to India and back!" (Director of Development).

Retail's IT leadership forced Supplier B to remediate at their costs, transferred their own people to staff the help desk, let the contract run out, and never engaged Supplier B again.

Supplier C has a rocky start, but soon recovers

Retail's third large Indian supplier – Supplier C – was invited to bid on two projects. One project required Supplier C to customize the accounts payable module within Retail's existing ERP system. The other project required Supplier C to help Retail redesign an accelerated close process, then execute the changes prompted by the new design by modifying the ERP module. Retail's IT management was confident – based on Supplier

C's claims of vast experience with the ERP package – that they would be ready for an applications project rather than a purely technical project. However, Supplier C assigned a person who was just recently promoted to manage the account. Although he had never worked for a client the size of Retail, he assured Retail's IT manager that he had plenty of experience with the ERP package. Eager to please Retail, he would never tell Retail's IT managers when he did not understand something. Retail soon discovered that the engagement manager's ERP experience was limited to the general ledger, not accounts payable. Furthermore, he had only done *execution* for another client on accelerated close, not *process redesign*. Retail's IT management tried to be patient, but according to the director of Corporate Systems, the Indian engagement manager "bid on project X but we wanted project Y. This happened three times."

Finally, Retail's IT leaders called senior managers at Supplier C and demanded a new engagement manager. This request required several iterations of explanation and face-to-face meetings. Finally, after nearly three months from the initial replacement request, Supplier C acquiesced and brought in a very experienced engagement manager. Ever since that change, Retail has enjoyed a good relationship with Supplier C. "We've been very happy with Supplier C" (Director of Corporate Systems).

Results from multi-sourcing

As Retail's engagements with offshore suppliers continue to mature, senior IT leaders remain committed to multi-sourcing. Retail maintains primary relationships with Supplier A and Supplier C. Retail now asks Supplier A and Supplier C to bid for work, rather than automatically assigning work to a supplier based on a predetermined area of expertise:

> Our philosophy is we're trying to drive prices down with competition. With big projects, we do a bid process [between Supplier A and Supplier C]. And Supplier A and C now have to show why we would bring them in. If the value is the same, then it comes down to pricing. (Director of Corporate Systems)

The parallel story: domestic contracting prices drop and headcounts dwindle

As Retail began building good relationships with offshore suppliers, Retail's IT managers began to question the high costs of domestic contractors. Why should Retail pay $100 for domestic workers when it can get the near equivalent for $25 offshore? The head of the PMO began to leverage his Indian supplier relationships to get domestic contractors to lower their prices. Domestic contractors were forced to significantly drop their prices or lose the Retail account. ERP personnel costs dropped from $100 to $80 per hour. Other programming skills fell from $100 to as low as $55 per hour! Thus, domestic contractors were forced nearly to cut their rates in half to compete with the growing Indian-supplier competition.

After seven years of offshoring, the CIO began to more closely inspect the sourcing strategy. Clearly, the quality of work by Supplier A and C was high. The CIO reasoned that 35 percent of Retail's development work could be done with offshore suppliers. The question was how to get there:

> A lot of my counterparts [other CIOs] mandate how and when to offshore. We did not take that approach. I challenged my staff to do the analysis, create a model and set targets on what we could transition to so we could provide the best value equation back to the company. (CIO)

By 2004, the headcount for offshore contractors exceeded the headcount for domestic contractors. Table 3.1 was created in 2004 and projects that the employment of domestic contractors will all but evaporate by 2007. The projections, for the first time, also predicted a decline in the internal staff as a percentage of total headcount. No layoffs were planned; just more new work would be given to the offshore suppliers.

The timing could not have been worse. In 2004, the media began to portray offshore outsourcing as stealing American jobs. Offshore outsourcing became a major issue in the US presidential and congressional elections. Retail's IT staff – fully accustomed to offshoring since 1997 – began to

Table 3.1 Staff composition by headcount

	2004	2005	2006	2007
Internal staff	71%	70%	65%	59%
Domestic contractors	10%	5%	3%	3%
Offshore contractors	19%	25%	32%	38%

panic. Their reaction stunned Retail's IT management. The IT managers had to resell offshore outsourcing to the IT staff:

> I think the [IT staff's] reaction was, "We're losing American jobs and I'm going to lose mine." We pointed out that offshore outsourcing allows us to retain your job because it's lowering our prices. We have to find a better way to communicate that as we roll this out [the increased use of offshore outsourcing]. Who is losing is the domestic contractor. (Director of Contract Management)

In response to the question about the IT staff's concern, the CIO said simply, "When you start the conversation with 'we are eliminating zero jobs,' you can have a pretty short conversation."

Concerning the domestic contracting firms, Retail has been pruning relationships since its peak in the late 1990s from 35 domestic contracting firms to 14 in 2004, with plans to reduce to four suppliers by 2008. The pruning was handled carefully, with plenty of notice to domestic contracting firms.

Increasing the role of the PMO

In 2004, the CIO saw a need to increase the role of the Program Management Office (PMO). Until then, the PMO only had one dedicated person, with many ad hoc teams to address issues such as negotiating with a new supplier:

> Our Program Management Office is going to have to be more robust. You know, we have one dedicated resource to the PMO today and then a whole lot of ad hoc. I see us in the future with a group dedicated to the excellence in this area and managing not only the vendor assessment and acquisition and contract negotiations, but the project assignments, evaluations, and best practices. (CIO)

Concerning the tracking of projects, each Retail director was using their own systems to track project costs. Some directors used Microsoft Project, some used Excel spreadsheets, some used SAS, and some used combinations of these applications. The CIO wanted the PMO to implement a uniform, total cost of ownership approach to track projects, including an overall management dashboard.

Lessons learned on engagement models

Retail's longstanding use of offshore suppliers offers many lessons for client stakeholders. As noted in Chapter 1, there are many ways for clients to engage offshore suppliers within the fee-for-service approach. In our research, we found that fee-for-service engagement models can be quite complex, but can be generalized along a continuum of increasing supplier responsibility (see Figure 3.1). On the low end of supplier responsibility is a pure staff-augmentation approach in which the client treats their offshore staff as a substitute for domestic contractors. Anchoring the other end of the continuum is business-process outsourcing. With this engagement model, the offshore supplier is responsible for a discrete, end-to-end business process. Along the continuum are four other commonly used engagement models.

Retail offers a rich context for assessing each engagement model because Retail has used all six models identified in Figure 3.1. Seven years after the initial engagement with Supplier A, Retail's senior IT leadership created a task force comprising 21 Retail employees to evaluate the offshore outsourcing program. The team interviewed a total of 45 employees who had worked with the offshore suppliers. One of their responsibilities was to assess the overall effectiveness of six engagement models. As we discuss below, some of the task force's prescriptions were counter to the views of the people we interviewed. We extracted the principles that stakeholders agreed upon and depict them in Table 3.2. *The key learning point is that an engagement model not only must fit with the type of work, but also must match the client's capabilities and the supplier's capabilities.*

1. Staff augmentation engagements: offshore suppliers supplement in-house teams with staff located both on- and offshore. For this model, clients engage offshore suppliers to provide supplemental IT staff – such as engagement managers, developers, and programmers – to in-house teams. Typically, the contracts are based on time and materials (invoiced

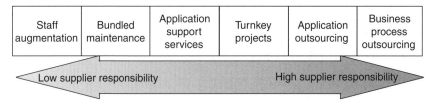

Figure 3.1 Fee-for-service engagement models

Table 3.2 Matching engagement models to type of work, client capabilities, and supplier capabilities

Engagement model	Description	Type of work	Client capability	Supplier capability
Staff augmentation	Offshore supplier supplements in-house teams with staff both on and offshore	IT work in which the requirements cannot be fully known upfront, but in which concrete tasks can be incrementally assigned to the supplier as requirements become more clearly defined	Client must learn to *manage* work, not people, but client must *monitor* invoices for people, not work	Supplier must commit to keeping a solid delivery team offshore and not use this approach as a training ground for new people at the client's expense
Bundled maintenance	Offshore supplier handles small maintenance items and minor requests handled through an IT intermediary	Non-critical applications for which users may want quick responses to minor items such as ad hoc reports to which the internal IT department lacks resources for timely response; maintenance work must entail enough offshore coding to generate overall cost savings	Client must commit to comprehensive knowledge transfer about the client's application and technical platform Client-side project manager must detail requirements before assigning work to offshore supplier	On-site engagement manager must be exceptional at business, people, and technical skills Offshore delivery team must have requisite technical skills
Application support services	Offshore supplier works directly with users and IT to support existing applications	Non-critical, stable applications with enough users and enough volume of transactions to gain economies of scale with outsourcing	Client must commit to comprehensive knowledge transfer about the client's business processes, application, and technical platform; client must know how to write a solid contract with strict service-level agreements	Entire supplier team with client-facing roles must have exceptional communication skills; supplier managers must have good succession planning to ensure knowledge is not lost

			Client requirements	Supplier requirements
Turnkey projects	Offshore supplier responsible for management and delivery of project	Purely technical projects (platform or programming language switches or upgrades) or application projects with very clearly defined requirements	Client can clearly articulate and detail comprehensive requirements upfront Client devotes enough internal people to review work coming from offshore Client ensures supplier will transfer knowledge about new system back to client	Supplier can submit realistic bids to ensure deadlines are met; supplier shares internal CMM/CMMI reports and updates with clients to forewarn of any problems
Application outsourcing	Offshore supplier responsible for IT systems associated with a business process	Non-critical, stable IT systems that can be moved physically, legally, and politically (Retail only used this model to support systems scheduled for elimination or replacement)	Client must commit to comprehensive knowledge transfer; client must know how to write a solid contract with strict service-level agreements	Supplier has strong application, IT, and domain knowledge capabilities
BPO	Offshore supplier responsible for entire end-to-end business process	Discrete business processes that have few interfaces to internal IT systems	Business and IT work together to define and craft contract	Supplier has deep domain expertise; supplier commits to standard processes where possible

each month) or based on a retainer model (the client pays $x in advance for y hours of work). Staff augmentation was the primary approach used by Biotech in Chapter 2. At that company, the staff augmentation model was a poor fit with Biotech's culture of close user/IT relationships and informal requirements gathering. Retail, however, had more success with this approach as discussed below.

When Retail uses this model, a Retail IT manager directs a team comprised of Retail staff and offshore-supplier staff. According to the offshore task force report, this model requires a change of mindset from managing people to managing work. The task force recommends that Retail's IT managers define specific tasks for the supplier employees and should ensure a steady stream of tasks so that the offshore team is never idle. Retail's IT managers should focus on testing the deliverables coming from offshore, rather than directly interacting with offshore team members.

According to some project managers, however, the transition from managing people to managing work sometimes backfired. Retail's IT managers who were responsible for large projects comprising 40 offshore team members said they needed to know exactly who was working offshore and for how many hours to properly verify supplier invoices. Some project managers said that this model motivated the supplier to staff the project with new hires because Retail subsidized a new supplier employee's learning curve. Also, supplier employees who were unproductive took more hours to complete tasks, again reflected in Retail's bill.

Thus, we see some different opinions among stakeholders regarding the client's capabilities to manage staff augmentation engagements. Their opinions can be reconciled with the statement: *for staff-augmentation engagements, project managers must learn to manage work, not people; however, project managers must also monitor invoices for people, not work.*

Concerning the main advantages of staff augmentation, all client stakeholders agreed that this approach enables (a) the ability to quickly ramp staff headcount up or down and (b) provides the easiest exit. Overall, the offshore task force rated this model as "has shown to be effective" provided the supplier doesn't start to replace offshore staff with inexperienced people.

2. Bundled maintenance engagements: the offshore supplier works with the client's IT leads to handle small maintenance items and minor requests for existing applications. This model requires significant upfront knowledge transfer from the client to the supplier about the applications and technical platforms. At Retail, this engagement model was managed by a technical lead from Retail to control the application architecture and design. The supplier's on-site engagement manager attended all client-facing meetings with Retail's technical lead to ensure that the supplier understood business requirements. The main advantage of this engagement model was the ability to refocus internal staff on more strategic activities. The main disadvantage was that cost savings only occurred when the maintenance required considerable coding that could be done offshore. Overall, the offshore task force rated this model as "viable" provided that expectations are clearly defined in the contract, including concrete service-level agreements.

3. Application support-services engagements: the offshore supplier works directly with users to support existing applications. This is the first model in which the offshore supplier works directly with users to support existing applications. Compared to the first two models, this model required more upfront investment in knowledge transfer from the client to the supplier. It could take one year before the supplier could independently handle the work.

Retail had mixed results with this model. One supplier proved to effectively deliver on this model. However, another supplier failed due to poor language skills (users complained they could not effectively communicate with their Indian support person), fire-fighting rather than planning, and frequent calls to Retail analysts for help (recall the disaster with Supplier B's merchandising application help line). When the engagement model worked, it helped to free up internal resources on more strategic work and provided support at a lower cost. Overall, the offshore task force concluded that this model "is attractive but we have had problems implementing in our environment." The task force provided five caveats to this model:

- The supplier on-site engagement manager must be exceptional.
- The supplier on-site engagement manager must attend meetings with business sponsors, users, and IT project managers.
- The support area must have enough coding work to ensure cost savings.
- Retail must communicate and enforce standards to ensure maintenance work does not harm the overall design or structure of the system.
- Retail and the supplier must plan for frequent knowledge transfer as supplier staff is rotated on and off the assignment.

4. Turnkey project engagements: the offshore supplier is responsible for the management and delivery of a predefined project. This model entails discrete engagements for a single, predefined project with specific deliverables from beginning to end. Because the price is typically fixed, the supplier can best decide how to staff the project to meet their contractual obligations while maximizing their own profit margin. The supplier is incentivized to put their most productive people on the project to increase their margin. Among our cases, this engagement model worked well when the client could provide detailed, realistic, and comprehensive requirement specifications to the supplier. Most of our companies could successfully do this only for purely technical work, such as platform upgrades or programming language upgrades. Retail was typical in this respect.

Retail used this engagement model primarily for technical projects, like COBOL version upgrades. If the Retail employees excelled at writing comprehensive specifications, then this model worked well. This engagement model was implemented with the highest percentage of offshore resources because requirements were defined and work was primarily technical. Thus, good cost savings was achieved with this model. The main disadvantages of this approach were that (1) Retail often lacked enough people to "catch" work coming from offshore and (2) Retail sometimes failed to learn about the new technologies and thus had to award the supplier a support contract after the development project was complete. For example, Retail's senior managers would not invest in new Java skills, so Retail's in-house staff could not support the new assortment planning system. Support went to the offshore supplier. Because of this risk, the offshore task force rated this model as "has shown to be effective" provided that the project requires standard offshore resources – not costly, highly specialized skills.

5. Application outsourcing engagements: the offshore supplier is responsible for supporting IT applications associated with a business process. When Retail used this model, Retail kept the business process and application hosting inside the client organization, but the entire support of the IT applications was outsourced. The supplier must excel at client-facing roles, must be willing to co-invest in knowledge transfer, and must have good succession planning to ensure knowledge is not lost due to either planned or unplanned supplier turnover. This option expands the bundled maintenance option to include service levels for call-center support, application response time, and application availability.

At Retail, this model is used on a very limited basis to support IT systems that are scheduled for elimination/replacement. By having the outsourcing supplier keep the application going in the interim, Retail can focus in-house resources on building the application's replacement. The offshore task force concluded that use of this engagement model should be "extremely rare."

Why doesn't Retail use this model more frequently when it is so prevalent in other organizations? According to the CIO, he has evaluated this model of outsourcing several times and concluded that Retail can do it cheaper than outsourcing providers. He also noted the difficulty of relying on suppliers for long-term technical provision: "The other factor against outsourcing is staying current with technology. What ends up happening with outsourcing, the technology becomes stale and there is no perfect way to get subsequent technology" (CIO).

Another possible explanation for Retail's limited use of outsourcing is the "Wal-Mart" effect. Nearly every large retail company perceives Wal-Mart as best-in-breed concerning strategic use of information technology. Retail's CIO noted that Wal-Mart considers IT to be a core competency and it avoids large-scale outsourcing because it wants 100 percent control over IT. In mimicking the practices of best-in-breed, Retail may also be predisposed against application outsourcing, particularly for core applications that support its retail and catalogue businesses.

6. Business process outsourcing (BPO) engagements: the offshore supplier is responsible for an entire end-to-end business process. The supplier typically owns, operates, and maintains all associated IT systems within the business process. The supplier must have deep domain expertise, a deep knowledge of supporting applications, and a commitment to providing standard processes to prevent cost escalation.

Retail uses this model on a limited basis for credit-card processing, payroll, and benefits administration. Retail, like other companies we studied, successfully used a BPO engagement model provided that the business sponsors and IT managers partnered upfront. In some cases, the business units bypassed Retail's IT department without realizing that the business process had a number of interfaces with other in-house IT systems. The offshore task force concluded that BPO can be effective, but that the "business must have an open dialog with IT on each of the processes they are considering outsourcing very early in the conceptual phase."

Summary of engagement models

Client firms have a variety of engagement models to consider when engaging an offshore supplier. We highlighted six models and discussed the model's fit with type of work and required client and supplier capabilities to realize each model's potential. Of course, we recognize that many companies mix models and that reality is more complex than depicted in Figure 3.1 and Table 3.2. We believe, however, that the general principles are sound, as experienced by Retail and our other client firms.

The next section shifts focus from managing the relationship at the engagement level to managing the relationship at the project level.

Lessons learned on project management

Whereas the decisions to engage offshore suppliers are made by the senior IT leadership, it is the project managers who are most responsible for making the relationship work on a daily basis. While project managers noted many positive experiences related to working with offshore suppliers, there were also new challenges. Client project managers often complained that their hours of work were considerably extended because of the offshore component. Many project managers went to work very early to attend conference calls. And project managers often felt isolated because they could not officially complain or be seen as rejecting senior IT leadership's offshoring initiative. This section addresses the specific changes to the project manager's role when offshore suppliers are engaged.

Project managers experienced several benefits from working with offshore suppliers

We begin with project managers' positive experiences with working with offshore suppliers. In general, project managers reported that offshore suppliers favorably contributed to their projects in four areas.

1. Faster staffing of projects. Most project managers we talked to – both at Retail and elsewhere – welcomed the offshore suppliers initially because their projects were staffed quickly: "Supplier C is great at finding people. Before them, I would be scrambling within Retail trying to find more people. Nobody had anybody available. So, I can just go to Supplier C and say send me three people and they are here" (Applications Development Manager).

A supplier's deep bench of available talent was certainly a positive attribute from the project manager's perspective.

2. Faster development when time-zone differences were coordinated. Some Retail IT project managers said that their projects were completed more quickly because of the offshore supplier. For example, one development director said his large system was built in three months with the help of an offshore supplier instead of the estimated six months for internal development. His project manager synchronized work so that the

Indian employees were working on the project while US workers slept, and vice versa. Although there were more bugs (in his opinion) with offshore than in-house development, the delays caused by fixing more bugs were still offset by an overall shortened development cycle. On this project, "follow the sun" development was possible because of good project management. However, other project managers found that time-zone differences hindered their projects. When the timing was not well coordinated, employees in India remained idle for an entire work day while waiting for the US team to respond to a query, review work, or update a database.

3. Access to scarce skills. At Retail, and in other client companies, project managers were delighted to have access to the offshore supplier's scarce technical skills. At Retail, for example, one development director noted that the large Java-based assortment planning application could not have been done without the offshore supplier. Retail simply lacked the critical mass of in-house Java programmers. The same was true of DBA skills, which are expensive and in short supply onshore.

4. Offshore supplier employees are bright and eager to please. Even though there are significant cultural differences to understand between US and India, nearly all US project managers noted that Indian employees are intelligent, pleasant, have good senses of humor, and are eager to please their clients, as shown by a sample quote from Retail: "Most of the Indian folks who worked for me during my career – they're very hard-working and very bright. I mean they really catch on and they do very well" (Applications Development Manager).

Changes to the project manager's role

Despite the many positive experiences of working with offshore suppliers, project managers were often unprepared for the changes required in their roles. Table 3.3 highlights the 20 major effects of offshore suppliers on the roles of project managers. The effects are categorized by six areas of concern: organizational support, project planning, knowledge transfer, CMM/CMMI processes, managing work, and managing people.

Organizational support for the project manager

Ideally, project managers should not be assigned to lead projects with offshore suppliers unless they have strong organizational support in the form of a helpful Program Management Office and extensive training on how

Table 3.3 Effects of offshore suppliers on project managers

Area of concern	Effects of offshore suppliers on project manager's roles
Organizational support for the project manger	1. Project managers had to fill many of the roles that should have been performed by the PMO. 2. Project managers needed a mentor the first time they managed a project with offshore resources.
Effects of offshore suppliers on project planning	3. Project managers needed to thoroughly verify offshore suppliers' work estimates, which tended to be optimistic. 4. Project managers experienced higher transaction costs, which threatened their ability to deliver projects on budget. 5. Project managers experienced project delays, which threatened their ability to deliver projects on time.
Effects of offshore suppliers on knowledge transfer	6. Project managers had to do more knowledge transfer upfront. 7. Project managers were often forced to short-cut the knowledge-transfer process because of deadlines set by senior IT managers. 8. Project managers had to ensure that knowledge transfer was successful by testing the supplier employees' knowledge. 9. Project managers had to ensure that the supplier followed pre-agreed knowledge-renewal practices. 10. Project managers had to ensure that supplier's knowledge about the new applications or technologies was transferred to the client. 11. Project managers had to gain knowledge about new applications or technologies independent of suppliers to insure that the supplier's information and bids were valid.
Effects of offshore suppliers' CMM/CMMI processes on the management of work	12. Project managers had to provide greater detail in requirement definitions. 13. Project managers had to integrate the suppliers' CMM/CMMI processes into their own project-management processes. 14. Project managers had to ensure the supplier's employees were fully trained as promised by suppliers.
Managing work, not people	15. Project managers had to motivate the supplier to share bad news about work status. 16. Project managers needed to set more frequent milestones. 17. Project managers needed more frequent and more detailed status reports. 18. Project managers needed more frequent working meetings to prevent client-caused bottlenecks.
Managing people, not work	19. Project managers accompanied offshore suppliers to all client-facing meetings. 20. Project managers had to make offshore suppliers feel welcome and comfortable.

to manage offshore suppliers. In the 25 companies we studied, no organization initially provided the ideal level of support for project managers. PMOs were typically understaffed. Most client companies did hire outside firms to conduct cultural awareness training, but few project managers received training on how to manage offshore suppliers. The lack of organizational support effected project managers in the following ways:

1. Project managers had to fill many roles that should have been performed by the PMO. Project managers frequently mentioned that the launch of their offshore teams was delayed by internal structural issues they had assumed the Program Management Office had previously addressed. The most frequent issues that caused delays were

- the inability to quickly obtain visas;
- the inability to set up log-on IDs;
- the inability to let offshore personnel access client systems or data remotely.

It was highly inefficient for project managers to address these issues. Such universal ramp-up issues should have been handled by the PMO. In client companies we studied, the PMO staff was initially so busy with finding destinations, interviewing suppliers, and negotiating contracts, that these internal processes were neglected. PMO staff wanted to help project managers, but resources were typically scant in companies just initiating offshore programs. In one organization, project managers banded together to convince the CIO to allocate more resources to the PMO. The CIO heeded the advice from the trenches. In mature organizations we studied, PMOs helped project managers track projects, learn lessons from prior offshore projects, monitor suppliers, validate invoices, and deal with workforce issues such as getting suppliers to replace inferior personnel (see Chapter 1 for the 15 roles of a PMO). Good PMO support freed the project manager to focus on more productive work.

In lieu of the ideal forms of organizational support (a strong PMO and extensive training), project managers said the following practice was one of the most useful and least expensive forms of support.

2. Project managers needed a mentor the first time they managed a project with offshore resources. Mentors provide expertise to less experienced people in order to help them succeed in their careers. Although mentors are traditionally "senior" to the protégé, the key characteristics of a good mentor for offshore outsourcing were (1) a project manager who had served in a similar role, (2) someone not in the protégé's chain of command, (3) someone the protégé trusted implicitly, and (4) someone who offered positive advice rather than merely commiserated.

Effects of offshore suppliers on project planning

Although project plans are often negotiated with business sponsors, capital budgeting committees, IT planning committees, and suppliers, project managers are responsible for delivering those projects on time, on budget, with promised functionality. The inclusion of offshore suppliers, particularly for the first time, challenged many project managers to deliver projects on time and on budget. Project plans were often unrealistic. False assumptions about costs and schedules were not uncovered until the project was already under the project manager's control. In this section, we highlight project managers' experiences with cost escalation and project delays when offshore suppliers were involved.

3. Project managers needed to thoroughly verify offshore suppliers' work estimates, which tended to be optimistic. Several project managers said that Indian suppliers underestimated the amount of work required to complete a task. At Retail, the offshore task force identified three reasons for this. First, suppliers underestimated work because they did not fully understand what Retail needed. Second, suppliers were unfamiliar with complexities of Retail's technical environment. Third, suppliers underestimated because they are inherently optimistic or wanted to please the client.

To counter-balance this tendency to underestimate, some project managers had frank discussions with their offshore-supplier managers and said, "This estimate is too low." They had to reinforce that they wanted the "most likely" forecast, not the "most optimistic" forecast. Some project managers simply added a buffer by increasing time estimates 30–50 percent.

4. Project managers experienced higher transaction costs, which threatened their ability to deliver projects on budget. Although clients called these "hidden costs," hidden costs are actually transaction costs clients fail to full identify during project planning. All client-side stakeholders – from the CIO down to team members – underestimated the transaction costs associated with offshore outsourcing. These costs included additional travel costs, infrastructure costs, monitoring costs, costs prompted by rework, or a poorly trained staff. Overall, the CIO at Retail said: "The biggest piece of learning about offshore to me was the hidden costs. The labor arbitrage is so attractive initially you almost tended to dive in. You really need to consider the infrastructure costs, training, the scale-up, and all the transition activities and knowledge transfer."

The additional costs for software licenses provide one concrete example of "hidden" transaction costs. Several project managers said additional software license fees were not included in their budgets. On large projects with 50 people offshore, software licenses proved to be quite costly. The project managers had assumed the suppliers held licenses for most products, but suppliers did not:

> I'm buying licenses for my offshore team and I'm buying licenses for my onshore team because both teams have to be able to troubleshoot and test the same piece of code. Seems like they should foot the bill for this but their expectation was that we would pay for those licenses. (Director of Development)

Another example of "hidden" transaction costs was infrastructure costs not included in the project budget. For example, some project managers at Retail had to unexpectedly replicate the testing environment. The offshore suppliers could not effectively use the testing environment at Retail's headquarters because it was too slow. So a shadow testing environment had to built offshore. In addition, the testing data had to be frequently updated, shipped to India, and synchronized with the US. All this contributed to cost escalation.

5. Project managers experienced project delays, which threatened their ability to deliver projects on time. In addition to unidentified costs, project managers also experienced unidentified delays. For example, some project managers experienced project delays because of the lack of client-side readiness, such as obtaining visas, log-on IDs, etc. Another source of delay was the offshore supplier's holidays and personal events. Project managers said that official holidays are not as well documented in foreign countries as they are in the United States:

> It seems India declares holidays – I don't want to say spur of the moment – but, for example, the elections were not on the calendar. I hear, "Oh, it's election time so it's a day off for us." Or an extended holiday is written as 11 days but it turns out to be 13 or 14. (Application Development Manager)

Some US project managers did not understand that certain personal events take much longer in other cultures. For example, weddings in India are frequently two-week events. As another example, an applications development manager at Retail explained that one of her male Indian teammates said he was taking off work for the birth of his child. She had assumed this meant he would be absent a day or two. However, he was not back after a week. She inquired and found out that the birth event extended 11 days after the birth, to when the baby was officially named.

The next section addresses the effects of offshore suppliers on knowledge transfer.

Effects of offshore suppliers on knowledge transfer

Offshore suppliers need to understand the client's business requirements, technical platforms, and internal practices and procedures before they can be assigned actual work. In comparison to transferring knowledge to new internal IT employees or to domestic contractors, project managers had to learn new ways to transfer, test, and renew knowledge to/from offshore suppliers.

6. Project managers had to do more knowledge transfer upfront. When team members comprised only internal IT staff and domestic contractors, project managers transferred knowledge incrementally. However, when a project included offshore employees, knowledge transfer occurred in a more concentrated timeframe. Some members of the offshore delivery team were only on-site for a few weeks, so the project managers planned for intensive knowledge transfer:

> When you have an internal person, you give them a little bit because you know they are around. They can come up and ask you a question. When you bring in someone offshore, knowledge transfer is more structured. We have to invest more time. When you know they are going back offshore, you need to take advantage of those three to four months and give them as much information as you can. (Applications Development Manager)

7. Project managers were often forced to short-cut the knowledge-transfer process because of deadlines set by senior IT managers. Unfortunately, some senior IT leaders mandated that knowledge transfer must be completed within a certain timeframe. In one telecommunications company, for example, senior IT leaders said that project managers had eight weeks to transfer knowledge before turning control over to the offshore supplier. The project managers said they needed four to six months. Senior IT leadership enforced the mandate. After eight weeks, the work was outsourced to the offshore supplier and client-side project managers were re-assigned or terminated. Quality deteriorated. The supplier kept trying to track down the reassigned project managers to ask for help. Two months later, a substantial system bug made it through the supplier's testing phase, causing the client company financial losses and loss of goodwill with their external customers. This anecdote alone may help project managers persuade their senior IT leaders to let them determine the timetable for knowledge transfer.

8. Project managers had to ensure that knowledge transfer was successful by testing supplier knowledge. We heard from several project managers at Biotech, US Manufacturing, and Retail that Indian employees often do not express incomprehension. To ensure knowledge transfer has truly occurred, some project managers orally quizzed their Indian contractors: "During the knowledge-transfer portion, the project manager actually gave them oral tests every Monday based on what they learned. She quizzed them to see what they learned so she could tell 'Are they really picking up the knowledge?' And she'd say, 'yeah, they did well!'" (Applications Development Manager).

Of course, "quizzes" were not official tests, but rather frequent and detailed conversations to ensure that supplier employees understood the business requirements.

9. Project managers had to ensure that suppliers followed pre-agreed knowledge-transfer renewal practices. Once a client made an initial upfront investment in knowledge transfer, the client had to ensure that the supplier reinvested in knowledge transfer for new people assigned to the project. Retail – and other companies we studied – ensured knowledge renewal by including a contractual clause that required the supplier to have replacements shadow incumbent employees for a period of two to four weeks, depending on the nature of the work. The problem was that the project managers often had no good way of verifying that the work shadowing actually occurred, particularly on large projects. A few project managers suspected that new hires were assigned to projects and billed to clients before the required shadowing period took place.

10. Project managers had to ensure that supplier knowledge about new applications or new technologies was transferred to the client. With domestic contractors, knowledge transfer from the supplier to internal IT staff was frequently informal. Internal IT staff literally looked over a domestic contractor's shoulder or sat by their side to learn about the domestic contractor's deep technical expertise and to understand the systems they were building for clients. In contrast, offshore contractors were located remotely from internal IT staff, thus informal knowledge transfer did not take place. This meant that project managers had to lobby for formal transfer of knowledge or the client risked not being able to support applications built by offshore teams. Suppliers charged the clients for formal knowledge transfer, thus project managers had to convince their superiors of the need.

11. Project managers had to gain knowledge about new applications and technologies independent of suppliers to ensure that the suppliers' information and bids were valid. Retail's senior IT leaders realized that Retail needed to make their own informed opinions about new technologies from sources other than their suppliers. One solution implemented at Retail is to gain independent expertise. Retail's senior IT leaders and project managers keep abreast of emerging technologies by attending symposiums, engaging independent research firms, taking courses, and talking to other client firms. As one Retail manager put it, "We need to know what we think."

Effects of offshore suppliers' CMM/CMMI processes on the management of work

One of the most interesting aspects of talking with offshore suppliers is their pride in their high levels of Capability Maturity Model (CMM) or Capability Maturity Model Integrated (CMMI). Suppliers believe high CMM or CMMI levels signal quality. Among our client interviews, however, the uniform message we heard is that CMM/CMMI are indicators of quality *potential*, but not guarantees of quality. For example, consider the following quote from a Retail participant:

> CMM 5, I shrug that off. It doesn't mean anything to me in reality because obviously there are good projects and bad projects. Their CCM 5 certification didn't guarantee that I was going to have a faultless implementation with 0.5 defects per 1,000 lines of code. We know that didn't happen. That's why I am always leery of those things. CMM may be a predictor of performance but it is not a guarantee of performance. (Senior Development Director)

What CMM/CMMI means to client project managers, is that they must learn to package work in a format that supplier employees are ready to execute. First and foremost, project managers must learn to provide very detailed, written specifications.

12. Project managers had to provide a greater level of detail in requirement definitions. Project managers who have extensively worked with domestic suppliers understood the importance of defining requirements. However, in the context of offshore outsourcing, even more details had to be provided. One project manager said he was surprised when a financial statement came back with the dollar fields left justified. The supplier responded, "You didn't say you wanted them right justified." This anecdote provides a concrete and real example of the level of detail often required in functional requirements that are transferred offshore. Certainly, Retail's project managers were surprised about how much they needed to define requirements:

> It's been a real shift for us to have to deal in the level of detail that this offshore model requires. I'm used to delegating something to very knowledgeable people who could fill in details. With offshore, you first have a high-level design called a use-case. My folks [at Retail] can take that use-case and run with it. [With offshore] you have to turn use-cases into detailed requirements. (Director of Development)

When project managers didn't plan enough time upfront to detail requirements, more rework delayed projects downstream. When the supplier did a fixed bid, extensive rework severely eroded the supplier's margins, which is something no client wants. (Significant research shows that when suppliers seriously miss their margins, the client consequently experiences lower quality.) Some project managers decided to use the supplier's templates. This gave the client-side project managers a good idea of what the supplier employees needed. Also, the supplier delivery teams were used to working from these templates, which reduced the need for rework.

13. Project managers had to integrate the suppliers' CMM/CMMI processes into their own project-management processes. Besides the complaint that CMM/CMMI required more detailed requirements, project managers also complained about other aspects of CMM/CMMI. For example, simple change requests such as moving a button triggered a 20-page impact statement at one financial services firm. At Retail, one project manager said the supplier's CMM processes meant that errors replicated faster. CMM places a lot of emphasis on the reuse of coding modules. On one of his large projects, a small error in one module was replicated 100 times in the application. The error ate up CPU cycles and crashed the system. From the supplier's perspective, however, once the error was diagnosed, it was much simpler to fix. All the supplier had to do was fix the small error in one module and roll the fix throughout the system. Among other things, this anecdote shows the different perceptions people have of CMM/CMMI. From the client perspective, one small bug created a huge issue because of CMM. From the supplier perspective, the bug was easy to fix because of their CMM processes.

14. Project managers had to ensure the suppliers' employees were fully trained as promised by suppliers. At Retail, one project manager said that Supplier B bragged about its CMM processes during sales and negotiations, but the supplier employees assigned to her team were slow to respond when she asked to see their code reviews, inspections, and test cases. After a significant delay, she would be handed something that was of inferior quality. After much probing, she found out Supplier B assigned new hires to her account before they completed their advertised "intensive CMM training." What annoyed this project manager most was that the new supplier people were not introduced as new. They were introduced as fully trained. It wasn't until the project was underway that she discovered their low level of experience: "We expected to get someone pretty experienced. They should be able to read a dump. And they should know what a soft seven is, that kind of stuff. On average, two were fine, but one couldn't answer very basic questions" (Applications Development Manager).

One signal that suppliers were using clients as training grounds was when suppliers requested generic log-on IDs, such as Supplier Staff1, Supplier Staff2. Project managers told us that the suppliers said that generic logons were quicker to process, but the project managers wanted to know who was doing what work using that log-on ID for security and control purposes. One remedy was for the client to require a one-to-one relationship between log-on ID and supplier employee. But of course, the project manager had no way to prevent offshore employees from logging in using someone else's ID and password.

Managing work, not people

This issue manifested itself during many interviews and in many contexts. In the discussion about engagement models, we have already addressed some of the controversial views on managing work instead of people. At Retail, for example, the offshore task force saw this as a guiding principle. However, some project managers found this principle impossible when they were dealing with very large staff-augmentation engagements. One director of development, for example, said he preferred fixed-price projects because he didn't have to micro-manage the supplier's staff. He could focus on work, not people. But he pointed out, that with a staff-augmentation engagement, he had to try to keep track of the offshore teams. He found this very frustrating: "I had no way of knowing – are we getting a mess of people at four hours a day because I don't want a mess of people four hours a day. I want fewer people working more hours a day so that I'm leveraging the knowledge base" (Director of Development).

In this section, we discuss the challenges project managers had when trying to managing work, not people.

15. Project managers had to motivate the supplier to share bad news about work status. One uniform complaint we heard is that the Indian suppliers did not like to report when they were going to miss a deadline. This makes it difficult to trust the supplier to independently complete a packet of work.

> They don't like to tell you that they're going to miss a deadline. I think they think they can make up for it and hustle and get there, but they can't. So you find out very shortly before the deadlines that they are going to be missed. (Director of Development)

One development director had a very frank discussion with the supplier. She said she needed advanced notice when a deadline might be missed. She would work with the supplier to determine the best way to address the issue. She said it was in his best interest to forewarn her because then she could not accuse him of being late because he made a decision without her. With advanced notice, the decision was made together. Furthermore, she said the supplier was losing money by pouring resources in, working the weekends, working nights, when some of this could be avoided if the supplier provided realistic status updates.

16. Project managers needed to set more frequent milestones. To help project managers manage work (not people) many project managers required more frequent milestones for work packets. Project managers at Retail created intermediate milestones and more frequent "code drops" so that project managers could better track progress. For domestic contractors, Retail typically has two or three milestones for an eight-month project. For offshore suppliers, some project managers went to weekly milestones.

17. Project managers needed more frequent and more detailed status reports. At several client companies, project managers requested more frequent and more detailed status reports from offshore suppliers than from domestic suppliers. At one US bank, the project manager required daily status reports using a form with very targeted and specific questions for the offshore team lead. She said that it was easier for the offshore team lead to report delays in written form. At Retail, two directors of Development also went from weekly status reports to daily updates: "When they first came, we were meeting weekly with them. We do it daily now. Every single day, on both projects, we spend an hour with them going over what they're doing. Every single thing" (Director of Development).

18. Project managers needed more frequent working meetings to prevent client-caused bottlenecks. On development projects, Retail's project managers became aware that offshore programmers halted work when they needed Retail to answer a question. On a large project, this became quite burdensome for the client: "When there are 50 people offshore and everybody has a very specific thing to do and they are stuck, they need a quick turnaround" (Applications Development Manager).

While Retail's project managers said the suppliers' questions were quite legitimate, they needed a better process to quickly gather all the minor issues and resolve them. One team had an hour-long meeting in the US every day with the engagement manager from 4:30 to 5:30pm. The engagement manager collected all the issues that had to be answered by the client. The project manager had an early morning meeting with her user group to get answers to questions by the end of the day in time for her next 4:30pm meeting.

Managing people, not work

While it was important for project managers to learn how to manage work (not people) when assigning concrete tasks to offshore teams, project managers could not fully escape managing people. The design, develop, support, and maintenance of IT applications are done by people, and the social capital issues as highlighted in the next chapter are enormous. For the project manager, we have already mentioned that at the engagement level, project managers monitored people to verify invoices for staff-augmentation projects. At the project level, they needed to manage people who came on-site for training and who served as on-site engagement managers. At Retail, two important "managing people" practices were learned.

19. Project managers accompanied offshore suppliers to all client-facing meetings. We asked participants, "Why not have the offshore engagement manager speak directly to users?" At Retail, project managers cited two reasons. One reason is the risk of scope-creep:

> Scope-creep? It was scope-explosion! If the client wants it, then that's a new project or something to that effect. Because they're so willing to do things and so willing to please, that's their culture, we were finding they were doing things that we couldn't afford. Now even though they may go to user meetings, there's always an IT person there. (Director of Development)

A second reason was that some users complained to the project managers about speaking directly to the offshore staff:

> The liaison group was bombarded with questions [by the offshore supplier]. It was frustrating for them. (Director of Development)

> There were a couple of occasions where Supplier A went directly to the person that had the issue and there was a language thing there. Why is this man calling me? I don't know what he is asking. I don't know his name. (Director of Development)

By accompanying on-site engagement managers to client-facing meetings, project managers (or their designees) served important social boundary-spanning roles. The IT liaison prevented scope-creep, ensured understanding, and fostered the user–offshore employee relationship.

20. Project managers had to make sure that offshore suppliers felt welcome and comfortable. Project managers appreciated that it was difficult for foreign workers to come to a strange country for extended periods of time. Project managers welcomed them by including them in social events at work and by being considerate of cultural differences. For example, one project manager said she made sure every work event included vegetarian meals when offshore employees were invited to attend.

Conclusion

Throughout this chapter, it is evident that Retail's engagements with offshore suppliers generally have been very successful. The success is largely attributed to Retail's willingness to build the necessary in-house capabilities to successfully engage suppliers throughout the learning curve. Retail's senior IT managers always examined their own abilities to select the right engagement models, to manage projects with offshore teams, to expand the role of the PMO, and to alter sourcing strategies to keep costs low and quality high. After ten years engaging offshore suppliers, the practice has become institutionalized within the organization.

As noted in Chapter 1, when a practice becomes institutionalized, it does not mean that the organization will forever continue with the practice. The possibility for managers to change course always exists. As we were concluding this chapter in 2007, Retail had just hired a new CIO. This change in leadership may alter Retail's sourcing strategy.

CHAPTER 4

A client's offshore outsourcing program becomes strategic by investing in social capital

Joseph Rottman and Mary Lacity

The importance of social capital

As evident in the previous chapters, decision-makers often rationalize offshore outsourcing by comparing hourly rates for domestic and offshore workers. This approach is dangerous because it assumes domestic and offshore workers are equivalent "factors of production". Once engaged in offshore outsourcing, senior executives are often disappointed. Many complain that offshore suppliers do not understand their business, deliver late, and produce poor-quality work. In reality, the problems are not caused primarily by the supplier – they are primarily caused by the client's naive focus only on costs and failure to invest properly in the relationship.

One of the best ways to improve overall value is to invest in social capital. Social capital is defined as "the advantage created by a person's location in a structure of relationships. It explains how some people gain more success in a particular setting through their superior connections to other people."[1] Social capital is simply the idea that knowledge and resources are exchanged, work gets done, and value is created through social relationships. In the context of outsourcing, *who* the supplier knows in the client organization is the key to ensuring *what* value the supplier delivers. Conversely, *who* the client knows in the supplier organization is the key to ensuring *which* supplier resources will be devoted to the client's account to ensure value. Research suggests that once social capital is built, many benefits follow. These benefits include increased efficiency, more cooperative behavior, higher levels of trust, less need for costly monitoring, and, most importantly, increased innovation.[2]

In this chapter, we explain how practitioners can invest the *right amount* of social capital to ensure that they get overall value from offshore outsourcing. If clients invest too little in social capital, they will not get the value they seek. At a minimum, clients must invest in social capital by

- laying the foundation for trust (called the relational dimension of social capital);
- creating shared language, codes, and systems of meaning among parties (called the cognitive dimension of social capital); and
- designing social linkages among people (called the structural dimension of social capital).

However, there is one important caveat: if clients invest too much in social capital, they will erode cost savings. For example, if clients bring all the supplier employees on-site to build close relationships, the travel costs and onshore rates would cancel out the cost benefits of outsourcing. Another risk of excessive investment in social capital is the transfer of too much intellectual property to the supplier. Clients must find the right balance in transferring the knowledge the supplier needs to know versus protecting its intellectual assets. Furthermore, clients must find ways to protect the social capital investment in the face of supplier turnover.

The practices for investing "the right amount" of social capital are illustrated through the case of a US manufacturing company. Among the 24 US client firms we studied, US Manufacturing leveraged social capital the best. Its social capital investment yielded the most strategic results from offshore outsourcing during Phase IV in the learning curve described in Chapter 1. US Manufacturing's suppliers are helping to build innovative products faster and cheaper than in-house provision alone. However, before achieving a strategic advantage with offshore outsourcing, US Manufacturing failed in its initial offshore initiatives because managers only focused on costs and ignored the social dimensions of outsourcing. After diagnosing the causes of its initial failures, US Manufacturing remedied the supplier relationships by investing the right amount of social capital. These social capital practices are:

Lay the foundation for trust:

1. Assure the internal IT staff that offshore outsourcing will not result in layoffs.
2. Demonstrate how offshore outsourcing will enhance internal IT career paths.

Create shared language, codes, and systems of meaning among parties:

3. Indoctrinate the supplier employees into the client's world of language and meaning through co-training.
4. Indoctrinate internal employees into the supplier's world of language and meaning by elevating internal CMM/CMMI processes to better match suppliers' processes.

Design social linkages between client and suppliers:

5. Know the suppliers' key power players.
6. Build strong ties with on-site supplier managers.
7. Engage multiple suppliers to broaden the social network.

Require suppliers to protect social capital investment through succession planning:

8. Require suppliers to have shadows for key supplier roles.
9. Require supplier employees trained on-site to train supplier employees offshore.

Protect intellectual property:

10. Divvy intellectual property across multiple suppliers.

While some of the practices to build social capital have been discussed during the Biotech (Chapter 2) and Retail (Chapter 3) cases, the entire feel of these practices is different at the US Manufacturing site. In comparison to Biotech and Retail, US Manufacturing exemplifies how clients can shift their view of offshore suppliers as "external providers" to offshore suppliers as "integral partners."

The next section provides an understanding of US Manufacturing's business and why management wanted to offshore outsource IT work.

US Manufacturing's background and offshore engagements

US Manufacturing is a Fortune 100 manufacturer of industrial equipment with over 75,000 employees spread across 20 countries. The successful social capital practices highlighted in this chapter are centered within US Manufacturing's Six Sigma-certified Software Center of Excellence (SCE). The SCE at US Manufacturing employs approximately 150 people and has an annual IT development spend of approximately $32 million.

The members of the SCE are responsible for the development and deployment of embedded software[3] systems that are highly integrated into US Manufacturing's core products.

To understand US Manufacturing's offshore journey, we interviewed senior managers within the Software Center of Excellence, including the manager of the SCE, a Six Sigma blackbelt, and the engineering supervisor. Additionally, we interviewed ten people who worked for US Manufacturing's largest supplier in Bangalore, India.

US Manufacturing's first attempt with offshore outsourcing

The Software Center of Excellence began its offshore journey in late 2000 with the hope of taking advantage of the lower labor costs available offshore. With the primary goal of saving money on development costs, they engaged one large Indian supplier to work on several projects.

One project involved integrating a new Global Positioning System (GPS) steering system into one of their larger product lines currently in production. This project required the offshore supplier to design and create the embedded software intended to control the steering systems and interface with the GPS satellites. The project involved new software tools, new interface systems and new processes for both the SCE and the supplier. For this project, all the supplier employees were located offshore to take greatest advantage of the labor rates. Primarily due to the fact that knowledge transfer was an afterthought, this project failed to produce any of the deliverables outlined in the statements of work. The project was ultimately pulled back in-house and completed well behind schedule and over budget. According to the engineering supervisor:

> It didn't succeed. We would get something back and it didn't do what we wanted it to do and we would have to redo the whole thing. We weren't very good at being outsourcers and the model of throwing a document over the wall and having a supplier magically give us what we want in the end – it didn't and doesn't work.

The GPS project was indicative of the many failures US Manufacturing encountered, which were related to social capital and knowledge transfer. Looking back, the manager of the SCE and his staff underestimated the need for extensive domain knowledge transfer about US Manufacturing's products, processes, and markets. According to the SCE manager: "We had to realize that our Indian vendors did not understand embedded software or even the equipment we manufacture. They didn't even know what our products looked like!"

Tacit knowledge cannot be transferred through documents

The first attempt showed US Manufacturing that they were not successful in transferring knowledge to the supplier. US Manufacturing needed to transfer specialized coding skills and manufacturing-domain knowledge. Concerning specialized coding skills, US Manufacturing's embedded software development requires skills not readily available in the offshore space. The "rules" for traditional software do not apply to embedded software. For example, requirements for response time, speed, power consumption, and correctly interfacing with the external environment are much greater for embedded software. Concerning the manufacturing-domain knowledge, successful creation of embedded software requires an intricate and detailed knowledge of the equipment that will house and interact with the software. Such rich knowledge cannot simply be transferred by passing documents from the client to the suppliers. Rather, the offshore suppliers needed to see the equipment and understand how the software they were building worked.

Discouraged, but hopeful, US Manufacturing tries again

Despite the failures, US Manufacturing did see some promise in offshore development. While the projects themselves were not completed, SCE managers noticed that code quality improved over the life of the projects. They were confident that the offshore developers might be able to reduce the project backlog if US Manufacturing was able to better share knowledge and expertise with the suppliers. The SCE managers decided to move forward with the offshore model, even though one said: "I must admit, it was a tough sell."

US Manufacturing's second attempt with offshore outsourcing

In January 2004, the SCE used the lessons it learned and re-launched its offshore effort. SCE managers chose different suppliers in round two and used better practices to build social relationships to facilitate knowledge transfer.

The client selected suppliers with better capabilities

The supplier selection and engagement process was very different in round two for US Manufacturing. The failures in round one showed US Manufacturing that it was critical to find offshore suppliers with at least some embedded software expertise. They also needed partners willing to invest in a long-term relationship. In round two, US Manufacturing selected two large Indian suppliers that had already exhibited some expertise in the embedded software market, primarily in the automotive industry. In addition, they selected a boutique firm that specialized in embedded software in the manufacturing market. This prior experience with the embedded software development process was a critical success factor that was overlooked in round one. The SCE manager said:

> We really didn't understand how different we (embedded software development) were until we saw the failures in round one. We now know that our vendors need a very specialized skill set and we now know how to identify and test for those skills. We are much better at vendor selection and talent assessment.

Even though suppliers had some knowledge of embedded software, the SCE still had to train suppliers about their unique embedded software practices. For example, US Manufacturing has a unique way of wiring electronic control units that contain the embedded software.

On-site visits acclimated offshore suppliers to SCE people and processes

The second attempt focused on building closer relationships with suppliers. This time, nearly half of the suppliers' delivery teams spent time on-site at US Manufacturing's headquarters prior to working on the outsourced projects. According to the manager of the SCE:

> What we saw was the benefit and real value of actually bringing those people here for a short time to bring them up to speed. Let them

see how an application works and work right next to the team doing the development. That is the real benefit to the teaming aspect.

Intensive face-to-face training and shadowing exchanged tacit knowledge from client to supplier

Beyond the offshore supplier delivery teams' short visits to the US, some higher-level offshore supplier employees were given extensive training. The training sessions were delivered by US Manufacturing's architects and project leads to the suppliers' project leads, as well as to US Manufacturing's internal IT employees ready for the next phase in their career development. Essentially, these two groups were trained together as peers.

Once trained, the supplier employees who held leadership roles would typically remain on-site at US Manufacturing for six to 18 months. SCE managers did not want to migrate the trained supplier employees offshore too soon because it would create a talent and knowledge vacuum on-site and sever many professional and personal connections that were created. SCE managers also used these on-site supplier employees to educate the next batch of supplier employees. The next group of supplier employees would come over from India and shadow the incumbent supplier employees for three and six months. While this approach is expensive, the two on-site supplier employees are able to (a) establish common frames of reference and (b) transfer social relationships and connections to the new employee. Additionally, because the new supplier employee is trained by the incumbent supplier employee, US Manufacturing's architects and project leads were free to engage in higher-level activities. Once the incumbent supplier employees migrate offshore, they then transfer the knowledge obtained during their on-site time to the offshore employees.

Short visits by supplier delivery teams and face-to-face training/work-shadowing for supplier project leads were successful in building the social capital necessary for knowledge transfer. However, these practices are costly. The hourly onshore rates are three to four times higher than offshore rates. SCE managers had to be careful about not completely eroding cost savings with these practices. At the time of our interviews, the suppliers provided about 15 people on-site and 35 people off-site. The SCE's ultimate goal is to have a 20:80 ratio of supplier employees onshore versus offshore. This ratio will provide the near-perfect balance between the costs and benefits of establishing relationships for knowledge transfer.

The outcome of round 2: lower costs, better quality, higher value

As of 2006, US Manufacturing paid the two large suppliers and one boutique firm about $3.4 million, or 10 percent of the SCE's annual budget. The three engagements are all increasing in dollar value and headcount.

Thus far, SCE managers have declared offshore outsourcing a success. The suppliers are helping US Manufacturing to develop embedded software quicker and cheaper than in-house provision. The manager of the SCE summarized round two by stating:

> I think we are now doing it right and the data we are gathering support that idea. Our vendors are not only providing a lower-cost talent pool, but they are helping us strategically. We keep looking for ways to increase the engagements. Our costs are down, productivity is up, and the quality is as good, if not better, than what we can do in-house.

Evidence of increased value from offshore outsourcing can be found in the detailed metrics US Manufacturing maintains to track the offshore engagements. As an example of their detailed metrics, consider the costs for one large project comprised of three teams. Figure 4.1 shows the costs per activity for the three teams: the in-house project team, a large supplier team, and the small supplier team. The project was started in July 2003

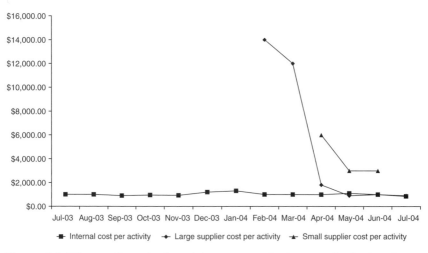

Figure 4.1 US manufacturing's activity cost metrics by team for Project A

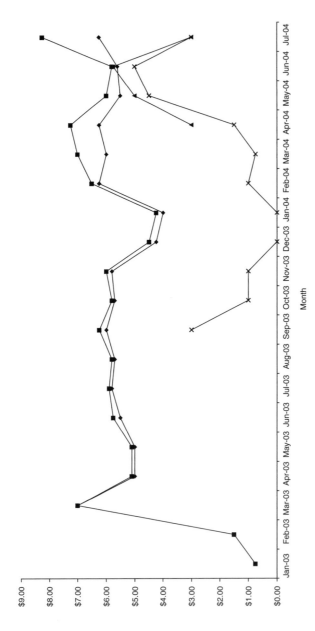

Figure 4.2 US manufacturing activity cost by team by person for Project B

and ended July, 2004. The average cost per activity for the internal team remained constant over this time period – about $800 per activity. The large offshore supplier team initially had the highest costs per activity – around $14,000 per activity. The costs were initially high because of the investment in social capital (visits, training, and shadowing). But benefits of this investment rapidly emerged, as evidenced by the severe decline of costs per activity to $800 within four months. The small supplier team only had a three-month assignment, but the data also show a rapid decline in costs per activity from $6,000 to $3,000.

Whereas Figure 4.1 tracks costs per activity per team, Figure 4.2 tracks cost per activity per team per person. This figure shows the four teams on Project B: (1) the internal team, (2) a large supplier team, (3) the small supplier team, and (4) a blended team comprising both internal and offshore employees. Among these four teams, the team consisting of only internal staff had the highest cost per activity! The smallest supplier team had the lowest costs, partly because they initially charged only offshore rates for onshore employees. The blended team (comprising both internal and external employees) had lower costs per activity per person than the internal team, but higher costs than offshore supplier teams.

These metrics not only helped the SCE manage the engagement and understand the costs structures, they also motivated the team. According to the manager of the SCE: "We can't wait for the next month's metrics to come out and see where the points are. We are seeing real cost benefits to the supplier's people coming on board and making real contributions to the tasks and projects!"

Practices for building and protecting social capital

The US Manufacturing case provides an opportunity to explore how clients can invest the right amount of social capital to ensure offshore outsourcing success. For US Manufacturing, investing in social capital was the best way to transfer knowledge, and knowledge transfer was the best way to ensure value. In this section, we discuss seven practices that build social capital by (a) laying the foundation for trust, (b) creating shared language, codes, and systems of meaning, and (c) designing social linkages among parties. Next, we present two lessons that require the supplier to protect the social capital investment through succession planning. The final lesson shows clients how to transfer knowledge to suppliers while still protecting intellectual property.

Lay the foundation for trust

Research has shown that workers will not share tacit knowledge without trust.[4] Furthermore, a lack of trust may lead to "competitive confusion about whether or not a network firm is an ally."[5] In the context of offshore outsourcing, client IT staff must be willing to share their knowledge with offshore supplier employees. People are only willing to share knowledge if they believe that overall benefits of sharing outweigh the risks. US Manufacturing laid a foundation for trust through the following two practices.

1. Assure the internal IT staff that offshore outsourcing will not result in layoffs. US Manufacturing, like most of the US client firms we studied, were using offshore outsourcing to "do more with less." US Manufacturing did not intend to reduce internal headcount through outsourcing, but planned to use offshore outsourcing to reduce the immense backlog of work. This message was strongly communicated to the internal IT staff, which assuaged their fears and made them more willing to cooperate with offshore suppliers. In addition, this message was shared with offshore suppliers so they did not have to worry about replacing US workers.

At US Manufacturing, the plans to explore offshore outsourcing were met with optimism and relief by the internal staff of the SCE. Facing a three-year backlog and a flat staffing forecast, employees welcomed the possibility of a decreased workload. According to the manager of the SCE:

> My people were tired of working 60-hour weeks. We communicated that offshore was a way to better manage our project pipeline since we were not going to add a bunch of expensive North American resources to meet the demand and then lay them off later, we had to find other ways of being able to add flexibility to our workforce. And so they are not worried about losing their job. They just see this as a way of getting back to some kind of normal 40- to 50-hour work-week and, even more importantly, as a way for them to move up in their level of responsibility.

Once the internal IT staff's fears were assuaged, they willingly worked with offshore suppliers. For example, according to the engineering supervisor: "I was amazed at how open our developers were with the supplier's team. Once they realized that the quicker they [the offshore team] were up to speed, the sooner they could share the load, there was no 'turf' to protect, or 'secrets' to keep."

While the lesson to share this positive message seems obvious, in other US client firms we studied, senior managers decided to keep experiments with offshore outsourcing "low key" even when no layoffs were planned. We found that secrecy *always* resulted in the internal IT staff panicking and sabotaging the experiments by being uncooperative. In Chapter 5 we present lessons on how to communicate with internal staff when offshoring will lead to layoffs. The message is the same – communicate the strategy honestly – but it requires special practices to ensure redundant employees cooperate until their employment ends.

2. Demonstrate how offshore outsourcing will enhance internal IT career paths. US Manufacturing realized that if their second attempt was to succeed, internal IT employees needed to understand how offshore outsourcing would affect their career paths. On the surface, offshore outsourcing is often touted as allowing internal IT staff to focus on more interesting, higher-value work. This was certainly true at US Manufacturing because higher-value roles such as architects, project managers, and database administrators would always remain in-house. But in reality, low-level tasks (such as routine programming) are used to train future project managers. So how will those managers gain their skills and expertise if offshore suppliers are now doing routine work?

SCE managers answered this question by creating a clear vision for IT career paths. From past experience, SCE managers knew that about one-third of programmers are promoted to higher-value roles. So, for example, if SCE managers project that they will need five architects in three years' time, they hire 15 new programmers internally. Even though these internal programmers cost more than offshore equivalents, the SCE managers know they need to provide entry-level experiences to groom future IT leaders: "We have made the business case to management that even though internal programmers are not as cost efficient as sourced programmers, we need to maintain a certain level of expertise internally."

As suggested by this practice, the SCE needs an accurate forecast of future IT needs. To accurately predict the human resources (HR) demand requires significant knowledge of the HR environment, past HR trends, and the current staffing constraints. US Manufacturing created an intricate staffing model based on the current and past project staffing data, the current internal talent pool and the projected demand.

The staffing plan is openly communicated to both internal IT staff and suppliers. By communicating the plan with internal IT staff, US Manufacturing's developers were not worried that they were "building their own guillotines" by working closely with the suppliers' teams. Instead, trust was established and enhanced by the internal employees seeing a clear and obtainable career path. By communicating the plan with offshore suppliers, the offshore suppliers could better plan for its staffing needs and better predict its future revenue generation. Such predictability enabled suppliers to stop selling and start working. According to the manager of the SCE: "Initially, the suppliers seemed to have one eye on the current project and one eye on what was coming next. Once we were able to share our forecasts with them, the attention turned to the current tasks."

The open communication of the vibrant internal career path and long-term commitment to suppliers laid the foundation for trust among the parties. Both sides saw the benefit of the relationship. As predicted by theory, the atmosphere of trust contributed to the free exchange of knowledge between committed exchange partners.[6] Trust is but one prerequisite for knowledge transfer. Another prerequisite is creating shared language, codes, and systems of meaning.

Create shared language, codes, and systems of meaning among parties

Effective communication requires that parties not only share common languages and codes but that language and codes are interpreted through a shared schema.[7] In the context of offshore outsourcing, the "common language" of software development is often only superficially understood between clients and suppliers. For example, clients and suppliers may share the terms "functional requirements," "statements of work," and "code testing" but the meaning of those terms may be vastly different among parties. To a client, "functional requirements" may mean documenting high-level business processes, which are immersed in the client's idiosyncratic business jargon. To a supplier, "functional requirements" may mean detailed, technical programming specifications.

Both clients and suppliers must interpret language similarly, but this is not easy. We witnessed many clients and suppliers clinging to their own interpretations with awkward translations to bridge the gaps. For example, many of the suppliers we studied are committed to the Software Engineering Institute's Capability Maturity Model (CMM). When US clients passed their own versions of functional requirements to offshore suppliers, the first thing the offshore suppliers did was to translate the US requirements into its CMM formats. The translations were then sent back to the client for validation. Such iterations are wasteful and expensive. Two practices avoid this issue by creating shared language, codes, and systems of meaning.

3. Indoctrinate the supplier employees into the client's world of language and meaning through co-training. One of the best ways to create shared language, codes, and systems of meaning is to provide shared experiences. US Manufacturing did this by co-training new internal employees and supplier employees who would serve as project leads. Both sets of stakeholders took facility tours and training classes on engine architecture, production software, equipment simulation products, operating guides for various lines of equipment, quality-assurance processes and an overview of all of the various manufacturing products and platforms. They were introduced to various software development tools, the development environment, and embedded development tools. For the supplier employees located offshore, the classes were recorded and streamed to India. According to the manager of the SCE: "We couldn't ship an engine or a piece of large equipment over to India, so we did the next best thing: we videotaped many equipment pieces in action and showed what the ECUs [Electronic Control Units] were designed to do."

The result of co-training was that both internal and offshore supplier employees understood US Manufacturing's business and IT development terms. Both sets of employees now spoke the same language. Furthermore, they understood the context of the language – both sets of employees understood the manufacturing process and how the SCE developed software for key parts. For this lesson, US Manufacturing primarily indoctrinated the offshore employees into its world of language and meaning.

While training obviously facilitated knowledge transfer about US Manufacturing's products and processes (the cognitive dimension of social capital), an additional benefit surfaced: team members became friends. According to the manager of the SCE:

> I mentioned that our strategy is to bring some of their folks here on-site to be trained in our processes. We did not plan on this, but it turns out that through the course of bringing them here for that training they get to be friends with and get to know all of the people here and the people here get to know them. So when they go back to India they're not some nameless face that's just working on software. They're friends of the people who are here. They know them and trust them to some degree, and there are relationships that have been built that it turns out are important, or add to the success of that kind of work.

4. Indoctrinate the client employees into the supplier's world of language and meaning by elevating internal CMM processes to better match suppliers' processes. In this lesson, US Manufacturing became indoctrinated in the suppliers' world of language and meaning. The SCE managers understood that the suppliers had more mature software development processes. They sought to improve their own process maturity by learning from suppliers' superior CMM capabilities. By agreeing on the same processes, work transitions were smoother. According to the manager of the SCE:

> That's actually another reason why we're trying to climb the CMM ladder ourselves is so we have enough structure in our organization that we can exploit, we can use other suppliers to do work for us and get predictable results. Not that it's their fault, but if we know that we have to improve our process act. During our first trip offshore the likelihood that we could successfully manage external work was very low, and so we are now climbing up that ladder and are better at managing ourselves and now we can more successfully manage outsourced labor.

Design social linkages

Thus far we have discussed building social capital by laying the foundation of trust and creating a shared system of language, codes, and meaning. The missing element goes to the heart of social capital: designing social linkages. Clients must consider which employees in both the client and supplier organizations need to establish social ties.

There are two types of social ties to ponder: strong ties and weak ties. Strong ties require people to spend a considerable amount of time together and are characterized by emotional intensity, and intimacy.[8] Strong ties between people increases trust, knowledge exchange, learning, environmental adaptation, and technical performance.[9] The downside is that strong ties require high levels of investment.

In contrast, weak ties[10] are typically equivalent to acquaintances – people who have met face-to-face and understand the knowledge and resources each possesses. Weak ties have one remarkable strength: they are much more likely to transmit new, relevant information than a strong tie![11] The reasoning is that a weak tie is more likely to generate a non-redundant connection between different social circles.[12] The classic example of this phenomenon is a job search. If a person seeking employment only shares this desire with her strong network ties, it is unlikely her close friends have relevant job opportunities. When this desire is disseminated through weak ties, information spreads rapidly to other people in other social networks who are much more likely to have relevant employment opportunities.

In the context of offshore outsourcing, SCE managers had to determine which client and supplier employees needed strong ties and which needed only weak ties. SCE managers could not afford to build strong ties between all SCE and supplier employees because of the high costs of travel, lodging, and onshore rates. They built weak ties with the offshore delivery teams and supplier senior management from the large suppliers. They built strong ties to the suppliers' project leads and engagement managers. In addition, SCE managers built strong ties to the senior partners at the small Indian supplier. These relationships are discussed below.

5. Know the suppliers' key power players. One of the fundamental benefits of social capital is that network ties provide access to resources.[13] For clients, a considerable challenge is building close relationships with the supplier's key power players to ensure that the best resources are devoted to the client's account. For example, one CIO we talked to said she could not get the right resources on her account. After continual frustration with the supplier's appointed liaison, she repeatedly tried to call the supplier's CEO. He never called her back. Then she got creative. She discovered that the supplier worked closely with a strategy professor at Harvard. She called that professor and he immediately called the supplier's COO on her behalf. The COO met with her, solved her problem, and the relationship significantly improved.

The opportunity to know the supplier's key power players is largely a function of the supplier's size. For suppliers the size of a Wipro or Infosys, their top managers cannot possibly build close relationships with all their clients. In many instances, clients may never even meet the supplier's senior management. One advantage of selecting a smaller supplier is a greater opportunity to build closer relationships with top management. At US Manufacturing, its engagement with the small, specialized supplier shows the advantage of establishing strong ties with the supplier's leadership team.

The small supplier was founded by senior managers from an embedded software division at a large Indian supplier. These entrepreneurs realized that in order to grow their new company, their approach needed to focus on responsiveness and high-quality talent. US Manufacturing built and nurtured strong relationships with the principal partners of the small supplier and leveraged these connections to gain access to the supplier's top talent. In addition, the small supplier was willing to invest its own money in the relationship by charging off-site rates for the on-site training at US Manufacturing headquarters. This investment improved the supplier's own domain knowledge while showing a commitment to US Manufacturing.

According to the manager of the SCE:

> It is great dealing with the managing partners at [small supplier]. They know our offshore history and we know their goals for growing their firms. We can call them and talk directly with decision-makers about talent levels, ramp up needs, upcoming projects etc. Those relationships helped improve our training models (especially costs) and they have an engagement with a premier client to help market their embedded software skills.

So how can clients build relationships with senior executives from large suppliers? One of the best ways is to go visit the supplier delivery team offshore. The supplier delivery team can often arrange for visiting clients to meet their own senior managers. When the manager of the SCE finally made the trip to Bangalore, the supplier delivery team arranged meetings with supplier senior managers. Beyond the value of finally establishing ties to the large supplier's top executives, he developed much closer ties to the supplier's delivery teams. He said:

> I can't believe I waited two years to meet the people I have been only emailing and seeing in video conferences! What a difference this trip has made. Now, I know my team. I should have done this at the very beginning. I now have faces, and more importantly personalities, to go with names and titles. This trip was worth every penny.

6. Build strong ties with on-site supplier managers. Our research found that offshore suppliers working on client sites are often viewed with fear and even contempt. For example, the program managers at one Fortune 100 firm witnessed the internal IT staff's open hostility towards offshore supplier employees.

US Manufacturing made a concerted effort to welcome and integrate the offshore supplier employees who would remain on-site for up to six months. Long engagements away from home can leave these workers feeling alienated and lonely. The managers of the SCE invited offshore supplier employees to social events such as birthday parties and happy hours. The effort to increase the social ties between internal and supplier employees paid dividends at US Manufacturing. The line between "us and them" blurred. The suppliers' employees (both on- and offshore) were viewed by US Manufacturing employees as team members and they all shared in the successes and challenges of the projects. According to the group project manager at one of US Manufacturing's large Indian suppliers:

> Of all of our embedded systems clients, [US Manufacturing] has worked the hardest to make our employees feel very much part of the team at [US Manufacturing]. Our customer satisfaction ratings from [US Manufacturing] show the value of this integration. Our employees have internalized the mission and values of [US Manufacturing]. It is a highly coveted assignment to work on the US Manufacturing account.

7. Engage multiple suppliers to broaden the social network. The SCE within US Manufacturing distributed work among three suppliers (two large and one boutique). While maintaining engagements with multiple suppliers did increase transaction costs, the benefits included protection of intellectual property and the creation of a competitive environment to keep costs low and quality high. The use of multiple suppliers also created larger social networks, thus increasing US Manufacturing's ability to both create social capital and manage knowledge transfer. While it may seem counter-intuitive that increasing the number of suppliers would increase the social capital within teams, the SCE found that exposure to divergent engagement models, suppliers with different work processes and styles, and suppliers with unique expertise, broadened the outlook of the internal employees. Specifically, internal teams were able to enhance their own skill sets and increase their levels of expertise and confidence by working with developers from multiple suppliers. The manager of the SCE concluded:

> In our first try, we only used one vendor and we did not learn much from them and they did not help us. When we spread work out [across suppliers], our processes improved, as did the exposure of our internal people to multiple viewpoints. It also helped us to "keep alive" multiple vendors – we were spreading the development around.

Require suppliers to protect social capital investment through succession planning

The practices to build social capital require a significant financial investment for clients. Clients must ensure that their investment is protected in case of unscheduled supplier turnover. Two practices can help.

8. Require suppliers to have shadows for key supplier roles. Employee turnover can have a destabilizing effect on a social network. As Inkpen and Tsang (2005) found, "personnel turnover affects intracorporate knowledge sharing, which often takes place through formal or informal exchanges on an individual basis. Maintaining a stable pool of personnel within a network can help individuals develop long-lasting interpersonal relationships."[14] To mitigate the risks associated with supplier employee turnover, the SCE managers required suppliers to overlap key people, like project leads, at the client site. Depending on the role, the required shadowing period was three to six months. This overlap period had two major social-capital and knowledge-transfer benefits. First, the knowledge transfer was done predominately between the supplier's employees, thus freeing up the SCE's valuable architects and leads. Second, the incumbents were able to ease the impending transition by introducing their replacements to US Manufacturing's business units and staff and subsequently transferring more social aspects of the arrangement. This helped to maintain the social contacts and connections that were created during the engagement. According to the engineering supervisor:

> Once we started overlapping the liaisons, our customers felt much better about rolling people off the project. The outgoing liaisons made our job much easier since they took their initial training and subsequent learning and were able to convey it to their replacement much, much better than we can.

Figure 4.3 shows the relationship between the supplier's on-site projects leaders and the offshore team.

9. Require supplier employees trained on-site to train supplier employees offshore. While the engagement contracts between US Manufacturing and its suppliers did not specifically detail the cost structures and/or penalties for unplanned turnover, both US Manufacturing and its suppliers realized the risks associated with turnover. As mentioned earlier, US Manufacturing needed to ensure that the resources invested in on-site training could be protected in the event of unplanned turnover. According to the manager of the SCE:

> I know [the supplier] will experience turnover, but they will be responsible for transferring the training from one person to another. For example, let's say that we got ten people from [the supplier] working on this domain. When those ten people return from our training, I expect that [the supplier] will actually add other people to the team and train them. The net number will still be ten, but it may be different people as they have other people moving into other roles. As long as they are retaining and passing on that domain knowledge to the new people, that's great. We don't expect those ten individuals to stay tied to this domain forever. We just expect them [the supplier] to now be shepherds of the training we gave them and be able to transfer that to the new folks that they want to add to that team.

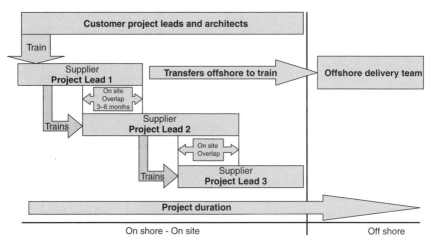

Figure 4.3 US manufacturing's use of supplier employee shadowing

While the informal agreements helped to alleviate some fears associated with lost domain expertise in the suppliers' teams, US Manufacturing acknowledged that risks still existed. They were building formal remediation methods into the future contracts. According to the engineering supervisor:

> We're trying to build enough domain knowledge in those suppliers in the areas they work in that if one or two guys leave it's not a problem, but we know if the whole team left then we're in big trouble. We would have to go retrain a bunch. So we are working with them now to protect that investment by working with the suppliers to prevent that and structuring the contracts to address the issue if it happens.

In other companies we studied, clients require suppliers to reimburse training costs if supplier employees do not remain on the account for a certain period of time. From the client perspective, this is a best practice for protecting investment in social capital, although suppliers will likely resist.

Protect intellectual capital

Due to significant amounts of product and process knowledge the suppliers needed to successfully develop software, the SCE chose to co-train both internal and supplier developers. However, the co-training of internal employees with supplier employees creates significant trade-secret and intellectual-property risks. The amount of information passing from the client to the supplier can lead to a divulging of proprietary intellectual property or an unbalanced relationship with one supplier. US Manufacturing used the following practice to balance the need to transfer knowledge to suppliers against the need to protect its intellectual assets.

10. Divvy intellectual property across multiple suppliers. Whereas Lesson 7 addressed the use of multiple suppliers to increase the social network, this lesson focuses on the use of multiple suppliers to protect intellectual property.

Considering the proprietary nature of the software the SCE developed, US Manufacturing faced an interesting problem: how to transfer enough knowledge to enable successful product development while protecting their trade secrets. To mitigate this risk, the SCE (1) unitized projects into small segments of work and (2) dispensed these segments among three offshore suppliers to effectively distribute the intellectual property. They viewed their intellectual property as a puzzle. By distributing small pieces among three suppliers, no one supplier can assemble the puzzle on their own (see Figure 4.4).

The first part of the practice involved the unitization of tasks to be sourced. US Manufacturing segmented large projects into smaller, well-defined tasks. These tasks were typically five to seven business-day activities that had clearly defined objectives and requirements. While the transactional overhead of this strategy was considerable, the manager of the SCE claimed the transaction costs were more than recouped by such close monitoring:

> In our first round [the failed attempt at offshore sourcing], projects were allowed to creep and the only people who saw the creep were the accounts payable people on our end and the accounts receivable people at the supplier. Now, each task has an owner and we watch the projects from a functional perspective, not an accounting perspective. By using this strategy, we are seeing much less rework and the quality has improved considerably!

The second part of the strategy involves multi-sourcing. While maintaining engagements with multiple suppliers did increase transaction costs and management overhead, the benefits included protection of intellectual property and the creation of a competitive environment to keep costs low and quality high.

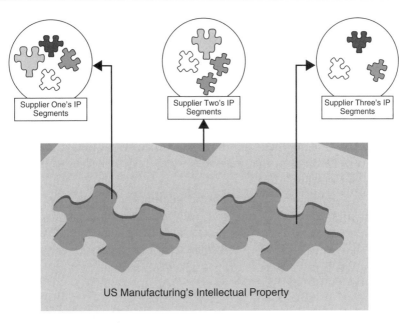

Figure 4.4 Intellectual property divided among suppliers

Social capital as a business asset

Many managers like to call their outsourcing deals "strategic." In reality, much of outsourcing is still about cost reduction in back-office services. For us, the term "strategic outsourcing" is restricted to circumstances for which suppliers play a key role in helping clients deliver innovative products to the market faster and cheaper than competitors. Under that definition, US Manufacturing is using its offshore suppliers strategically.

As the US Manufacturing case illustrates, strategic use of outsourcing requires a considerable social investment in suppliers. Clients must establish trust, create shared language and meaning, and design social ties. However, we have shown that building social capital requires significant financial resources and time before benefits are realized. Consequently, clients must approach offshore outsourcing as a long-term commitment with carefully selected suppliers in order to earn a return on that investment.

Most importantly, social capital must be viewed as a business asset. While friendships among client and supplier employees are pleasant, the real purpose of social capital is to add business value. Social capital enables knowledge and resource exchanges that add value in terms of increased efficiency, better quality, and more innovation. Because work gets done through people, relationships matter.

Notes

1. http://en.wikipedia.org/wiki/Social_Capital
2. Nahapiet, J., and Ghoshal, S. (1998), "Social Capital, Intellectual Capital and the Organizational Advantage," *Academy of Management*, Vol. 23, No. 2, pp. 242–66.
3. Embedded software is software that is embedded in mechanical parts on pieces of equipment to provide task-specific functions. Embedded software is found in many devices, such as thermostats, cell phones, cars, and elevators.
4. Lin, C. , "To Share or Not to Share: Modeling Tacit Knowledge Sharing: Its Mediators and Antecedents," *Journal of Business Ethics,* Vol. 70, 2007, pp. 411–28; Inkpen, A. and Tsang, E. "Social Capital Networks and Knowledge Transfer," *Academy of Management Review*, Vol. 30, No. 1, 2005, pp. 146–65.
5. *Ibid.*, p. 154.
6. *Ibid.*
7. Nahapiet and Ghosal, "Social Capital, Intellectual Capital and the Organizational Advantage."
8. Granovetter, M.S., "The Strength of Weak Ties," *American Journal of Sociology*, Vol. 78, May 1973. pp. 1360–80.
9. Kale, P., Singh, H. and Perlmutter, H. (2000), "Learning and Protection of Proprietary Assets in Strategic Alliances: Building Relational-specific Capital," *Strategic Management Journal,* Vol. 21, pp. 217–37; Larson, A., "Network Dyads in Entrepreneurial Settings: A Study of the Governance of Exchange Processes," *Administrative Science Quarterly,* Vol. 37, 1992, pp. 76–104; Rosenkopf, L. and A. Nerkar, "Beyond Local Search: Boundary-spanning, Exploration, and Impact in the Optical Disk Industry," *Strategic Management Journal*, Vol. 22, 2001, pp. 287–306.
10. Weak ties can also occur between people who have never met but have a third person with whom they have a strong tie in common. In theory, the strength of a tie is formally defined as a *continuum* (Granovetter, 1973). In the offshore outsourcing context, we are treating the strength of a tie as categorical variable with values "strong" and "weak."
11. Granovetter, "The Strength of Weak Ties."
12. *Ibid.*
13. Nahapiet and Ghosal, "Social Capital, Intellectual Capital and the Organizational Advantage."
14. Inkpen and Tsang, "Social Capital Networks and Knowledge Transfer," p. 156.

References

Granovetter, M.S., "The Strength of Weak Ties," *American Journal of Sociology*, Vol. 78, May 1973. pp. 1360–80.

Inkpen, A. and Tsang, E. "Social Capital Networks and Knowledge Transfer," *Academy of Management Review*, Vol. 30, No. 1, 2005, pp. 146–65.

Kale, P., Singh, H., and Perlmutter, H. (2000), "Learning and Protection of Proprietary Assets in Strategic Alliances: Building Relational-specific Capital," *Strategic Management Journal*, Vol. 21, pp. 217–37.

Larson, A., "Network Dyads in Entrepreneurial Settings: A Study of the Governance of Exchange Processes," *Administrative Science Quarterly*, Vol. 37, 1992, pp. 76–104.

Lin, C. , "To Share or Not to Share: Modeling Tacit Knowledge Sharing: Its Mediators and Antecedents," *Journal of Business Ethics*, Vol. 70, 2007, pp. 411–28.

Nahapiet, J., and Ghoshal, S. (1998), "Social Capital, Intellectual Capital and the Organizational Advantage," *Academy of Management*, Vol. 23, No. 2, pp. 242–66.

Rosenkopf, L., and Nerkar, A., "Beyond Local Search: Boundary-spanning, Exploration, and Impact in the Optical Disk Industry," *Strategic Management Journal*, Vol. 22, 2001, pp. 287–306.

CHAPTER 5

A client's award-winning global shared services

Mary Lacity, Jim Fox, and Joseph Rottman

The promise of shared services

According to Accenture, shared services is defined as "the consolidation and redesign of business processes into a standalone service."[1] Organizations create shared services to dramatically reduce costs, improve service, and even increase revenues. Studies have shown, however, that organizations do not always achieve the full benefits they expect from shared services. IBM, for example, found that the results of shared services have been "mundane rather than magical" among a survey of 210 senior finance managers.[2] Another study of 140 executives in North America and Europe found that expected benefits exceeded actual benefits in the majority of cases. Overall, the survey also found that 67 percent reduced costs, 66 percent improved performance, 56 percent increased productivity, and 42 percent increased customer satisfaction. Among the 67 percent who reported cost savings, the average cost savings was only 14 percent.[3] Furthermore, the average time to fully implement shared services was two years in Europe and twice that long in North America. Given the time and investment required, senior managers question, "How can we realize the full potential of shared services?"

In this chapter, we help answer this question by presenting detailed, actionable practices learned from a global financial information services firm. This company, assigned the pseudonym FIS, spent five years reducing financial costs and improving financial services through global shared services. FIS's journey comprises two overlapping periods. From 2001–4, FIS was able to reduce financial costs from 2.3 percent of revenues to 1.8 percent of revenues by moving much of the decentralized business support services to six existing regional service centers. This initial effort reduced the financial staff from 1,077 employees to

702, while simultaneously improving service levels and financial controls. From 2003–6, FIS further reduced costs by redesigning the regional service centers, erecting a new captive center offshore, and outsourcing specialized financial services to third-party suppliers. In February of 2005, FIS opened its Global Service Center in Bangalore, India, and hired and trained 150 Indian employees within six months. In 2006, the second effort reduced the financial staff from 702 employees to approximately 573. FIS experienced a second success, by delivering the promised savings within $100,000 of the targeted $6.5 million. In addition, FIS won a number of shared services awards for Best New Shared Service Organization, Best Use of Technology for Shared Services, and Best Shared Services Leader.

Such victories are never easy, and this chapter explains the choices FIS made, the lessons they learned, and what they would do differently with the benefit of hindsight. Unlike platitudes such as "secure top management support," and "manage change," this case offers explicit lessons that will provide meaningful insights for other executives seeking to create global shared services. These lessons are:

1. Integrate within silos before integrating across silos.
2. Consider a blended transformation approach.
3. Ensure management support until stability has been obtained.
4. Invest in enabling technology first.
5. Analyze costs, attributes and readiness of process activities to identify contenders for shared services.
6. Reassemble activities to ensure seamless end-to-end delivery.
7. Make the sending end accountable for successful migration.
8. Coach – don't police – business-unit clients.
9. Envision the future for retained employees.

The next section provides an understanding of FIS's business and why top management wanted to create global shared services.

The background context for shared services

FIS Group was founded in Europe over a century ago. Throughout its entire history, FIS embraced new technologies to facilitate organic growth. Throughout the 1980s and 1990s, FIS grew through both organic growth and through a number of acquisitions. As might be expected, the rapid growth resulted in redundant back offices, leading to high financial costs and integration concerns.

During the late 1990s, the company that had always embraced technology was also bitten by it. The proliferation of the Internet commoditized some of FIS's core content. For example, companies were buying information from FIS and widely distributing it over the Internet. During the late 1990s, competition was also increasing. FIS had always enjoyed the largest market share in Europe and Asia, but was experiencing increased competition. Although competitors were only grabbing a small percentage of FIS's market share, the overall effect of increased competition was falling prices. Also, FIS only had 20 percent of the world's largest market – the US. Increased profitability became the primary charge of FIS's senior management team.

In 2002, for the first time since FIS went public, FIS recorded a pre-tax loss. Revenues also dropped by 2 percent. Early in 2003, the company announced a formal three-year program to achieve a total cost savings of nearly $1 billion. This program proved effective. In 2005, FIS generated nearly $4 billion in revenue and earned significant positive income. In 2006, revenue and profitability again increased, thus indicating FIS's overall recovery. As of 2007, FIS remains a leading provider of financial services to support equities, fixed income, foreign exchange, money, commodities, and energy markets.

FIS's migration to shared services occurred in two major phases. The next sections detail those phases and the challenges FIS faced.

Phase I: regional shared service centers

In 2001, FIS's finance leaders were concerned about FIS's inefficient finance operating model and relatively high costs – which exceeded 2.3 percent of revenues. At that time, best-in-breed financial costs were approximately 1.5 percent of revenues. How could finance costs be reduced? The CFO began to look closely at the structure of the finance organization.

In 2001, FIS employed approximately 1,077 financial people, distributed in 60 countries. The financial staff worked in one of three organizations:

1. Corporate finance. 115 finance employees worked in the corporate finance group in the London headquarters. Their roles included financial reporting, internal audit, group treasury, group tax, and reporting to the Audit Committee.

2. Decentralized business units. 869 finance employees worked in decentralized business units in 60 locations. They supported all the financial processes such as strategic analysis, business planning, financial management, investments, budgeting and forecasting, and payroll.

3. Non-integrated subsidiaries. 92 finance employees worked in independent subsidiaries. In 2001, these independent businesses were completely separate from the Corporate Finance group and were thus outside the scope and control of the shared services initiative.

The CFO thought he could significantly reduce financial costs and improve finance effectiveness by launching a global sourcing initiative and migrating many services from the decentralized business support groups into new regional service centers. He reasoned that many services could be consolidated, standardized, and automated.

He assigned some of his top leaders to work full time on the shared services initiative. To obtain the needed cost savings, the shared services team needed to standardize finance policies, implement a standard, global ERP and workflow systems, and move a significant amount of work from the decentralized business units to six regional service centers. The six regional service centers were located in London, New York (later moved to St. Louis), Amsterdam, Buenos Aries, Nicosia (in Cyprus) and Singapore.

Much of the shared services team's initial efforts focused on standardizing finance policies and migrating the entire company to one single instance of Oracle ERP. Oracle was implemented in the United Kingdom in 2000. FIS hired a management-consulting firm to help Finance and Human Resource functions roll out Oracle and launch the shared service initiative. The consulting firm brought in a team of 25 people and was instrumental in defining the shared service operating model and supported the IT function in the global installation of Oracle. Most of the installation was completed by December 2002.

The shared services team estimated that half of the work in the decentralized business units provided direct value to the business or was required to remain local, including strategic analysis, budgeting and forecasting, performance management and financial reporting, statutory and tax accounting, payroll, and project investment management and analysis. These processes were not initially moved to the regional service centers. However, the shared services team estimated that the other half of their work provided only indirect value. These activities included purchasing, payables, cash application and management, account entries and reconciliations. Many of these processes were moved to the regional service centers.

Significant changes to finance policies and finance systems – combined with the relocation of many finance services – obviously posed some change-management challenges. *As expected, the business units often resisted the changes caused by the re-engineering of business processes.*

The purchasing activities within the source-to-payment process were the most difficult to change. The sourcing and shared services team needed to implement unfavorable policies such as "no purchase order, no payment" to nearly 2,000 employees with purchasing authority. Local business units preferred to buy from their local suppliers, even though some of the suppliers had no warrantee. In some cases, controls were ineffective and there was little accountability for spend. Often, the business process changes moved local financial support to regionalized purchasing in shared services. Some of the people from the local business units believed that the regional service centers did not understand their unique spend requirements. An example of a change resisted by local business units was the standardization of allowable travel and entertainment policies. Local practices differed significantly. For example, some countries paid for family support costs when employees traveled for business. Some countries had generous and expensive health club policies. As expected, business-unit employees resisted losing perks.

The shared services team overcame user resistance to change by following four practices: buy-in, stewardship, incentives, and gentle enforcement. First, the shared services team made sure that the local CFO and HR director fully supported the new changes. Second, after the CFO/HR buy-in, the team positioned themselves as stewards – not owners – of the new policies. The team's message was, "These are not my policies, these are our policies. Your senior management has bought into these policies and it's just our job to implement them." Third, the team tried to create a culture that valued change by creating awards for best, continuous improvement. Any FIS employee could submit ideas, but the team found that the best ideas came from the business users, not from their internal team members. The awards were very visible and prominent, thus serving as a positive motivator of behavioral change. Fourth, the team enforced the policies with a forgiving rather than policing hand. If an employee broke a policy, the team addressed the first infraction by re-explaining the rule and gently cajoling the perpetrator by saying, "I'm sure now that you know the rule, it will never happen again." This last practice evolved after a few members of the shared services team unsuccessfully tried to enforce policies with a heavy hand. Clearly, cooperation and buy-in were more effective than mandates.

Some finance employees did not want to move from business units to the regional service centers. Users were not the only stakeholders to resist the changes. Many finance employees did not want to move from the decentralized business units to the regional service centers. Some members of the financial staff simply did not want to relocate. Other members of the financial staff perceived the changes in their roles as deskilling from client-facing services to transaction processing. In the end, about 60 percent of the staff in the regional service centers were new hires.

In hindsight, the shared services team felt that they should have proactively articulated the vision and career paths for the financial staff to prevent so much resistance. The feared deskilling did not occur. Quite the contrary occurred because the regional service center staff expanded their roles to service more clients across more business units.

The results of Phase I: reduced financial costs, better cost controls, and better service

By 2004, FIS reduced the financial service staff by 375 people (35 percent) and reduced financial costs from 2.3 percent of revenues to 1.8 percent of revenues. Table 5.1 shows the distribution of financial staff by the end of 2004. The regional shared service centers were launched in 2000 and grew to 251 finance people in 2004. The decentralized business units shrunk from 869 finance people in 2001 to 340 finance people in 2004. The corporate finance group reduced staff by 28 people over the three years. (FIS sold several of the non-integrated subsidiaries, so the reduction of financial staff from 92 to 24 is primarily a result of divestiture, not shared services.)

More impressive than the obvious reduction in financial costs was that FIS also improved controls and services during Phase I. Key controls

Table 5.1 Approximate number and location of finance employees from 2001 to 2006

Organizational unit	Financial services headcount before Phase I (2001)	Financial services headcount after Phase I (2004)	Financial services headcount after Phase II (2006)
Corporate headquarters	115	87	59
Decentralized business units	869	340	192
Non-integrated subsidiaries	92	24	12
Six regional shared services		251	97
Captive center			174
Outsourced partners			39
Total employees	1,077	702	573

standards were concurrently implemented under a global template. On the one hand, key controls added challenges to the implementation, but on the other hand, key controls later served as the foundation for the Sarbanes-Oxley (SOX) program and other process standardization initiatives. In addition, customer service was measured throughout the program. FIS shared services was regularly recognized for enhanced user experience, improved self-service functions, and improved quality of information and reporting. Moving from local purchasing to e-procurement in one region reduced the number of vendors from 10,000 to 6,000 and improved purchasing controls and helped reduced prices. Prior to the expansion of the regional shared service centers, FIS had nearly 600 finance processes. Afterwards, the number of financial processes was reduced to 359.

Phase II: redesigning global shared services

In late 2003, the shared services team and finance leaders met to plan the business goals for 2004. The team was celebrating the success from years of hard work, which resulted in a much-improved finance operating model and six efficient, customer-centric, regional service centers. However, the celebration was short-lived. FIS's profitability was still not where it needed to be. Senior management needed an extra 33 percent cost savings over two years with no lapse in control or service levels. For the next two days, the shared services team began brainstorming options. They initially considered six options.

Six options for shared services

Option 1: continue to improve and automate. This was the most conservative option. This option entailed growing the shared services organization by transferring more processes, such as HR, to further drive efficiency through process improvement and technology enablement. This option also proposed finding opportunities for more automation. The team evaluated this option by examining the best technologies in the financial automation market and leveraging best practices to improve economies of scale further. They quickly concluded that the option could only deliver 5–10 percent cost savings, and was eliminated.

Option 2: consolidate six regional service centers into one "transaction center of excellence." This option would migrate the work from six regional service centers (London, Nicosia, Singapore, St. Louis, Amsterdam,

Buenos Aires) all to a Center of Excellence. The team considered locating the Center of Excellence in Singapore due to its lower cost structure and opportunity for scale. Locating the Center of Excellence in one of FIS's existing centers offered the added benefit of moving quickly enough to meet the team's two-year time requirement. But the team questioned whether Singapore's costs were low enough to meet the aggressive 33 percent targeted cost savings. They needed to closely evaluate this option.

Option 3: nearshore from six regional service centers to three. This option entailed moving financial support services from higher-cost regional service centers to existing nearby lower-cost regional service centers. Work from London and Amsterdam would be moved to Cyprus, work from St. Louis would be moved to Buenos Aires, and work from Singapore would be moved to India. The team questioned whether Buenos Aires and Cyprus had enough local resources to accommodate more services. Other risks included higher inflation, lower tax incentives, and less political stability than other destinations. They needed to evaluate this option more closely.

Option 4: redesign regional service centers, erect a captive center, and engage outsourcing partners. This option would entail moving some higher-value work that remained in the decentralized business units to the six regional service centers, and moving many of the standardized processes now in the regional service centers to a lower-cost captive center located offshore. Selective use of outsourcing partners would fill in gaps in FIS's capabilities. This option became a candidate because the director of Shared Services began to question whether Option 2 (consolidate six regional service centers to Singapore) would just be a half-way step to an eventual move to China or India. Clearly, Singapore's prices were higher than these two alternative destinations. Independent of the shared services team, other units within FIS were looking at Bangalore and Bangkok. As the team started pursuing this option, they quickly narrowed the location of the captive center to Bangalore. The team selected Bangalore because of available talent and because they thought they could piggyback off another FIS presence in that city. This option entailed multiple moves and needed closer inspection.

Option 5: outsource to an offshore supplier. This option entailed attracting a supplier to move financial services to India and to continue supplying services once the transformation was completed. A few suppliers did show interest, but they required significant upfront management fees. The team was also worried that an outsourcing supplier would not be able to manage the global complexity. This option was thus eliminated early on.

Option 6: commercialization. Because FIS considered its financial service support as best-in-class, the team was very excited about the possibility of exploiting this asset through commercialization. Like Procter & Gamble, who sold their shared service operations, the team evaluated this option as well. FIS faced the problem that its shared services operation was too small to excite a serious buyer. While Procter & Gamble is a $40 billion company and had a few thousand people in its shared service center, FIS is only a $4 billion company with a few hundred people in its shared services. This option was thus eliminated.

By January 2004, the team had narrowed the choices down to Options 2, 3, and 4.

Analysis of the remaining three options

The shared services team conducted four assessments on the remaining three options:

1. Strategic assessment: The extent to which the option met the vision, objectives, and timeline for accomplishing a 33 percent reduction in costs.

2. Operational assessment: The extent to which the option would protect service levels and the extent to which the processes could be standardized, packaged, and redistributed.

3. Financial assessment: The total financial benefits versus the costs for each option. The cost assessment was comprehensive and included technical, communications, administrative, employee package, training, travel, and capital outlays. The outcome of this analysis showed that the captive center would generate the most savings ($6.5 million) and would have the fastest payback period (2.03 years) (see Table 5.2).

Table 5.2 Financial assessment of shared services options

	Sourcing option		
Financials	**Consolidate six regional service centers to one transaction center of excellence**	**Near-shore from six regional service centers to three**	**Redesign regional service centers, erect a captive center, and engage outsourcing partners**
One time investment	$10 million	$10.8 million	$13.5 million
Total savings	$3.2 million	$2.9 million	$6.5 million
Payback period	3.05 years	3.75 years	2.03 years

4. Risk assessment: The extent to which the options had high or low risks for 11 risk factors. These risks were: systems and communications, stability of the location, whether "all the eggs were in one basket," whether FIS has end-to-end process control, time-zone differences, language coverage, business-case delivery, scale opportunities, continuous improvement, flexibility/agility, and strength of governance.

The shared services team then assessed each of the 11 risks on a scale from 9 (indicating high risk) to 0 (indicating low risk) for the remaining three options. Each team member's vote was public and each team member had to defend their number. With this procedure, the team held each other accountable but, more importantly, they completed the risk assessment by December 2003. (Some companies take up to six months to complete a risk assessment.) The result of this analysis is found in Table 5.3.

Table 5.3 Risk assessment of shared services options

	Options		
	Consolidate six regional service centers to one transaction center of excellence	Near-shore from six regional service centers to three	Redesign regional service centers, erect a captive center, and engage outsourcing partners
Systems/communications	2	8	6
Location stability	1	5	3
Eggs in one basket	8	4	7
E2E process control	6	3	7
Time zone support	5	2	3
Language coverage	5	2	7
Business case delivery	3	7	4
Scale opportunities	3	6	3
Continuous improvement	3	6	3
Flexibility/agility	2	3	2
Strength of governance	3	5	2
	3.727	4.636	4.272

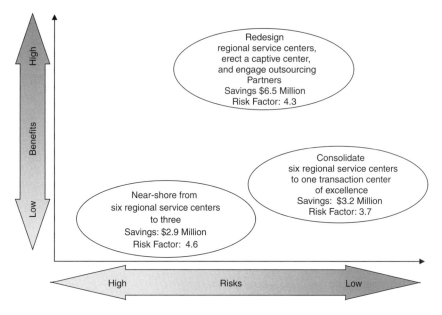

Figure 5.1 Risks and benefits of shared services options

The three options were presented to a meeting attended by shared service leadership, including the executive sponsor of Shared Services, the director of Shared Services, and the shared service leaders in late January 2004. Figure 5.1 shows the relative benefits and risks of the three options. The mood of the room was that it was an election year (US and UK elections) and the media and popular sentiment was very anti-offshoring. The director of Shared Services said the move to India is inevitable a few years from now, so he lobbied that FIS should "take the higher risk, do it once, do it right." The vote was taken. The group selected Option 4 for recommendation to the FIS CFO for approval.

Implementation of redesigned regional service centers, captive center, and outsourcing

The director of Shared Services charged his team with the move. He was adamant that FIS would not let the drastic move erode service quality. According to the former senior vice resident of Americas Shared Services at FIS, the director told his staff that, "We are going to build this service so we can look our customers in the eye and say the service is not going to be compromised."

The vision for the new finance-operating model is found in Figure 5.2. The model comprises the corporate center in London to provide compliance and governance, the decentralized business units to retain local financial staff for client care and support, and the business service centers, which would now comprise three areas:

Six regional services centers. The regional service centers would be redesigned to assume more responsibility for certain controllership services, the so called "greyzone," which currently remained in the decentralized business units. The greyzone included activities such as preparing baseline budgets and forecasts, creating standard management reports, and standard accounting functions such as recoveries, statutory, tax, and payroll processing. Over the next two years, the shared service team wanted to move these greyzone activities from the decentralized business support

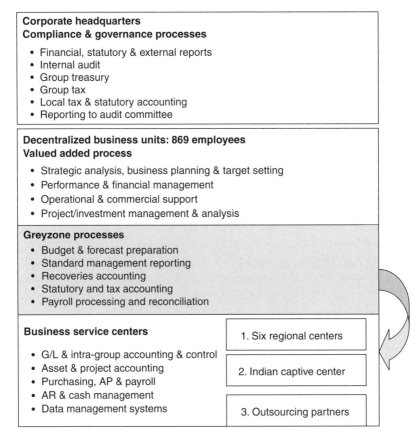

Figure 5.2 Vision for shared services

organizations to the six regional service centers. The migration of the greyzone activities further enabled the business-support functions to focus a greater proportion of their time as strategic business partners in support of profitable growth. The regional service centers would also do processes that required physical proximity to customers, processes that required specialist knowledge, and processes that frequently change.

However, despite this increase in responsibility for "higher-value" work, the overall headcount in the six regional service centers would decline. The plan was to consolidate and move the standardized processes currently performed in the six regional centers to the new captive center.

The global captive center in India. The captive center would provide standardized transactional processes, optimized processes, structured processes, automated processes, processes with low error rates, and processes that would benefit from economies of scale.

The outsourced partners. Selective use of outsourcing partners would provide processes that required deep functional expertise, specific technology requirements, and geographic support capabilities.

To realize this vision, the team spent a considerable amount of time analyzing the best location for providing each financial service. The team had to consider not only the ability to reduce costs by relocating a process, but also the operational feasibility and organizational readiness to relocate a process. The team developed an original analytical method, which they call the "strategic activity-based analysis," to help make the optimal decision for each process. This method is explained below.

The strategic activity-based analysis. The team spent a considerable amount of time analyzing the financial processes that could be relocated. For example, they spent ten days in each of the six regional centers to understand exactly what each location processed. The team identified a total of 359 processes, of which 279 were fairly standardized because of FIS's previous decision to implement a global template supported by a standard Oracle ERP system. However, about 80 processes were completely localized, such as the requirement in Italy to keep cash application transactions within the country's borders.

The complete inventory of 279 standard processes is found in Table 5.4. The processes are listed at a high level, and within each process a number of activities are performed. For example, there are six activities within the statutory accounts preparation process: provide information checklist for local statutory, provide additional reports, create statutory tax provision

Table 5.4 Inventory of standard FOA processes

	Number of processes
Order to cash	**Total: 76**
Data management	12
Debt collection	2
Processing receipts (credit card)	2
Customer and invoice creation	10
Cash management	17
Processing receipts (EFT and cheques)	14
Processing receipts (direct debit)	1
Debtor maintenance, balances, and adj.	10
Management reporting	8
Record to report	**Total: 93**
Transaction processing	18
Completeness and accuracy of accounting data	21
Management reporting	11
Statutory reporting	8
Corporate reporting	3
Intragroup	9
Fixed assets	23
Procurement to pay	110
Expense processing and audit	13
Customer service desk	16
Invoice processing	48
Payment processing	7
Purchase order processing	26
Record to report	93
Transaction processing	18
Completeness and accuracy of accounting data	21
Management reporting	11
Statutory reporting	8
Corporate reporting	3
Intragroup	9
Fixed assets	23
Procurement to pay	**Total: 110**
Expense processing and audit	13
Customer service desk	16
Invoice processing	48
Payment processing	7
Purchase order processing	26

for local audit, reconcile local statutory accounts with FIS group, prepare draft statutory accounts, and translate draft accounts to English.

The next task was to identify which activities within the 279 processes could be relocated. Rather than just assessing the costs of a process, they also assessed the attributes and readiness at the activity level within each process. The model focused the team on reducing the cost of low-value activities within core processes.

The **process attributes assessment** identified activities for offshoring within the 279 processes using the following criteria:

- repetitive and transactional;
- few touch points with internal customers;
- highly structured;
- rules-based;
- standardized inputs, outputs, and technology;
- low material business impact on internal customers;
- independent of third parties;
- virtual communications;
- simple, low skills transfer;
- language neutral (only one-time translation of forms required);
- local language independent (did not require extensive oral or email communications);
- legally possible.

This analysis funneled about 80 percent of the activities within the 279 processes to go through the next assessment step of **process readiness**. This step identified candidates for relocation based on whether the process was

- documented,
- stable,
- built on common service levels,
- technology-ready,
- politically acceptable,
- within an acceptable error rate,
- understood from a legal perspective,
- based on good-quality data.

This assessment eliminated about 40 percent of the remaining activities within the 279 processes. The activities that would remain in the regional services centers included purchasing and call center activities. The shared services team knew that purchasing was the most politically sensitive process, so they had to be careful which purchasing activities would transfer and when. The shared services team also kept the call-center activities within the six regional service centers because they believed they needed stability in the first line of communication between internal customers and shared services. The call centers would also serve as the best mechanism for spotting trouble and identifying opportunities for continuous improvement.

The team also had to ensure that the sequencing of activities made sense. For example, they did not want a process that resulted in a sequence of activities "onshore, offshore, onshore, offshore, onshore."

The three assessments (cost, attributes, readiness) resulted in a three-layer model of "process value tiers" (see Figure 5.3). At the top of the tier are the high-value, high-cost processes called "relationship and control" processes. These processes require high levels of client interaction, decision support, and risk management. The team was also delighted to discover that the "relationship and control" processes were also Sarbanes-Oxley control points. FIS would keep these processes in the decentralized business units and in the downsized regional centers. The next layer in the tier involves the "solution and support" processes. These processes are mid-cost, mid-value. These are sourced to the regional service centers if they are not ready to be moved, or to the captive center if they are ready.

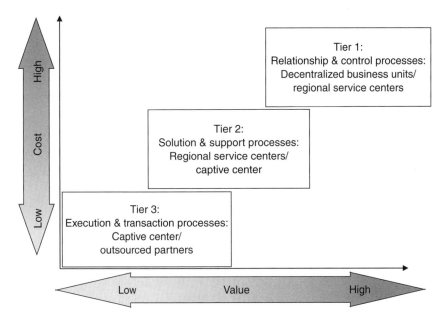

Figure 5.3 Best sourcing the process value tiers

The lowest level in the value tier is made up of the "execution and transaction" processes. These are both low value and low cost. Processes from the lowest-level tiers would be relocated to captive center and outsourced partners. (Of course, reality is more complex than depicted in Figure 5.3, and there are exceptions to the mapping of value tiers to locations.)

Creating the global captive center in India

The shared service transformation team in charge of erecting the captive center comprised mostly internal people. The shared services transformation team was developed by pulling 20 key people from their jobs to work on the project. The team included FIS's top shared service leaders, including three directors from shared service organization, line managers from various service centers, and key people from the business. To fill the void caused by the reassignment of top talent, each team member promoted someone from below to fill their roles. They used temporary workers to fill the lowest-level jobs left vacant by the promotions.

By the end of February 2004, the team needed to announce the transformation program to the FIS staff. Management had a clear desire to be transparent. The decision was made to officially announce the program to the employees in March 2004. The employees were told that the team did not know exactly who would be impacted, but that everyone would know by 31 July 2004. Some employees would be included in the succession and some employees would be given severance packages. The employees appreciated the advanced notice. Some employees had 18 months' advance notice that they would no longer have a job at FIS.

FIS hired a new manager to lead the captive center in Bangalore in July 2004. He had tremendous experience because he spent three years establishing a 300-person captive center for a Fortune 500 company. Unlike other applicants who managed captive centers with 1,500 or more people, this man knew how to efficiently and effectively manage a smaller center.

In January of 2005, FIS started hiring Indians to staff the Bangalore center. FIS's new Bangalore director was under pressure to hire 150 people within six months at a pace of 30 employees per month. (174 people were actually hired, as explained in Lesson 3 below.) To attract good people, FIS promised that employees would work normal hours, unlike many US-centric Indian support centers (only nine employees work the night shift). Also, FIS offered slightly higher than market rates. Another business unit within FIS was in the early stages of building a facility to support data management and development. At first, the shared services transformation team thought finance could share this facility with the other unit.

However, the other unit had plans for all the available space in the building. Thus, there was no room for the new finance hires! The shared services transformation team had to procure a building and implement the entire technology and communications infrastructure in four months. They used their internal IT department for the latter, which helped contain costs.

Once hired, the Indian employees were fully trained via courses delivered on-site in India, as well as traveling to FIS's locations in cities around the world for knowledge transfer. New hires shadowed the workers they would replace for two to four weeks to learn all about the business processes, clients, technology, and procedures.

Engaging the outsourcing partners

FIS needed a number of outsourced partners to enable the new financial operating model. The shared services team engaged the help of outside experts to make sure they created a solid RFP and selected the right partners. In hindsight, FIS's management believes their supplier selection principles were valuable. These principles were:

- Define the scope and schedule before approaching suppliers. (Prior research has found that clients need to perform 22 key activities before approaching suppliers.[4])
- Select suppliers based on value, not just price.
- Review the suppliers' past experiences with established clients. (In our prior research, we found that it is best to interview clients with some relationship problems to determine how suppliers deal with conflict. Conversely, honeymoon clients – clients who recently hired the supplier – make poor references.[5])
- Base supplier payments on delivery of outputs, not inputs.
- Create a global services agreement but allow local deviations for valid exceptions.
- Measure with detailed service-management tools, but manage with key-performance indicators.
- Ensure suppliers will benefit from the relationship – don't let suppliers experience the "winner's curse."[6]
- Define communications and escalation procedures.
- Trust your instincts – even if the spreadsheets indicates "yes," do not engage a supplier if it doesn't feel right.

Applying these principles, FIS selected one major outsourcing partner, several specialty partners, and expanded relationships with their existing banking partners. FIS selected the major outsourcing partner to provide services for statutory accounting and tax and filing that could not be moved across borders. FIS leveraged this partner's truly global presence to provide country-specific processes rather than trying to retain and develop deep functional expertise in specialized areas throughout the world. This outsourcing partner took over the responsibilities for the work of approximately 40 full-time equivalents. The partner either hired FIS staff or leveraged their existing staff to fulfill FIS's needs. In addition to the major outsourcing partner, specialty partners were engaged to perform very specific processes like scanning, facilities administration, and local taxes. The shared services team also expanded existing relationships with banking partners to ensure that global shared services could handle payment transactions across borders and across partners.

The outcomes of Phase II

In the end, FIS has achieved its vision for effectively and efficiently delivering financial services. The six regional service centers, now downsized, focus on higher value-added processes that require close proximity to customers, specialist local knowledge, and non-optimized processes that would have high error rates without special care. The Indian captive center provides the standardized, transactional processes that have already been automated and optimized in terms of having low error rates. The captive center adds value by providing these processes at a lower cost because of lower wages and economies of scale created through the consolidation. The outsourcing partners fill critical gaps in FIS's capabilities.

The global shared services effort resulted in reducing costs within $100,000 of the targeted $6.5 million. Some of the savings came from a reduction in finance staff from 702 employees in 2004 to about 570 employees in 2006. In addition, service has been excellent. FIS won a number of shared services awards for Best New Shared Service Organization, Best Use of Technology for Shared Services, and Best Shared Services Leader.

Lessons learned

There are four widely known practices to successfully create shared service organizations. These practices are (1) secure top management vision and support, (2) provide adequate upfront investment in technology, facilities, and people, (3) move standard, reliable stable processes to shared services organizations, and (4) aggressively manage change to prepare all stakeholders. In practice, however, we have found that these practices are frequently preached, but it is not always clear how they can be implemented. This case offers managers advise in the form of nine specific lessons. FIS planned for and purposefully executed some of these lessons, some lessons emerged during the move to shared services, and some lessons were identified with the benefit of hindsight.

Secure top management vision and support

This practice is a critical success factor for any organizational initiative that requires large-scale change. At FIS, the vision of a global shared services organization was supported by the CEO, corporate CFO, and eventually the business-unit CFOs. During Phase II, these top managers assigned their best talent to the shared services transformation team and allocated sufficient investment funds to implement the vision. Top management focused on shared services within silos first (Lesson 1) and used a blended transformation approach (Lesson 2). However, once the captive center was open, top management disbanded their shared services team before stability was achieved (Lesson 3). Each lesson is discussed in more detail.

Lesson 1. Integrate within silos before integrating across silos. FIS is like several companies we have studied in that top management mandated cost reductions from each back-office director simultaneously. Back-office directors frequently meet the mandate by creating shared service organizations and by implementing other cost-reduction tactics within their own functional silos. Given that all the directors share the cost-reduction mandate, it is logical to question: should companies create shared service organizations across functional silos to gain better efficiencies? The answer is not simple. The amount of change management required within the functional silos is enormous. Trying to coordinate across functional silos would require agreeing on locations, addressing vastly different client needs, different types of work, and different types of capabilities. This is perhaps why FIS, and other companies we have studied, erect shared services within silos first.

Although this chapter focuses on financial services, other functional areas within FIS – most notably IT and HR – were also making drastic changes at the same time. For example, IT Product and Software Development was erecting centers in Bangkok and Hong Kong as Finance was moving to Bangalore. For the IT department, Hong Kong was a good base due to the high quality of available IT talent and close proximity to major exchanges that IT supported. In 2006, IT Product and Software Development erected another captive center in Beijing. By 2007, 40 employees worked in that facility, which is predicted to grow to a few hundred by 2009/2010. The next logical step may be integration of shared services across functions. By 2007, FIS was expanding its presence in Bangalore by offshoring some analysis and procurement. Some organizations – such as Procter & Gamble – eventually unify most back offices into one global shared services organization.

Lesson 2. Consider a blended transformation approach. The creation of shared services requires major capabilities to manage large-scale change, reorient staff, redesign processes, technology-enable, establish and enforce standards, and reorganize. Senior managers must consider the right approach towards transformation. In the inaugural book in this Palgrave series on Technology, Work, and Globalization, we discussed six approaches for creating shared service: (1) do-it-yourself, (2) hire management consultants to manage the change, and four outsourcing approaches: (3) net-sourcing, (4) fee-for-service outsourcing, (5) joint ventures for commercialization, and (6) transformational outsourcing through enterprise partnerships.[7] Rather than pick one approach, FIS selected a blended approach that relied primarily on "do-it-yourself," supplemented with management consultants to help with the global ERP, and fee-for-service outsourcing for global coverage of country-specific processes. Blending approaches is becoming recognized as a best practice, as found in IBM's survey of 210 senior finance managers. The benefit of a blended approach is access to the "best of breed" source for the myriad of capabilities needed to create shared services. The caveat, of course, is that the additional transaction costs associated with coordinating work across parties can be significant. In retrospect, FIS found that the benefits of a blended approach outweighed the costs.

Lesson 3. Ensure management support until stability has been obtained. At FIS, part of the estimated cost savings for global shared services came from less management. The power players on the shared services team knew they were planning for their own redundancies. The senior vice president of the Americas Shared Services said: "We actually did put our business case to management and said, 'You don't need the same-level management layer you have today. You need a strong management layer in India, and you need the solid customer center management layer on shore, but you don't need us.'"

They could not go back to their old roles because they were filled by successors, and indeed their old roles were no longer the same. In September of 2004, senior management wanted the plan accelerated by three months to capture and additional $500,000 in savings. As a result, some members of the shared services transformation team were moved to other programs or left the company prior to stabilization of the new service model.

This decision accelerated the cost savings but at the price of a loss of focus. The shared services transformation team had always envisioned that the captive center would be staffed with supervisors who acted as process experts and who would be responsible for the execution and quality of service delivery. However, the new manager hired to run the captive center had a different vision, aligned more with the Indian business culture. He organized the captive center so that supervisors were primarily responsible for managing the staff and for allocating work to the staff. Initially, the captive center suffered from the lack of grooming of subject-matter experts and higher than expected staff turnover. (See Chapter 7 for evidence that Indian professionals prefer supervisory and client-facing roles rather than routine work.) FIS had to hire 24 more people in India than anticipated to provide a buffer for turnover and because the new workers were not as experienced or as efficient as the displaced financial staff. But because Indian employees are so much cheaper to hire, the additional headcount did not significantly erode the anticipated savings.

Provide adequate upfront investment in technology, facilities, and people

In our prior research, we found that many senior managers are not willing to make an upfront investment in shared services. This is why many senior executives use transformational outsourcing to create shared services because suppliers make the upfront investment on behalf of the client. But if companies are pursuing the "do-it-yourself" option, they must invest upfront in technology, facilities, and people. In addition to the investment in setting up the original shared services model and related technologies, FIS spent $13.4 million to create the new shared service model. We have already discussed the investment in people in terms of the shared services team and the 174 new hires in India. We also discussed the erection of the captive center facility in India. In this lesson, we discuss the details of the crucial investments made in enabling technologies.

Lesson 4. Invest in enabling technology first. FIS found that technology is a critical enabler of shared services. FIS discovered that their best initial investment was a global, single-instance ERP system. As one informant said, "This is worth investing in before anything else." FIS invested in Oracle applications for Financials and HR. The global ERP system drove process standardization and was the "engine" of the shared services. Besides the ERP system, FIS also invested in systems for invoice scanning, approval workflow, and electronic employee expenses. These technologies helped FIS create a paperless office and enable geographical independence. FIS also customized existing systems to enable language transition workflow. This application reduced the risk around language dependency.

FIS also custom built four applications. Two applications – electronic invoice uploads from major suppliers and accounts receivable cash application automation – were built to reduce error rates. FIS also custom built a help-desk logging and workflow application to track incidents across geography and functions. Finally, FIS built an automated straight-through processing and approval of payments to ensure security and control. Overall, technologies support global shared services by enabling the following:

- Standardization.
- Paperless office.
- Increased control.
- Reduced error rates.
- Reduced reliance on decision-making.
- Security.
- Self-service applications.

Move standard, reliable, stable processes to shared services organizations

Common wisdom suggests that processes that are candidates for shared services are standard across units, reliable in terms of low error rates, and stable in that the processes do not require frequent rule changes. While FIS's management agrees with these guidelines, they offer a much richer process assessment. Lesson 5 provides a way to analyze candidates for shared services at the activity level. Here, processes are pulled apart and component activities are examined by costs, attributes, and readiness. Once candidate activities for shared services are identified, the activities are reassembled into end-to-end processes (Lesson 6).

Lesson 5. Analyze costs, attributes and readiness of process activities to identify contenders for shared services. At FIS, management assessed costs, attributes, and readiness at the activity level. Processes were inventoried, including the major activities within each process. FIS's management was open to the idea that activities within a process could be sourced in different locations. FIS's management assessed the costs, attributes, and readiness of activities through a set of conceptual funnels. The first funnel tested activities for costs: can moving this activity save us money? The second funnel tested for activity attributes: is this activity suited for shared services in terms of standardization, language dependency, and so forth? The third funnel tested for readiness: could this activity be moved? Activities that were ready were well documented, stable, optimized (low error rates), had common service levels, were technology-ready, and were politically acceptable to move. The strategic activity-based model is depicted in Figure 5.4.

Once activities within a process are mapped to their optimal source, the process has to be reassembled to ensure a seamless end-to-end delivery.

Lesson 6. Reassemble activities to ensure seamless end-to-end delivery. Because different activities within a finance process could be

Process 1-Activity 1.1, 1.2, 1.3, 1.4, 1.5,
Process 2-Activity 2.1, 2.2, 2.3, 2.4, 2.5,
Process x-Activity x.1, x.2, x.3, x.4, x.5,

COST:
Which activities provide opportunities
to reduce costs?

Process 1-Activity 1.1, 1.2,
Process 2-Activity 2.1, 2.3, 2.4,
Process x-Activity x.1, x.2, x.3, x.5,

ACTIVITY ATTRIBUTES:
Which activities are suited for shared
services?

Process 1-Activity 1.2
Process 2-Activity 2.1, 2.3
Process x-Activity x.2, x.3, x.6

READINESS:
Which activities
are ready to be
moved to shared
services?

Process for activities shared services

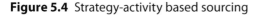

Figure 5.4 Strategy-activity based sourcing

sourced by three types of service centers (regional, captive, or outsourced), the shared services team had to build solid controls and interfaces across service centers and to/from business clients. Each process was fully documented, including the process name, process reference, author, service imperative, SOX control requirements, process narrative, and all process activities. The processes were fully diagramed showing inputs, automated process steps and substeps, manual process steps and substeps, control process steps and substeps, decision points, and outputs. Clear lines of responsibility were drawn around the diagrams, indicating the duties of each party. Service levels described the quality and timeliness of outputs.

Aggressively manage change to prepare all stakeholders

Companies seeking to establish global shared services obviously need to manage change by preparing all stakeholders, including business-unit clients, staff to be retained, staff to be hired, and staff to be made redundant. FIS managed change exceptionally for business-unit clients, redundant staff, and new hires – but somewhat neglected the retained staff during Phase I. Three change-management lessons are discussed below.

Lesson 7. Make the sending end accountable for successful migration. In many organizations, companies find it difficult to solicit cooperation from employees targeted for redundancy. FIS found a way to ensure that the redundant employees were accountable for the success of the migration. FIS built into the retention package a requirement that the employee facilitate and sign off on the transfer of their work. Part of this responsibility was letting the new Indian workers or third-party supplier workers shadow them in their daily jobs. In order to receive their full redundancy benefits, the person from the sending site had to agree that their shadows were ready to take over the process. "If you remember nothing else from the transition process, remember this: let the people that are giving away the work give it away. Make them responsible for it. They know the job the best and most will enjoy the process of teaching what they do everyday" – (Programme transformation leader).

Lesson 8. Coach – don't police – business-unit clients. FIS prepared and involved the business-unit stakeholders in the implementation of shared services. The shared services team understood that many business-unit clients would likely resist the changes brought about by global shared services. Users naturally prefer to have services located in close proximity. Rather than coerce the business-unit clients to accept the change, the shared services team acted as coaches. Coaches evangelized the vision set by the "owners" (in this case the CEO, corporate CFO, and business-unit CFOs). As coaches, the shared services team constantly conveyed the message, "This is your unit's vision – we are here to help." Before implementation, business-unit clients were significantly involved in acceptance testing. This gave users the opportunity to test the end-to-end process and the quality of deliverables. After the implementation, if users were caught violating the new procedures – such as bypassing the shared services organization to procure on their own – they were coached, not policed. The "offender" was gently reminded of the vision and rules. Once coached on the sidelines, the users played by the new rules.

Lesson 9. Envision the future for retained employees. FIS management succeeded in getting users to accept the change, hiring new employees, transitioning staff to third-party suppliers, and ensuring that redundant employees were motivated to train replacements. FIS also ensured that redundant employees were treated fairly and helped them with employment transition. However, during Phase I, the senior leaders in shared services did not adequately articulate the vision of the new career paths in shared services. In the end, we noted that about 60 percent of the staff in the regional data centers were new hires. Ironically, the resultant culture in these regional centers was strong and the financial staff relished their expanded roles of servicing more clients across more business units. During Phase II, senior leaders did not repeat this mistake. Senior leaders identified early in the process who would remain at FIS and more clearly envisioned career paths for retained staff in the finance organization.

In conclusion, we hope that senior executives will be able to learn from FIS's experiences to ensure that the full benefits of shared serviced can be realized. Whereas the average cost savings from creating shared services is only 14 percent,[8] our case company achieved cost savings of 33 percent in Phase II. This financial result is even more impressive because it followed another cost savings program that had already reduced the financial staff from 1,077 employees to 702. The senior leaders were so successful because they were committed to the vision of shared services, dedicated the right resources to create shared services, and managed both the project and change management details.

Notes

1. http://www.nasact.org/onlineresources/downloads/2005_NASC/p1_wilson.pdf

2. IBM Business Consulting Services, "Finance Shared Services and Outsourcing," http://www-935.ibm.com/services/uk/bcs/pdf/g510-6143-finance-shared-services.pdf
3. AT Kearney Report, "Success Through Shared Services," http://www.atkearney.com/shared_res/pdf/Shared_Services_S.pdf
4. Cullen, S., Seddon, P., and Willcocks, L., "Managing Outsourcing: The Life Cycle Imperative," *MIS Quarterly Executive*, March 2005, pp. 229–46.
5. See Willcocks, L., and Lacity, M., *Global Sourcing of Business and IT Services*, Palgrave, 2006.
6. The "winner's curse" occurs when a supplier wins the bid but does not make the profit it expected. In an analysis of 85 of our outsourcing cases, we found that when suppliers do not earn their expected profit margins, the client also suffers negative outcomes in terms of costs and quality. See *ibid.* for a thorough analysis of the winner's curse phenomenon.
7. Netsourcing is more about using outsourcing to *build* shared services rather than to *transform* existing services. In the netsourcing model, the client pays a fee to the supplier in exchange for a product or service delivered over the Internet or other networks. This model may be more familiar to readers under the name "application service provision." With fee-for-service outsourcing, the client signs a contract, which specifies the fees it will pay suppliers to perform services. This model is also extensively covered in Chapter 1 and Chapter 3. With a joint venture for the purpose of commercialization, a client searches for a supplier interested in exploiting the client's world-class services into a separate business focused on external revenue generation. With an enterprise partnership, the client and supplier create a jointly owned enterprise that both services the client investor and seeks external customers. However, enterprise partnerships are different than joint ventures. The first difference is the primary purpose for joining together. With an enterprise partnership model the main focus is delivering cost savings and better services to the client investor. The client's back office is not world class, so it seeks a supplier to help transform the function through better management, better IT systems, and better processes. External sales are merely a bonus. In a joint venture, on the other hand, the primary purpose is revenue generation through sales to third parties. Essentially, the client views its function as world class and believes it can gain more revenues by selling to competitors than keeping the advantage to itself. It seeks a supplier to help with commercialization. In our experience, however, the venture often becomes so preoccupied with providing service to the client investor that it has no resources for external sales.

In instances where clients truly had a competitive offering, a spin-off has been a more successful vehicle for creating a venture. See three relevant publications: *ibid.*; Lacity, M., Feeny, D., and Willcocks, L., "Commercializing the Back Office at Lloyds of London: Outsourcing and Strategic Partnerships Revisited," *European Management Journal*, Vol. 22, No. 2, April 2004, pp. 127–40; Lacity, M., Feeny, D., and Willcocks, L., "Transforming a Back-office Function: Lessons from BAE Systems' Experience With an Enterprise Partnership," *MIS Quarterly Executive*, Vol. 2, No. 2, 2003, pp. 86–103.
8. AT Kearney Report, "Success Through Shared Services."

References

AT Kearney Report, "Success Through Shared Services," http://www.atkearney.com/shared_res/pdf/Shared_Services_S.pdf

Cullen, S., Seddon, P., and Willcocks, L., "Managing Outsourcing: The Life Cycle Imperative," *MIS Quarterly Executive*, March 2005, pp. 229–46.

IBM Business Consulting Services, "Finance Shared Services and Outsourcing," http://www-935.ibm.com/services/uk/bcs/pdf/g510-6143-finance-shared-services.pdf

Lacity, M., Feeny, D., and Willcocks, L., "Transforming a Back-office Function: Lessons from BAE Systems' Experience With an Enterprise Partnership," *MIS Quarterly Executive*, Vol. 2, No. 2, 2003, pp. 86–103.

Lacity, M., Feeny, D. and Willcocks, L., "Commercializing the Back Office at Lloyds of London: Outsourcing and Strategic Partnerships Revisited," *European Management Journal*, Vol. 22, No. 2, April 2004, pp. 127–40.

Willcocks, L., and Lacity, M., *Global Sourcing of Business and IT Services*, Palgrave, 2006.

CHAPTER 6

Can China compete with India in the global ITO/BPO market?

Joseph Rottman and Hao Lou

Introduction

With over 2 million IT workers, 1.3 billion potential consumers and a booming economy, China has gained the attention of multinational corporations as an offshore destination for IT work. Those firms wanting to complement India as the preferred location for software development and back-office centers also look at China as a growing market for their products and services. This chapter looks at China's ability to compete with India in the global ITO/BPO market. A national, concerted effort by the Chinese government involving ICT infrastructure investment, the creation of a national ITO/BPO image and efforts to attract foreign investment is underway. As this chapter shows, even with China's impressive growth in the market, it is not quite ready to capture a significant portion of the global market. China's service providers are currently immature, small and fragmented. Additionally, intellectual property concerns and lack of English proficiency hamper China's current efforts to compete for North American and European business. However, the government and suppliers are actively addressing these challenges, thus CIOs should keep an eye on China.

China's 1,000, 100 and 10 Project

Since the beginning of 2007, a slogan frequently used in the Chinese media, "From Made in China to China Service," has been added to China's national strategy for encouraging foreign investment in China. As a result, "China Service" was the theme of the 2007 China International Software and Information Service (CISIS) Fair held in Dalian, China, in June 2007.

The conference, highlighting China's efforts to increase their share of the global outsourcing market, was attended by over 50,000 people and had over 800 exhibitors. As evidence of China's *national* movement towards service provision, leaders from the Chinese government, including the Vice Minister of Commerce, the Vice Minister of Information Industry and the Vice Director of the State Council Information Office, attended and presented the government's views on the Chinese service industry. In addition to the national Chinese officials, over 40 local government leaders attended.

Despite the relatively small size (about 3 percent of the global sourcing market), the $2 billion Chinese market is expected to grow to $7 billion by 2010, a 38 percent[1] compound growth rate.

Much of this growth is due to China's national plan for expansion of its ITO/BPO market. This plan, called the "1,000, 100 and 10 Project," calls for the creation of 1,000 local large and medium-scale service-outsourcing enterprises, attraction of 100 multinational corporations to invest in China's growing ITO/BPO market by establishing service centers in China, and the establishment of ten cities designed to attract ITO/BPO investment. This is the 11th five-year strategic plan (2006–10) for China.

This chapter will follow the "1,000, 100 and 10 Project," but in reverse. It will first describe the offshore environment of Dalian, China, one of the ten outsourcing destination cities in the ITO/BPO market. The chapter then proceeds with a look at the captive centers and investment by multi-national firms into China and finally it explores several Chinese software development firms.

The key takeaways from this chapter are: 1) China lags behind India in the maturity, size and scale of solution providers, but may fill the role of a complement to India, 2) China's infrastructure (ICT, road system, electrical grid, sanitation, etc.) is more stable and advanced than India's, and 3) China's outsourcing offerings will continue to grow and should be monitored.

Phase I: develop ten cities designated as outsourcing service cities

To understand the overall picture of the emerging Chinese market and the environment of development cities like Dalian, interviews, tours and site visits were conducted with over 35 people in Dalian, China, in June 2007. The participants in this phase of the study included employees of five Chinese software development companies, three captive centers from US-based corporations, and nine officials from the Dalian Chamber of Commerce, technology and development zones, and software parks. Additionally, the authors attended two outsourcing conferences and toured development zones and software parks.

First-hand observations of Chinese and Indian infrastructure

After spending three weeks traveling throughout Bangalore, Hyderabad, and Mumbai, India (all popular sourcing destinations) and ten days in Dalian, China, important distinctions and similarities become clear.

The infrastructure and environment in Dalian surpasses that found in Bangalore, Hyderabad and Mumbai. The power grid, road systems, and airports are more modern and reliable in Dalian. For instance, during a lengthy layover in Bangalore, the electrical power for the entire airport was lost no less than six times in four hours. During these outages (that did not seem to bother anyone other than the first author of this chapter), the entire airport would shut down with the only light coming from the terminals of the customer service agents. Clearly, the airlines had their own generators, batteries and/or power supplies. In the city of Bangalore, the power would routinely (at least once every two days) go out for two or three minutes. These outages seemed normal. In ten days in Dalian, the authors experienced one 30-second outage in the hotel.

The road and transportation systems are also better in Dalian than India. The roads are in better shape and traffic is far less congested in Dalian. Additionally, Dalian does not have the abundance of the motorcycle-based taxicabs that proliferate in India. The lack of these also reduces noise and improves the air quality on and near major roads. The public transportation systems (buses and trains) also appear to be less crowded and congested in Dalian. The road system also seems more likely to accommodate growth than that in India and the airports in Beijing and Dalian are more modern and in better repair than those in Bangalore and Hyderabad.

Both cities do share an incredible rate of new building construction. While the number of new buildings going up in India is amazing; the amount of construction in Dalian is almost impossible to comprehend. The sky is filled with skyscrapers under construction and construction cranes. The major reasons for this incredible growth in construction are the extreme growth in the Chinese economy (estimated to sustain its fourth year of 9.5 percent growth[2]) and the need to house 1.3 billion people.

The countries also "felt" very different. A major reason for the difference in the feel of the cities could be seen by the lack of shanty housing and open garbage in Dalian. In India, the poor and the rich seem to coexist in what appear to be adjacent, concentric circles that do not intersect. For example in India, you will see a brand new, beautiful building constructed of marble and glass being built right next to a slum. Or a beautiful, manicured park next to a large, open garbage pile. In Dalian, there were dilapidated buildings and poorer sections, but they were not nearly as evident as in India. Dalian is a more modern and comfortable city than Bangalore.

Another major difference in the environments of the cities is the evidence of poverty. While the authors did not venture to the countryside (where poverty is more extreme in both India and China) in either visit, the amount of clearly destitute people was ubiquitous in India while almost non-existent in China. This may be due to the differing levels of government control, but the amount of begging on the streets in India, especially in Mumbai, was staggering. There was strong competition among the destitute for "better" places from which to beg. The first author of this chapter did not witness a single episode of begging in China. While this may be due to stricter government control in China, it is most likely due to the fact that China's *per capita* income is 2.5 times as high as India's.[3]

There are also differences in the ICT and educational infrastructures as well. According to a report by the CTO of Neusoft citing experts from the EUCTP (Europe–China Trade Project) and expert reports from multiple sources, China surpasses India in many aspects of ICT capacity, including teledensity and Internet subscribers. Table 6.1[4] details these differences.

However, despite the improved infrastructure in China, Table 6.1 also shows that India far surpasses China in export of IT and related services. As evidenced by the wide gap in IT and related services, what India lacks in infrastructure, it makes up for in the maturity of its software industry and its level of English proficiency. Having interviewed large firms in both

Table 6.1 China and India ICT capacity

	China 2005	**India 2005**
Teledensity	57%	11.43 %
Total subscribers	750 million	123.85 million
Internet subscribers	103 million	6 million
IT workforce	2,386,000	830,000
Export of IT and related services	$1.98 billion (2004)	$17.2 billion

Source: see note 4

India and China, a clear distinction is evident. The campuses and available resources of the large Indian firms are far more advanced than those of Chinese firms. Physical facilities are newer and in better shape. The more advanced facilities are augmented by the clear advantage India has for interfacing with English-speaking countries and clients.

Skills and education

China does have a reported advantage in the number of college graduates. The National Bureau of Statistics in China reports that, in 2006, China had 4.76 million graduates from colleges and universities.[5] According to a report by *Forbes* magazine,[6] India graduated 2.5 million students. However, due to differences in accounting procedures for both Chinese and Indian universities and colleges,[7] comparing these numbers to US numbers is challenging.

English proficiency

The CISIS (China International Software and International Service Fair) and CSIO (China International Software and Information Service Outsourcing Summit) conferences the authors attended in Dalian in June 2007 and the India Outsourcing Summit the first author of this chapter attended in Bangalore in October 2004 provide further proof of the distance China needs to come to compete with India for North American and European business. As China's national media campaign for attracting multinational firms to invest in China, the CICIS and CSIO brochures themselves suffered from poor English translation of the Chinese content. Additionally, the live translation of the Chinese presentations was often incoherent, as were the translated PowerPoint slides. While poor translation of marketing materials may seem like a trivial observation, it does indicate a significant need for far better English skills across the Chinese ITO/BPO market if they wish to compete with India.

What China, as a whole, lacks in English proficiency, Dalian, China makes up for in Japanese-language proficiency. A primary reason that 80 percent of the outsourcing revenue in China comes from their neighbor, Japan, is the historical connection Japan and China have held. While this connection has certainly not always been positive (two obvious examples are the China–Japan War 1894–5 and subsequent Japanese occupation of Dalian and the Nanjing Massacre, 1937), it has created a significant number of Japanese-speaking people in China, and Dalian in particular. According to the Vice Director and Legal Counsel for the Dalian

High–tech Industrial Zone, the city of Dalian has 50,000 fluent Japanese speakers and the majority of the 3.2 million people in the city of Dalian are conversant in Japanese. Dalian has 2,100 Japanese majors in Dalian universities and those graduates help to staff the Japanese BPO and ITO call and development centers.

Our research has also uncovered some interesting techniques that US multinational corporations are using to help increase the English proficiency of their Chinese employees. Oracle's captive center in Dalian, profiled later in this chapter, employs a unique system of incentives and fines. As part of Oracle's Global Model, English is the standard language for all of Oracle's centers around the world – except when talking to a non-English-speaking customer. In other words, Oracle business is conducted in English and support is conducted in the language of the customer. To make sure Oracle's business is conducted in English and English skills are continually improved, if a manager at the Dalian center "catches" an employee speaking Chinese or Japanese to a colleague, they are fined one Chinese yuan (about 13 cents). However, if an employee catches a manager committing the same mistake, they can fine the manager *10 yuans*. The money is collected in a central fund and spent on office parties and gatherings. This system of fines is an attempt to stress the importance of English while maintaining a fun environment. As the general manager said, "The fines won't place hardship on any of the employees, but lets them know that English skills are key and the only way their skills will get better is to practice every day, all day."

High-technology development zones and software parks

A further indication of China's national movement towards a service-based economy, is the regional technology development zones and software parks that are being created. Through national initiatives, individual cities are chosen to house Special Economic Zones, or SEZs. The Liaoning province, which encompasses Dalian, is one of the growing number of provinces housing SEZs. Within the SEZs are High-tech Industrial Zones, which are under regional government control. Figure 6.1 shows the hierarchy.

The Dalian High-tech Industrial Zone covers 24.6 square kilometers and has 1,700 companies, including 380 international enterprises. It is within the Dalian Special Economic Zone that Intel has chosen to invest $2.5 billion in a new nano chip manufacturing plant. This represents the largest investment to date in Dalian and will house 2,000 people, of which 1,500 will be from Dalian. According to the director of the Economic and Trade

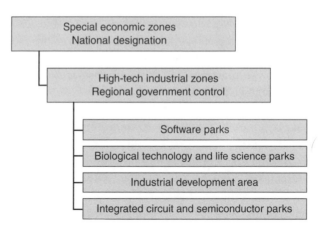

Figure 6.1 Hierarchy of high–tech industrial zones and software parks

Bureau, Mr. Li Xiao Yang, Intel cited tax incentives, solid infrastructure, including the road system and electrical grid, and a good relationship with the Dalian government as major reasons to choose Dalian over the seven other international cities that competed to house the factory. To support the needs of the 500 international employees, two international schools, one Canadian and one American, will educate the children of the employees. Additionally, the housing needs of the international employees who prefer individual houses as opposed to the Chinese tradition of apartments, is being addressed. Negotiations between Intel and Dalian took two-and-a-half years, while construction will take 20 months for Phase I of the factory.

In addition to industrial zones, software parks similar to those found in Hyderabad and Bangalore house software development firms. The Dalian Software Park (DLSP) was established in 1998 and covers 11.6 square kilometers. This makes it the largest software park in China, as well as the largest export base of software to Japan. As of May 2007, 375 companies (of which 30 are part of the Global 500) were located in the DLSP. The second phase of the software park under construction will have an additional 4 million square meters of rental space.

While the software park in Dalian is impressive, with its foreign investment, growth, and bustling population of young IT professionals, it does pale in comparison to those in Bangalore and Hyderabad. The major differentiators are facilities and scale. Having visited the campuses of three large Indian suppliers in Bangalore and Hyderabad, the first author of this chapter noticed that the infrastructure within the parks was far superior in India when compared to those in China. The parks were better organized, more modern and the technology within the Indian parks was more advanced. Additionally, the sheer size of the Indian parks is a differentiator. It seemed like the entire DLSP was equivalent to one firm's presence in Bangalore. A clear difference in scale of the number of employees is also obvious. For example, Neusoft, China's largest software company, has 12,000 employees. Infosys will add that many people in six months!

To sum up China's appeal, the CTO of China's largest software company, Neusoft, states six major reasons multinational companies should consider China, and Dalian in particular, for their outsourcing needs.

1. Well-established, stable, and scalable infrastructure of ITC, roads, power, and utilities. China invested over $50 million in ITC in 2006.
2. Large, well-educated workforce.
3. Huge potential market for services and products.
4. Booming economy. As proof of that, Wal-Mart is scheduled to open 2,000 additional stores in China.
5. Prime location for Asian customer service centers.
6. Significant government support for external investment.

Phase II: attract 100 multinational corporations to China

To understand the reasons why multinational corporations are investing in China by setting up captive centers, individuals from three US-owned captive centers were interviewed. Table 6.2 shows the firms, the major participants interviewed, and their current headcount in Dalian.

Table 6.2 Research participants from captive centers in Dalian

Firm name	Titles of participants interviewed in China	Number of participants	Headcount in Dalian
Oracle	1. Senior vice president	2	100
	2. General manager		
Financial services 1	1. Branch manager	2	400
	2. Administrative manager		
Staff-augmentation firm	1. General manager	2	100
	2. Relationship manager		

Captive Center Profile 1: Oracle's center in Dalian, China. Oracle is a Fortune 500 database and enterprise application company with an annual revenue of $12 billion and 75,000 employees worldwide. To understand Oracle's plans in China in general, and Dalian in particular, we interviewed Mr. Henry Ong, General Manager, Oracle Global Support Center (GSC) in Dalian.

According to Mr. Ong, the Dalian center represents one small facet of Oracle's advancement into China. With over 2,000 people in China and 700–800 people being added every year, Oracle is committed to creating and maintaining a significant presence in China. The advancing presence is part of Oracle's "Golden China Plan." Currently in the second phase of the Plan, Oracle is using the plan for three areas:

1. Investment in China. According to Mr. Ong, "In China, you have to pay to play." Success in China hinges on a clear interest in the long run, for both the investor and China. Oracle is not in China only for lower-cost labor; it views China as a partner on the research, employment, and, most importantly, Oracle sees China as a major customer.
2. Get closer to the customers. Oracle has placed both offshore development centers and global support centers in China to improve its Asian development efforts as well as customer support for Asian customers.
3. Invest in partnerships. Oracle views companies in China as potential partners and wants to nourish those relationships.

The global service center in Dalian is the 18th office Oracle has located in China. Oracle chose Dalian for three main reasons:

1. Resources: Oracle felt Dalian has a good supply of English- and Japanese-speaking, well-educated people. It also felt that growth could be sustained in Dalian.
2. Infrastructure: Oracle felt the sanitation, power grid and road systems were capable of sustaining growth. Additionally, local government support and support from the software parks and technology zones was very positive. Mr. Ong thought that, of all the 11 software parks they visited, Dalian was the most mature. Contract negotiation, site selection, leases, etc. were a smooth process, with most of the difficulty coming from Oracle's own lack of flexibility, not the levels of government bureaucracy or restrictions. To illustrate this point, Mr. Ong said, "One change in the structure or verbiage of the main contract and it has to go back to Oracle Legal. Then lawyers get locked in a room and never come out. For instance, indemnity clauses

can be very difficult to work out. But the Dalian leadership was great to work with."

3. Cost: While the lower employee costs in Dalian (compared to Shanghai or Beijing) did factor in to the decision to move to Dalian, pure cost was not the primary reason.

Mr. Ong has had a long career with Oracle and its China Plan. In China since 1996, Mr. Ong began his career with a "one-year-only stay" with Oracle after graduating from the University of Washington. His one-year stay has turned into a 17-year journey, which has led him from Seattle, to California, back to Singapore (his home) to Beijing and now to Dalian. He now calls Dalian home and has moved his family to Dalian.

The Dalian office for Oracle is part of the overall global model. The three facets of the Dalian impact on the global model are:

1. Investment in China (in Dalian in particular).
2. Support the North Asian customer base (China, Korea and Japan).
3. Mitigate business risk associated with reliance on India for global delivery and support centers.

Mr. Ong describes Oracle as a Mercedes–Benz; great brand name, reliable, and enviable but not swift. The growth of Oracle in China, and Dalian in particular, will be measured and rely on value. The brand recognition Oracle enjoys in Dalian has made recruitment of the current 100 Oracle employees in Dalian one of the easier tasks he has had to deal with. "I have been very happy with the recruitment practices and progress in Dalian. In most cases, I post openings on the Web and get many qualified applicants."

Oracle views their entrance into Dalian as the beginning of a new "ecosystem" centered on Oracle. "Cottage industries" such as manufacturing, support, components, etc., will grow in Dalian due to Oracle's entrance. Oracle helps the entire region when they enter. Large multinational companies with large presences in Dalian, such as American Airlines, China Mobile, Genpact, Sony, etc. are Oracle,Dalian, customers.

In its first year, Mr. Ong has built the Dalian office staff to about 100 people, spread across four areas: Global IT Infrastructure (15), Technical Support (20), Customer Care/Help Desk (55) and Critical/Premier Accounts (10). While the majority of the employees work in Customer Care for Asian markets, late-shift monitoring of the North American infrastructure in Austin, Texas, takes place in Dalian.

Oracle performed significant research prior to choosing Dalian for this global support center. Beginning in 2003, when Oracle first made contact with Dalian and other cities with economic development zones and software parks, Mr. Ong was impressed with the administration of Dalian's facilities and the "soft-sell" approach they took. Over the next three years of negotiation and due diligence, Mr. Ong said the negotiations went smoothly, with Oracle being more stringent and less flexible than the Chinese government.

To take advantage of the Dalian call center, Oracle employs an advanced, complicated customer call routing system. Once the customer enters their Customer Support ID (CSI), the routing system analyzes the customer profile, problem history, and geographic region to determine the appropriate call center to receive the call. The routing system also analyzes the current call volume and the capabilities (technical and language) of agents online to best match the needs of the customer with the skills of the agents. Of the skills needed for effective problem resolution, language skills are the most important.

As mentioned earlier in this chapter, having employees who are highly proficient in English is paramount to Oracle and they have taken a unique approach to encouraging "an English-only workplace." The system of fines and rewards described above helps to create a more relaxed atmosphere. This atmosphere is one of Oracle's strategies for improving both recruitment and retention of employees in the Dalian office. Of the current employees, about one half has come from referrals from current employees. This heavy reliance on referrals shows the importance of *guanxi* in China. *Guanxi* is a complex network of personal and business connections that facilitates relationships. It is the embodiment of the phrase, "It is not what you know, but who you know." *Guanxi* is evident in all aspects of social and business interactions in China. For a more complete definition of *guanxi* and its impacts on outsourcing relationships, see "The Implications of Chinese Guanxi for IS Sourcing Practices," by Chiasson and See (2007).[8] Oracle has used Internet job sites to recruit the remaining employees.

Mr. Ong says that salaries are rising in Dalian and this presents a problem for him in retaining employees. While Oracle is very competitive in its salary levels, they intentionally do not pay the highest salaries in the region. They monitor "market value" carefully and pay above market, but below the maximum for a specific level of skill and experience.

> As part of our global model, we follow this policy: If you pay the highest, you attract a person looking for the highest salary, not the best fit. Those people will continue to look for the "new highest" and move there. We rely on our solid reputation as a good company to work for

and consistently promote from within. I am a great example of this and I tell my employees this in every meeting. "I started 19 years ago in Customer Support and Oracle has made sure I have had the training and opportunities to grow." Each person I hire has those same opportunities and I will help them grow, even if it means growing outside of Dalian to another office. While their transfer may create a little work for me, it helps Oracle overall.

Despite his Asian roots, Mr. Ong mentioned that he experienced culture shock when he came to China. "Common sense does not have a global meaning." Mr. Wong says that "China makes you humble." The heavy reliance in China on *guanxi*, the rapid growth in the country, as well as the turnover of government officials, means "every four to five years things change. You get a new set of people to deal with. However, in China, the business card changes, but the face stays the same." *Guanxi* is only one cultural difference Oracle needed to address.

The differences between Western and Chinese cultures are many. An important difference Oracle had to concentrate on was the use of "side letters" in contract creation and negotiation. A side letter is a document outside of the official contract, which states, if you agree to the terms of main contract, a contingent agreement is also in place. For example, if you agree to a certain rate per square foot, then you also agree to using ABC contractor as the carpet installer. These types of letters are oftentimes illegal and are not used by Oracle. While Oracle did not experience this type of contract addendum in Dalian, they are popular in China and cultural awareness proves necessary in contract negotiation and implementation. Mr. Ong said that Oracle experienced many "growing pains" in its global expansion into China in the early 2000s and now all contracts are transparent and easy to audit.

Another cultural issue Mr. Ong had to understand was the idea of hierarchy and its impacts on the workplace. The Chinese culture is very in tune with who reports to whom, who the boss is, and the relative status of all persons involved in a situation. In many cases, the boss's views are to be followed and open discussion/debate is frowned upon. As two Asian sayings point out, "The tallest tree gets the most wind" and "The nail that sticks out gets hammered down." This idea of accepting authority and discouraging debate creates problems when open discussion is required. Mr. Ong openly encourages discussion and debate. He states he was quite lucky in starting with a blank slate in Dalian.

I had the luxury of hand selecting every employee we have hired. I tell them in each meeting that we are a team, and their opinions and differing thoughts are important and will help to improve Oracle, Dalian. But, this is a hard thing to change in China. Centuries of collective thinking is not something you change quickly. So, at every meeting, I give the same speech at the beginning. This speech is about teamwork and opportunities for growth and a career path. Those who have been here since the beginning are tired of hearing it, but it is important to repeat it. It takes about the first twenty minutes of each meeting for people to warm up and for the collaboration to begin. I encourage people to not only bring problems, but also solutions. Problems are easy to point out, but solutions are valuable.

Another cultural/governmental issue Oracle had to deal with is the Personal File of every Chinese worker. This file, which is maintained by the Ministry of Manpower, follows workers as they move from job to job. While employers know the status (in route, arrived, etc.) of the file, they do not see the contents. However, this file needs to be transferred from employer to employer for a person to change employers. This increases the time needed to bring new employees on-site. "We never know how long it will take for the P-File to move. Sometimes it is two days, sometimes it is weeks." In addition, Oracle conducts background checks using a third party and all gaps in employment must be accounted for.

The employment taxation situation is also different in Dalian. The Chinese equivalent of the US's Social Security costs is called Social Benefits. This tax on employees and employers is traditionally a percentage of the employee's salary and is used for housing costs subsidies, healthcare, retirement benefits, etc. To counteract the rising labor rates and the related expenses for the software industry in Dalian, the Dalian central government has appealed to the national government to change the calculation, thus benefiting all industries with rising salaries located in Dalian. Currently, instead of using an employee's salary for the calculation of the tax, they use the average for all employees of the Liaoning province. This has significantly lowered the Social Benefits cost for the multinational companies setting up shop in Dalian.

The ability to protect trade secrets and intellectual property in China is a major concern for firms wanting to explore China as a base of operations for Asia. China is notoriously lax in copyright protection for intellectual property such as software, music, and movies. Pirated versions of popular music CDs and software are readily available in stores and from vendors on the street. In fact, in 2005, the US State Department placed

China on its "priority watch list"[9] for intellectual property infringement and consulting firms caution corporations working in China that reliance on contracts or legal protection of intellectual property would be a serious mistake.[10] Mr. Ong acknowledges this concern. To protect its own intellectual property until the China market matures, Oracle does not do any "hardcore" development in China. Development, for the time being, is still not an activity that Oracle feels is ready for China's development centers. However, as Oracle grows its presence in China and Dalian, and the Chinese market matures, Oracle will continue to explore which activities are right for China and which aren't.

Mr. Ong plans to let the "value proposition" of Dalian set its growth rate. He envisions steady growth of about 100 people per year as the value of additional headcount can be shown. The majority of these people will be in Customer Support. He does not envision either BPO or development growing very quickly. He does think, however, that the level of customer care (Level 1, Level 2 etc.) will rise in Dalian. He is currently in the process of testing Level 3 and Level 4 customer support in the Dalian office. He initially set up the Dalian office with a "Full Operating License," so he can expand his operation to expand to fill any of Oracle's needs.

Since establishing the center in Dalian, Mr. Ong has been very satisfied with both the administration of the software park and the quality of the labor force in Dalian. He finds the new college graduates well equipped technically, with fairly good Japanese and English skills. To improve those skills, he is currently piloting a two- to three-month training program for new hires.

Globally, Mr. Ong sees India and China continuing their atmosphere of "friendly competition." The major difference he sees is in the focus of development efforts. India is still focused on external companies (i.e. outside of India), while China is still focused on internal companies (and some work for Japanese companies). While India has enjoyed the first position and will continue to do so for quite some time, he sees more R&D centers being set up in China. He sees the Chinese firms moving up the value chain to higher-valued tasks like R&D, and business process improvement.

He also feels that every company needs a "China Plan," and that concentration on the domestic market is a key to success. He also thinks that software parks need to be sure to take care of the current tenants and not give them any reason to leave. While still very happy in Dalian, Mr. Ong realizes his options are open. "All I need is bandwidth and I can set up shop anywhere. It will cost between 1 and 1.5 million to relocate, but my work here is very portable. But Dalian has meet all of our expectations, and we intend to stay."

Captive Center Profile 2: Financial Services. While Mr. Ong from Oracle was very open and frank about Oracle's captive center and global strategy, the two participants from Financial Services captive center in Dalian were not. While they did not require non-disclosure or confidentiality agreements, they did request anonymity for themselves and for their company. When asked why, they simply said, "We think it would be best."

Financial Services is a Fortune 100 firm with more than 300,000 people worldwide. As part of this research program, we have interviewed nine people from Financial Services, two people from their call center in Bangalore, two people from their captive center in Dalian, and five people from a US office.

Financial Services has a one-year-old captive center with 400 people. These employees are divided across three main areas, a call center, data possessing (BPO) and software development. Approximately 100 people work in the software development area and the remaining 300 are divided among the call-center and data processing areas. Similar to other captive centers in Dalian, all of the data processing and call-center work is for Japanese customers and employees of Financial Services' offices in Japan. However approximately 50 percent of the software development is for US divisions of Financial Services.

The call center handles both inbound customer inquiry calls for credit card account information and outbound collection calls. The software development area focuses primarily on Web development using .Net and Java. Additionally, the Software Development area creates and executes test scripts.

The two participants we interviewed, the branch manager and the administrative manager, felt it has been quite hard for the captive center to fully "fit" into Financial Services due to the differences in culture and experiences. This is due in large part to the business model they have with the Financial Services' offices in Japan. In general, the Japanese business units and IT staff completely design the software and submit detailed specifications and Dalian programmers then code to those specifications. This is a departure from the normal project lifecycle for Financial Services, where developers have a much larger role in design. According to the general manager, "The general feeling from outside is that we lack the skills needed to perform the higher-level roles of analysis and design. That is understandable, since up to this point we have only been given the lower-level tasks of coding and testing." The general manager also cited the relative newness of the Dalian center as a reason for the limited types of work being assigned to the center.

When asked for his major challenges managing the captive center, the general manager quickly mentioned finding people with language skills and managing the cultural differences. Despite the reported abundance of Japanese-speaking people in Dalian, he found it difficult to find the level of Japanese skills needed, especially in the call center. The cultural issues have more to do with Chinese culture than matching the Chinese culture with the Japanese culture. The management team feels that new hires are not as assertive as they need to be and leadership and management skills are difficult to teach.

Retention of employees, however, has not been an issue for Financial Services. While only based on one year of activity, the center has a very low overall (both call center and development) turnover rate, at 6 percent. This compares to the general manager's estimated 30 percent BPO attrition rate in Dalian. The low attrition rate seems to be due to a concerted effort by Financial Services to coach and mentor employees. The general manager and his senior staff implemented a detailed and measured mentoring program that acclimates new employees and helps them identify with Financial Services' global image. The training program also strives to address the lack of assertiveness and foster leadership skills.

To help manage and recruit staff members, the center categorizes employees into two pools: junior staff, those with less than five years' experience; and senior staff, those with more than five years' experience. Each category is both recruited and retained using different strategies. Junior employees are recruited from college job fairs and are assigned a mentor to aid in retention. Senior employees are recruited from social networks (*guanxi*) and Internet job sites, with promotions, increased responsibility, and raises used to increase retention. According to the branch manager, it is especially hard to retain and recruit senior staff in Dalian. Many of the people with greater skills or who are more senior live in "Tier 1" cities and are reluctant to move to Dalian, which is considered a "Tier 2" city. The general manager said, "It would be like asking a successful person living and working in New York City to move to St. Louis."

When asked about the planned growth for Financial Services' captive center, the general manager said they will double headcount in the next year. The ratios will stay the same with a total of 100 people in the software development area and 700 people in the call-center and data-processing areas.

Captive Center Profile 3: Staff Augmentation. Similar to Financial Services' captive center, the participants from Staff Augmentation also requested anonymity for both themselves and for their firm. Additionally, they requested that we not mention the name of their major client. We interviewed the general manager and a relationship manager who have the responsibility for establishing and managing the Dalian center.

Staff Augmentation is a 25-year-old, privately held company with more than 2,000 employees worldwide. Over the last 15 years, its revenue has grown 35 percent per year. It provides staff augmentation, consulting, and project management services for 95 percent of the Fortune 500 companies. It has offices in 40 cities worldwide.

The Dalian captive center provides staff augmentation for a Dalian subsidiary of a Fortune 100 technology and consulting firm, "TechUSA," almost exclusively. It represents over 90 percent of its revenue. The Dalian office has been open for 13 months and has three lines of business: staff augmentation (95 percent of the revenue), project services, and BPO consulting.

As mentioned earlier, the primary client for Staff Augmentation, Dalian, is TechUSA. In fact, TechUSA specifically asked Staff Augmentation to create a captive center in Dalian to help the company build its offices in China. TechUSA is growing so quickly in Dalian, it could not efficiently manage its recruitment and hiring processes itself and so engaged Staff Augmentation.

Staff Augmentation's value proposition centers on its successful recruitment and screening processes. It posts openings on Internet job sites, uses job fairs and has significant referral and joining bonuses. It relies heavily on the idea of "friends of friends," further evidence of the importance of *guanxi* in China.

The primary skills needed by Staff Augmentation are language and technical skills. It often finds that applicants have one, but not the other. Its primary goal is to offer TechUSA a "deeper bench" in a wide variety of technical skills. Due to the Chinese employment law that employers must offer employees a minimum of a one-year contract, changes in demand for TechUSA can better be met with Staff Augmentation's employees. Staff Augmentation also manages all visa application processing, background checks, and onboarding issues.

According to the branch manager, many of the new hires have strong Japanese-language skills (needed by TechUSA for its Japanese customers). They are primarily looking for applicants with one to two years' experience and they issue both language and programming tests to screen applicants. Then they will conduct face-to-face interviews and make the final decision. Once hired, the employees will transfer to the Dalian office of TechUSA.

Both the branch manager and engagement manager are very concerned about wage and housing inflation in Dalian. They cited 30 percent wage inflation in Dalian in 18 months. Housing costs are rising very quickly as well. However, the new labor law mentioned above is helping to lower the employers' "social security" costs. The general model is that the employer will pay up to 40 percent of the salary to the government for housing and social benefit. However, Dalian has a real advantage in that the employer will pay a percentage of the average salary in the province instead of percentage of an individual's salary. This results in substantial savings for both Staff Augmentation and TechUSA.

Considering the demand TechUSA currently has, Staff Augmentation plans to double its headcount each year for the next three years.

Phase III: cultivate 1,000 Chinese outsourcing companies

To understand the impact and structure of Chinese software development firms, interviews were conducted with five software firms. These included Neusoft, Dalian Hi-Think Computer Technology Co (DHC), NewLand, Crystal and Netai Techno. Table 6.3 below details the firms and

Table 6.3 Research participants from Chinese software development firms

Firm name	Titles of participants interviewed	Number of participants	Headcount	Total revenue 2006
Neusoft	1. Vice president and CTO	11	12,000	$470 million
	2. Vice president and GM of International Software and Services Division			
	3. Deputy general manager			
	4. CTO			
	5. President, Institute of Information			
	6. Vice president Institute of Information			
	7. Director, International Office			
	8. Project director			
	9. Member, International Office			
	10. Director, Propaganda Department			
	11. Associate marketing specialist			

Continued

Table 6.3 Continued

Firm name	Titles of participants interviewed	Number of participants	Headcount	Total revenue 2006
Dalian Hi-Think Computer Technology Co	1. CTO	1	2800	$70 million
NewLand	1. CEO	1	40	$800,000
Crystal	1. CEO 2. CTO 3. Project manager 4. Developer 5. Specialist 6. Graphics designer (3)	8	100	n/a
Netai Techno	1. CEO	1	40	n/a

participants. Of the five firms interviewed, this chapter profiles the two largest outsourcing firms in China, Neusoft and DHC, and a small start-up firm: NewLand.

Before discussing the Chinese software development firms, a view into the global market and the place China has is needed. As Table 6.4 shows, China lags behind in the size and maturity of its outsourcing and software development firms.[11]

China currently has a small share of the global market and the largest Chinese firms are much smaller than both the global and Indian firms. In fact, the entire headcount of the ten largest Chinese firms (34,627) is approximately the headcount of the fifth-largest Indian firm, HCL, and the total revenue ($424 million) for the top ten Chinese firms is approximately the revenue of the seventh-largest Indian firm, Patni. Additionally, the Chinese market is fragmented with many small firms battling for market share. The top ten firms hold approximately 30 percent of the market share, with the remaining firms with combined revenue of $994 million holding the rest.[12]

As Table 6.5 shows, Japan is China's largest customer for software development, with 61 percent of the revenues being generated by Japan.[13] The United States is second and showed the greatest increase (79.3 percent) between 2005 and 2006. Total Chinese software exports grew 55.4 percent in 2006.

Table 6.4 Global, Indian and Chinese Software and Outsourcing firms

Top ten global outsourcing firms			Top ten Indian outsourcing firms			Top ten software development and outsourcing Chinese firms		
Name	2006 Total revenue in billions	Headcount	Name	2006 Total revenue in billions	Headcount	Name	2006 Revenue from outsourcing in millions	Headcount
HP	$91.7	156,000	Infosys	$4.3	85,000	NeuSoft	$101	12,000
IBM	$91.4	355,766	Wipro	$3.5	66,000	DHC	$68	2,800
EDS	$21.3	131,000	TCS	$3.1	76,000	SinCo	$42	2,427
Accenture	$16.7	158,000	Satyam	$1.6	40,000	Worksoft	$39	2,400
CSC	$14.7	77,000	HCL	$.979	32,000	Inspur	$38	1,000
Cap Gemini	$10.6	75,000	Tech Mahindra	$.727	19,000	hiSoft	$37	2,300
Deloitte	$8.8	37,000	Patni	$.450	12,000	Chinasoft	$32	4,000
Atos Origin	$7.4	50,000	L&T	$.262	7,000	Insigma	$30	4,000
Unisys	$5.8	31,000	I-flex Perot Systems	Unable to determine	Unable to determine	Beyondsoft	$19	3,000
ACS	$5.0	58,000	TSI	$.175	9,000	VSC (Venus Software Company)	$18	700
Total	**$273.40**	**1,128,766**		**$12.76**	**346,000**		**$424**	**34,627**

Source: see note 11

Table 6.5 Chinese Software Development Export Revenue

Region	Chinese software development export revenue ($ million)		Increase	Percentage of exports to region	
	2005	2006	(%)	2005	2006
Japan	574	872	51.9	62.4	61.0
US	174	312	79.3	18.9	21.8
Europe	39	67	71.8	4.2	4.7
Others	133	179	34.6	14.5	12.5
Total	920	1,430	55.4	100	100

Source: see note 13

Chinese Software Development Firm Profile 1: Neusoft. To understand the structure and place in the market Neusoft has, we interviewed 11 Neusoft employees including the vice president and CTO, the president of Neusoft Institute of Information, the CTO for International Software and Services Division, and a project director.

Incorporated in 1991, Neusoft is named after the *alma mater* (Northeastern University, China) of its founder, Dr. Liu Jiren. With over 12,000 employees in four Chinese cities, Neusoft is the largest software company in China and was the first listed on the Chinese Stock Exchange. 2006 revenues of over $470 million were generated by three major areas of expertise: IT services (73 percent of revenue), medical equipment software (22 percent of revenue), and IT education (5 percent of revenue). Of the revenue, approximately one-quarter was generated by offshoring. Neusoft was the first Chinese company to receive both CMM5 and CMMI5 certifications, as well as the first to achieve ISO9001:2000 certification.

According to Walter Fang, Vice President and CTO, who joined Neusoft in 1997 after 27 years at IBM, Neusoft's major challenges come from managing its rapid growth: since 2000, revenues have more than tripled. One of these challenges in managing growth is ensuring a steady supply of talented people to fill positions. This is the reason that Neusoft has created three "Institutes of Information" in Dalian, Nanhai and Chengdu. These institutes have over 20,000 students and help Neusoft to manage its talent pipeline. The institutes help Neusoft address its three core human resource practices: recruit, retrain, and retention.

Of those 20,000 students on the three campuses, approximately 15–20 percent of those who graduate, come to work for Neusoft. The curriculum of these schools includes two years of "public curriculum" and two years of domain training.

While still very small in comparison to the large Indian vendors such as TCS, Infosys, and Wipro, Neusoft's growth is still impressive. Fang notes that the major difference in the current environment is the percentage of development revenue that is generated internally within China as opposed to generated externally. According to the CTO, for every $1 Neusoft makes offshore, they make $4 from the domestic market. This is in stark contrast to the Indian companies, who primarily target firms external to India.

A profile of two major customers of Neusoft, EMC[14] and CSC,[15] illustrates how Neusoft structures its engagements.

Neusoft has 50 people dedicated to EMC within a central Offshore Development Center. Within this center, there is an Offshore Development Team, an Offshore Task Team and an Offshore Location Team, which all report through the Offshore Development Center. Each of these teams is led by a bridge software engineer. Neusoft also has 150 people working in Japan on various accounts, including EMC, who act as customer-engagement managers, high-level design teams and business-requirement analysts, who work in gap analysis and requirement definition. The Japanese team members create specification to which the Dalian teams code.

For the CSC engagement, Neusoft does not work directly with the end users. Instead, they work with CSC to supply deliverables to CSC's customers. There are over 100 Neusoft employees on the CSC account.

Neusoft has experienced a much lower than average attrition rate. They have an overall 8 percent attrition rate and a 20 percent BPO attrition rate. Attrition that does occur is primarily due to two major reasons: family and salary. The family attrition is due to a boy/girlfriend not willing to relocate to Dalian. As for salary, they think an employee will only leave Neusoft for a minimum of a 50 percent increase in pay. According to Neusoft, attrition in Dalian is much less of a problem than it is in Shanghai and Beijing.

To compete for talent in Dalian, the recruitment and retention practices for Neusoft include a nice stock option package: 30 percent of the employees own stock and 30 percent of the stock is owned by employees. To avoid the "job-hopping" and talent-poaching Indian software companies are dealing with, Neusoft pursues any violation of the non-compete agreements employees sign. Additionally, the larger suppliers in Dalian are attempting to form an informal cartel to agree not to "poach" talent from each other and cause a bidding war.

Mr. Fang sees Neusoft and the other Chinese software companies continuing to grow, mature, and more effectively compete in the global ITO/BPO market. He sites the strong Chinese economy, large educated workforce, strong work ethic, and mature infrastructure as the main reasons the Chinese outsourcing market will move onto the global stage.

Chinese Software Development Firm Profile 2: Dalian Hi-Think Computer Technology Company Ltd. (DHC). DHC, a privately held company, has 2,800 people and, in 2006, reported $118 million in revenue.

Of this revenue, $68 million is from software exports. While currently in the process of going public, DHC is a joint venture between Microsoft (10 percent share), Japanese investment from NED and Hitachi (30 percent), and internal stock (60 percent). According to Mr. Limin Zhang, CTO, DHC is reporting a 30–40 percent annual growth rate.

As with many of our participants, Mr. Zhang, one of the founders of DHC, left China to study abroad (in the UK for three years) and returned in 1987. After working in Dalian for a state-owned enterprise, he founded DHC in 1996 with five other people. To staff DHC in its early stages, 30 people came from the "old firm," while they hired 30 new people.

As with the other software firms we interviewed, the majority of their work is done for Japanese customers with a very small US and European sector. They are still in the very early stages of exploring the US market and 80 percent of the revenue comes from Japan.

Their business comes from two main areas, domestic and overseas. The domestic work comes from the telecommunication, public, government, and industrial sectors, while the overseas work (primarily Japan) includes the logistics and financial sectors.

The average age of DHC employees is 27 and DHC recruits from universities (60 percent of new hires) and the experienced labor pool (40 percent of new hires). Many employees also go through internal training, in the form of courses lasting between six and 12 months. These courses offer training in language, technology, and management training. Most employees have computer science degrees and Mr. Zhang was satisfied with the training college graduates received prior to coming to DHC. However, as Mr. Zhang stated, "More is always better."

It is interesting to note that management training includes not only how to manage, but also how to be managed; for example, how to work in a team and how to show initiative. This was a consistent theme from all of the participants in Dalian; the need for Chinese developers and managers to show more initiative, leadership and individualism.

The major domestic competitors for DHC include HiSoft and Neusoft. However, multinational companies like Digital China, Accenture and IBM also compete for the same clients.

DHC has had both General Electric (GE) and Genpact as clients for over four years. DHC is a certified Global Delivery Center (GDC) for GE. An internal bidding system exists for GE and each of the other certified GDCs that compete for work. Many of these bids are fixed price, while a small percentage are time and materials. The key attribute of a winning bid is efficiency, since most of the GDCs are located in low-cost locations. GE currently represents only 2 percent of DHC's revenue, but Mr. Zhang is attempting to grow that share.

As with other senior managers in Dalian, Mr. Zhang is concerned about rising labor costs and the labor supply. In many cases, demand for talent exceeds supply and recruitment is a year-round effort. They send large recruitment teams to universities and conduct both written and technical tests. Of the students who attempt the tests, 30 percent pass the first test, and only 10 percent of those are recruited by DHC. DHC offers three major attractions for prospective employees:

1. A quality, reputable and stable company.
2. A clear career and growth path.
3. A medium to high pay scale.

According to Mr. Zhang, it is very hard for DHC to find and recruit top management and DHC follows a concerted effort to grow management internally through mentoring. They are hoping to promote from within and develop senior managers from existing employees.

Currently, Mr. Zhang feels it is much easier to focus on obtaining Japanese business as compared to US and European business because there is such a high demand in Japan for IT work and the costs in China are much less than those in Japan. Mr. Zhang states that DHC has a very solid reputation in Japan.

Mr. Zhang reports directly to the CEO and Figure 6.2 shows the partial organizational chart for DHC.

Quality of deliverables is important to Mr. Zhang and DHC. ISO and CMM standards permeate DHC's business processes. However, Mr. Zhang said that CMM compliance does raise development costs significantly due to documentation and overhead expenses.

The engagement model for DHC's largest customer base, Japan, is similar to traditional outsourcing engagements. Since offshore rates (in DHC's case, mostly Japan) are typically three to four times higher, they try to keep 90–5 percent of the resources for a particular engagement in Dalian.

Figure 6.2 DHC partial organizational chart

DHC creates a very clear interface between customers and developers and between the on- and offshore employees. This increases knowledge transfer requiring little overlap of resources.

Depending on the client, quality metrics differ. For Japanese clients, quality metrics consist of defects per 1,000 lines of code for both fixed price and time and material contracts. The most severe bugs come from post-implementation issues. For US clients like Genpact, quality metrics center on "first time right," response time, and time to completion. Most of those contracts are fixed price. Rarely are incentives or penalties part of the contract and penalties have never been exercised. As expected, DHC normally does not charge for rework unless it was due to the customer changing requirements or scope.

Looking forward, Mr. Zhang said that DHC's three-year plan calls for an increase to $223 million in annual revenue, of which 80 percent is outsourcing revenue and a headcount of 10,000.

Chinese Software Development Firm Profile 3: NewLand. To understand the role small, start-up firms are filling in Dalian, we interviewed Mr. Liu Jinbai, the CEO of NewLand, a new software development company. Started in April of 2006, NewLand is a very small software development firm with 13 internal employees and 27 employees spread across other partnerships. Housed in an "IT Incubator," NewLand receives reduced rent and tax breaks to encourage investment and innovation. Start-up capital came from investors and personal mortgages.

According to the CEO and founder, Mr. Jinbai Liu, NewLand's revenue for 2006 was $800,000. Half of the original employees transferred from Mr. Liu's previous firm and the other half were recruited. NewLand is focused exclusively on the Japanese software development market.

NewLand focuses on Java and .Net development for its Japanese companies and two-thirds of its revenue comes from .Net development. Primary clients include Japanese insurance and automotive companies, for which they offer both system integration and software development services.

According to the Mr. Liu, NewLand's greatest challenges are to grow the company while keeping both customers and employees satisfied. Another challenge is to grow the company with higher-yield customers and increasing the number of projects with existing customers.

The CEO feels that Chinese development companies are better suited than US or European companies to work with the Japanese firms since the cultures are similar. Chinese firms will find difficulty moving into the US market for the same reason; differing cultures.

Currently, the Japanese outsourcing market is very strong due to high demand for services and the high costs in Japan. Mr. Liu stated that development costs in Japan were three times as high as those in China, especially Dalian.

It is interesting to note, considering the heavy reliance on the CMM and CMMI certification of Indian suppliers, that in Mr. Liu's experience, Japanese customers do not require suppliers to be CMM certified.

While NewLand's profit margin is currently running at 15–30 percent of revenue, they feel the costs are rising in China, including Dalian. He sees a large shake-up coming in the industry with significant mergers and acquisition activity. He thinks large suppliers like Neusoft and DHC will battle for market share, while small suppliers like NewLand will continue to grow and focus on niche areas.

Conclusion

In conclusion, China is clearly well behind India in the outsourcing arena. Its development firms are small and immature and it currently lacks the scale to compete other than peripherally with India. However, it has many strengths and advantages worth watching. Its booming economy, solid platform for Asia-centric operations, strong infrastructure, a large educated workforce and significant government support will cause China's share of the outsourcing market to continue to increase. While executives should be cautioned about questionable intellectual property protection and the lack of English proficiency, China could well be an avenue to an increased Asian presence, as well as a complement to an Indian-centric sourcing strategy. For these reasons, "China – the world is watching" is our emerging trend in Chapter 8.

Notes

1. Bahl, S., Arora, J., and Gupta, A., "What's Happening in China?: A Curtain Raiser on the IT and Business Process Services Exports Market," Everest Research Institute 2007.
2. Smale, W., "China's Growth Looks Set to Continue," BBC News, 27 December 2005, available at: http://news.bbc.co.uk/2/hi/business/4528514.stm
3. Data obtained from various sources, including: the World Bank (www.worldbank.com) and Mengistae, T., Xu L. C., and Yeung, B., "China vs. India: A Microeconomic Look at Comparative Macroeconomic Performance," May 2006, available at: http://siteresources.worldbank.org/INTCHIINDGLOECO/ Resources/chinavsindia_draft2.doc

4. The data is from a report given by the CTO of Neusoft. It was also confirmed through various sources including:Li, Z., "China's Informatization Strategy and its Impact on Trade in ICT Goods and ICT Services," EU China Trade Project, available at: http://www.unctad.org/templates/Download. asp?docid=7910&lang=1&intItemID =4024 ; Foster, P. L., Wolcott, P., and McHenry, W., "The Internet in India and China," available at: http://www.firstmonday.org/issues/issue7_10/press/#p2; Kshetri, N., "What Determines Internet Diffusion Loci in Developing Countries: Evidence from China and India," available at: ritim.cba.uri.edu/wp2002/pdf_format/ Essay-Contest-2001-Kshetri-v3 percent5B1 percent5D.pdf; Kshetri, N., and Dholakia, N., "Drivers of the Broadband Industry in China and India: What Can We Learn?", available at: http:// www.ptc07.org/program/presentation/ M21_NirKshetri.pdf

5. "A Statistical Communiqué of the People's Republic of China on the 2006 National Economic and Social Development," National Bureau of Statistics of China, February 2006, available at: http://www.stats.gov.cn/was40/gjtjj_en_detail.jsp?searchword=students&channelid=9528&record=3

6. David, R., "India Struggles With Labor Shortages," Forbes.com, 11 July 2007, available at: http://www.forbes.com/2007/07/11/india-labor-shortage-markets-econ-cx_rd_0710markets2.html

7. See Ray, S., "US Holds Own Vs. China, India Engineer Grads," *EE Times*, 29 May 2006, available at: http://www.eetimes.com/showArticle.jhtml;jsessionid=JZ2AUITYFMLZOQSNDLPCKHSCJUNN2JVN?articleID=188500637

8. Chiasson, M. W., and See, E., "The Implications of Chinese Guanxi for IS Sourcing Practices," First Information Systems Workshop on Global Sourcing: Services, Knowledge and Innovation, Val d'Isere, France, 13–15 March 2007, available at: http://is2.lse.ac.uk/GlobalSourcing/papers/JIT06–209.pdf

9. See http://usinfo.state.gov/usinfo/Archive/2005/Apr/29–580129.html

10. Bahl, S., Arora, J. and Gupta, "What's Happening in China?"

11. "Managing Offshore, Strategies and Tactics for Global Sourcing," Volume 2.01, January 2005, available at: http://www.managingoffshore.com; "Top 10s in Outsourcing," by India Reports, published by Chillibreeze, October 2006, available at: http://www.indiareports.com; "Annual Research Report of Chinese Software Outsourcing Market 2005—2006," by CCID Consulting Company Ltd.; websites of top ten global, Indian and Chinese outsourcing companies.

12. "Annual Research Report of Chinese Software Outsourcing Market 2005–2006."

13. *Ibid.*
14. EMC is a large, multinational electronic storage company with $9.66 billion revenue in 2005 and over 31,000 employees worldwide.
15. CSC is a large, multinational software and consulting services company with $16.1 billion revenue in 2007 and 87,000 employees in 80 countries.

References

Bahl, S., Arora, J., Gupta, A., "What's Happening in China?: A Curtain Raiser on the IT and Business Process Services Exports Market," Everest Research Institute 2007.

Chiasson, M.W., and See, E., "The Implications of Chinese Guanxi for IS Sourcing Practices," First Information Systems Workshop on Global Sourcing: Services, Knowledge and Innovation, Val d'Isere, France, 13–15 March 2007, available at: http://is2.lse.ac.uk/GlobalSourcing/papers/JIT06–209.pdf

David, R., "India Struggles With Labor Shortages," Forbes.com, 11 July 2007, available at: http://www.forbes.com/2007/07/11/india-labor-shortage-markets-econ-cx_rd_0710markets2.html

Foster, P.L., Wolcott, P., and McHenry, W., "The Internet in India and China," available at: http://www.firstmonday.org/issues/issue7_10/press/#p2

Kshetri, N., "What Determines Internet Diffusion Loci in Developing Countries: Evidence from China and India," available at: ritim.cba.uri.edu/wp2002/pdf_format/Essay-Contest-2001-Kshetri-v3   percent5B1 percent5D.pdf

Kshetri, N., and Dholakia, N., "Drivers of the Broadband Industry in China and India: What Can We Learn?," available at: http:// www.ptc07.org/program/presentation/M21_NirKshetri.pdf

Li, Z., "China's Informatization Strategy and its Impact on Trade in ICT Goods and ICT Services," EU China Trade Project, available at: http://www.unctad.org/templates/Download. asp?docid=7910&lang=1&intItemID=4024

Mengistae, T., Xu L.C., and Yeung, B., "China vs. India: A Microeconomic Look at Comparative Macroeconomic Performance," May 2006, available at: http://siteresources.worldbank.org/INTCHIINDGLOECO/Resources/chinavsindia_draft2.doc

National Bureau of Statistics of China, "A Statistical Communiqué of the People's Republic of China on the 2006 National Economic and Social Development," February 2006, available at: http://www.stats.gov.cn/

was40/gjtjj_en_detail.jsp?searchword=students&channelid=9528&rec
ord=3

Ray, S., "US Holds Own Vs. China, India Engineer Grads," *EE Times*,
29 May 2006, available at: http://www.eetimes.com/showArticle.jhtml;
jsessionid=JZ2AUITYFMLZOQSNDLPCKHSCJUNN2JVN?articleI
D=188500637

Smale, W., "China's Growth Looks Set to Continue," BBC News, 27 December
2005, available at: http://news.bbc.co.uk/2/hi/business/4528514.stm

CHAPTER 7

Understanding turnover among Indian IS professionals

Mary Lacity, Prasad Rudramuniyaiah, and Vidya Iyer

Introduction

While much of this book focuses on offshore outsourcing from the client and supplier perspectives as experienced by senior and middle-level managers, this chapter focuses on the Indian IS professionals actually doing the work. In our research, we found that Indian IS professionals are often viewed as factors of production during the formulation of a client's initial business strategy for offshoring IT work. Clients largely justify sending work offshore because of the lower hourly wages for presumably equivalent work. When clients actually engage in offshore outsourcing, however, these "factors of production" finally become anthropomorphous. This is when the human resource issues enter the forefront of client–supplier relationships.

From the client's perspective, the biggest challenges we heard about regarding the Indian IS professionals actually doing their work were: (1) high turnover and (2) cultural differences, particularly when it came to status reporting on work to be done (see Chapter 2 for examples).

Concerning turnover, retaining IS professionals has been a major challenge for offshore suppliers. The environment of explosive growth combined with a shortage of Indian IS professionals has resulted in a particularly high turnover rate for Indian IS professionals with two to six years of work experience. One contribution we make in this chapter is to provide a better understanding of the causes of turnover among young, vibrant Indian IS professionals.

Although there are nearly 50 studies of IS employee turnover in Western cultures,[1] we are not aware of any research specifically addressing turnover among Indian IS professionals. To what extent are the determinants of turnover intentions the same or different for Indian IS professionals as compared to their US/Western counterparts? To help answer this question, the second two authors of this chapter interviewed 25 Indian IS professionals with 1.5 to ten years of work experience. The participants work for 13 different suppliers. We found similarities and differences for turnover intentions among Indian and Western IS professionals. The main findings, which are fully discussed in this chapter, are:

1. Indian IS professionals want challenging jobs, much like their US/Western counterparts. Our participants were eager to develop new software for clients, to learn new skill sets, to work on emerging technologies, and to manage other people. They complained about performing monotonous maintenance on a client's existing applications and merely coding and testing programs from predefined specifications. Moreover, the extent to which the Indian IS professionals were satisfied with their jobs determined their intentions to remain with their current employer.

2. Unlike US/Western counterparts, Indian IS professionals could not relate to the concept of "organizational commitment" as defined by the extent to which an employee feels emotionally attached to their organizations. Thus organizational commitment was not a major determinant of intentions to leave an employer among Indian IS professionals we interviewed.

3. Unlike US/Western counterparts, Indian IS professionals did not report that job stress/burnout was a major determinant of intentions to leave an employer. Overall, the majority of the Indians we interviewed reported low or only intermittent periods of job stress/burnout. This result may be cultural, as Indians generally do not perceive time in the same way as Westerners. The result may also be attributable to the fact that many participants were performing routine work.

4. Social norms as a trump card: **young Indian professionals are significantly pressured to reside in the same city as their parents**. Although we did not ask participants about the role their families played in their turnover intentions, it emerged as a major theme in 13 interviews.

5. The concept of organizational satisfaction – the extent to which an employee is satisfied with the organization in terms of management support, organizational culture, career development, supervisor support, and company policies – may be an important determinant of turnover intentions among Indian IS professionals. Organizational satisfaction is understudied in US/Western literature, thus it is difficult to assess whether this determinant is unique to Indian IS professionals.

However, among our participants, they could definitely describe their levels of organizational satisfaction and relate this satisfaction to their turnover intentions.

This chapter proceeds as follows. The next section describes the high turnover rates among Indian IS professionals and its effect on clients and suppliers. We then summarize the vast amount of research that identified the three major determinants of turnover for US/Western IS professionals: job satisfaction, organizational commitment, and job stress/burnout. We then describe our 25 Indian participants and present the five findings in more detail. We interpret the findings in light of cultural differences. The chapter concludes with some practices that clients and suppliers might consider based on this and other studies.

Turnover rates among Indian IS professionals

Turnover may be internal or external, voluntary or involuntary. Internal turnover involves employees leaving their current job to assume a new position within the same organization. External turnover involves employees leaving the organization, either for reasons of their own choice (voluntary) or for reasons not of their own choice (involuntary termination).[2] Internal turnover is planned by the organization, and therefore seen as less problematic than external turnover. However, in the context of outsourcing, internal supplier turnover may have similar affects as external supplier turnover from the client's perspective.

In India, the turnover rates in the IS services sector have been reported as high as 80 percent[3] and as high as 100 percent for Indian call centers.[4] For example, Wipro announced that it replaced 90 percent of its call-center and BPO workers in 2004.[5] The lowest rate we found reported on turnover in Indian software services was 30 percent.[6] No matter which turnover number one considers – the low estimate of 30 percent or the high estimate of 100 percent – there is no denying that turnover is a major issue to Indian suppliers and their global clients.

Supplier staff turnover delays the clients' projects, reduces quality, and increases costs.[7] Managers from both a supplier and client organization participating in this research confirm that supplier turnover is a problem for both parties: "Clients complain that the employees leaving at the supplier side cause unforeseen delays in project completion; it takes time and effort to ramp up the new entrant on what is happening, and for the knowledge transfer to be done" (Systems Architect for a global IS supplier).

[The small vendors] would take forever to find resources with the skills and levels of experience we were needing. The small vendors did not seem to be able to attract and retain good people. Then the other thing, too, when small companies lost a senior guy, it was 25 percent of their workforce. They had a huge black hole. That really hurt our projects – it took longer to ramp up and if there was unplanned turnover – we were dead. (IT Technical Lead, biotechnology company)

One structural factor contributing to high turnover rates is the gap between demand and supply for Indian IS engineers. By 2008, India is estimated to need over 1 million IS engineers, yet there are only 340,000 IS engineers in India in 2007. With such a large demand/supply gap, Indian IS professionals can quickly increase their salary by over 50 percent simply by changing organizations. This is particularly true in Bangalore, a city that delivers about 24 percent of Indian's exported software services. In Bangalore, salaries are 15 percent higher than in other Indian cities.[8]

To help retain staff, Indian IS suppliers have increased salaries by as much as 30 percent per year, which increases supplier costs and ultimately client prices. In 2004, the top Indian suppliers tried to enforce a "non-poaching" agreement, but this proved ineffectual.[9] Large Indian IS suppliers, like Infosys, have tried meeting the demand/supply gap by recruiting IS professionals from 30 countries. Although India is churning out more college graduates, recent graduates (called "freshers") require significant investment before they are productive. The co-founder of Infosys, Narayan Murthy, said that up to 75 percent of recent college graduates are "unemployable."[10] Turnover is highest among Indian professionals with two to six years' work experience. Suppliers do not want to spend two years investing in a recent college graduate who will quickly depart for another organization.

We have thus established that turnover rates among Indian IS professionals is high and that it negatively affects both clients and suppliers. The next section summarizes the vast amount of research on turnover among US/Western IS professionals. This research served as the foundation for our research on Indian IS professionals.

Determinants of turnover among US/Western IS professionals

In the US/Western academic literature, the main determinants of turnover intentions among IS professionals are job satisfaction, job stress/burnout (also called work exhaustion), and organizational commitment. These determinants are defined in Table 7.1 and depicted in Figure 7.1.

Table 7.1 Construct definitions

Constructs	Definition used for the interviews
Turnover intention	The extent to which an employee plans to leave the organization
Job satisfaction	The extent to which an employee likes his/her current job
Job stress/burnout	The extent to which an employee feels stressed about his/her job
Organizational commitment (affectual)	The extent to which an employee feels emotionally attached to his/her organization

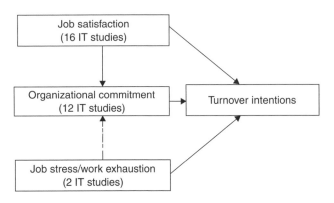

Figure 7.1 Major determinants of turnover intentions among US/Western IS professionals

Research has found that job satisfaction and organizational commitment are two of the best predictors of turnover intentions among US IS professionals.[11] For example, over 20 years ago, a survey of 229 IS professionals found that organizational commitment was the main direct determinant of turnover intention.[12] Fifteen years ago, a survey of 464 IS professionals found that among 11 tested determinants of turnover intentions, job satisfaction and organizational commitment explained the most variance.[13] Most recently, a study of 171 US IS workers found that organizational commitment directly affected turnover intention.[14] Two important studies also found that work exhaustion directly affects turnover intentions among US IS professionals. One study of 270 US IS professionals found that work exhaustion explained over 45 percent of the variance in employees' turnover intentions .[15] Another interesting finding from this study was that younger employees experienced burnout more often than older employees. Ahuja *et al.* (2007)[16] also found that work exhaustion, in addition to organizational commitment, directly affected turnover intentions in their study of 171 US IS workers. In addition, job satisfaction is a major determinant of organizational commitment among IS professionals.[17] These relationships are further described below.

Job satisfaction is negatively related to turnover intentions. Professionals with low levels of job satisfaction are more likely to have higher turnover intentions than professionals with high levels of job satisfaction.

Job stress/burnout is positively related to turnover intentions. Professionals with high levels of job stress/burnout are more likely to have higher turnover intentions than professionals with low levels of job stress/burnout.[18]

Organizational commitment is negatively related to turnover intentions. Professionals with high emotional attachments to their organizations are more likely to have lower turnover intentions than professionals with low emotional attachments.

Job satisfaction is positively related to organizational commitment. Professionals with high levels of job satisfaction are more likely to have higher levels of emotional attachment to their organizations than professionals with low levels of job satisfaction. Because organizational commitment takes longer to develop and is more stable than job satisfaction, turnover models suggest job satisfaction directly affects organizational commitment rather than the other way around.[19]

Job stress/burnout is negatively related to organizational commitment and job satisfaction. Professionals with high levels of job stress/burnout are more likely to have lower levels of organizational commitment than professionals with low levels of job stress/burnout. There is also a negative relationship between job stress/burnout and job satisfaction.

Beyond the literature, there is a vast amount of research from organizational behavior that also supports that the major determinants of turnover intentions are job satisfaction, organizational commitment, and job stress/burnout. For a more thorough academic version of this research, complete with review of prior literature, hypotheses, and detailed statistical analysis of the interview data, see Lacity, Iyer, and Rudramuniyaiah, 2007.[20]

With this understanding of the causes of turnover among US/Western IS professionals, we sought to interview Indian IS professionals to assess the extent to which the determinants were similar or different.

Our research participants

The two Indian co-authors interviewed 25 Indian IS professionals. We believed that they would elicit more trust than the American co-author due

Table 7.2 Demographics of 25 Indian IS professionals

Sex	Females: 7	Males: 18
Age	**Range:** 26 to 36 years	**Average**: 29.7 years
Years in current job	**Range:** 5 months to 6.5 years	**Average:** 23 months
Years work experience	**Range:** 1.5 years to 10 years	**Average:** 5.38

to higher homophily with Indian participants.[21] In addition, the IS professionals were selected based on mutual acquaintances of the Indian co-authors, which further served to elicit trust from the respondents. Although the sample is opportunistic, we believe it is better to ensure the trust and cooperation from an opportunistic sample than to attempt to solicit cooperation from an anonymous random sample because the topic is sensitive.

Interviews were conducted by telephone because the authors are located in the US and Indian IS professionals are located in India. The first eight interviews occurred in November/December of 2006. The next 17 interviews occurred between January and March 2007. The demographic information of the 25 Indian IS professionals is summarized in Table 7.2. The 25 Indian IS professionals, worked for 13 different supplier firms. (In the embedded quotes, the 13 supplier names have been replaced with S1 through S13.) Nineteen participants work in Bangalore, three in Pune, one in Hyderabad, and one in Delhi. The sample contained 13 different job titles, including senior software engineer, assistant project manager, project manager, analyst, developer, team lead, process lead, quality engineer, and quality lead.

The interviews were guided by questions suggested by the turnover research from the US /Western turnover literature. Participants were asked open-ended questions about their turnover intentions, job satisfaction, job stress/burnout, and organizational commitment. Participants were asked to share their reasoning behind their responses. The 25 interviews were tape-recorded and transcribed. Each participant was assigned an identifier labeled P1 to P25. Hypothesized relationships were tested using nonparametric statistics (see Lacity, Iyer, and Rudramuniyaiah, 2007).[22] The next sections describe the findings.

Determinants of turnover among our Indian IS professionals

Among our sample, 13 participants reported low intentions to leave their current employer, five reported moderate intentions, and seven reported high intentions to leave. For example, P3 had low turnover intentions. The following is an excerpt from her interview:

Author: Are you thinking of leaving this company?
P3: No, not right now.
Author: Where do you see yourself in one year?
P3: Hopefully in this company.

The five participants that reported moderate intentions to leave were hoping to switch jobs within their current organizations. They basically liked their companies, but not the current work they were doing. For example, P6 said, "There is a possibility I will be here or gone [one year from now]. As I said, in the next six months, if I don't get a position suitable inside S2, then I will have to look outside S2."

Seven participants reported high intentions to leave their current employer. For example, P16 said: "I have already resigned from the current organization. I will be moving shortly to the other organization."

In statistically analyzing the determinants of their turnover intentions, we found that the Indian IS professionals have both similarities and differences from their US/Western counterparts. Job satisfaction was the only determinant of turnover intentions from the Western literature that also was a major determinant of turnover intentions among our Indian participants. Job stress/burnout and organizational commitment were not determinants. Instead, two other promising determinants emerged: social norms (the employee's beliefs that their family thinks that he/she should remain with their current employer) and organizational satisfaction. Our model of turnover intentions among Indian IS professionals is found in Figure 7.2. Obviously, this model needs further testing, but it does suggest that retaining

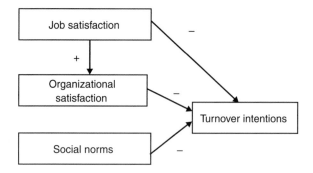

Figure 7.2 Major determinants of turnover intentions among Indian IS professionals in our study

Indian IS professionals requires particular attention to increasing employee job satisfaction, organizational satisfaction, and family support. The findings are explained below in more detail.

1. Indian IS professionals want challenging jobs, much like their US/ Western counterparts. Within the organizational behavior literature, job satisfaction has been extensively studied since the 1930s. Over 12,400 studies had been published on the topic by 1991.[23] Overall, there is strong evidence that job satisfaction among US/Western workers is negatively related to turnover intentions.[24] Among our sample of Indian IS professionals, job satisfaction was also a significant determinant of turnover intentions.[25] Furthermore, the major components of job satisfaction – compensation and job characteristics – were both important to Indian IS professionals, much like their US/Western counterparts. However, job characteristics were more important than compensation among our participants. Indian IS professionals prefer client-facing activities, design, and development work to application maintenance and support. Our interviews found that Indian IS professionals are not interested in routine or monotonous work. The evidence to support these conclusions is presented below.

Among our Indian IS professionals, five reported low job satisfaction, six reported moderate job satisfaction, and 14 reported high job satisfaction. Consistent with the US literature, the components of job satisfaction included compensation (salary, bonuses, benefits) and job characteristics such as task variety, task significance (its impact on other people), task identity (employee performs an entire piece of work), autonomy (employee has freedom to decide how to do tasks), and feedback on their work.[26]

Given the rising salaries among Indian IS professionals, we were interested to know how their perceptions of their current compensation affected their job satisfaction and ultimately turnover intentions. We asked four compensation questions pertaining to base salary, egalitarian bonuses (bonuses distributed equally among employees), performance-based bonuses, and benefits such as healthcare. Among the 25 participants, seven felt they were underpaid, but only two of these seven had low job satisfaction. *Fifteen participants were satisfied with their salaries even though they said they could increase their base salary if they left their current organization.* Furthermore, all but one participant said they could easily get a job in another organization because of the strong demand for IS talent. It is clear that salary is not the main reason for changing organizations among our interviewees.

Beyond compensation, a strong theme throughout the interviews was that Indian IS professionals want challenging jobs, just like their US/Western counterparts. Among the five professionals who were very dissatisfied with their jobs, four were mostly upset about the lack of task variety and low skill-set utilization. For example, P1 complained:

> I have been put into testing and coding and now it is kind of maintenance phase. Now I am not able to use my skill set much. I am not satisfied with the kind of work I am doing. Every alternate day I go to my manager and I tell him that I am not satisfied with the kind of work I am getting and I need more challenging work so I can improve my skills.

P2 complained about merely maintaining a client's application. He says he just, "fixes errors in the application and monitors the jobs … I utilize only 20 percent of my knowledge."

P10 reported very low job satisfaction as a technical analyst because most of his job entails writing emails. He said, "I am not happy with my job. I am dissatisfied. It has become very dull, very monotonous. There is no variety." He wants to find a job in applications development.

P24 is a female who loves her organization, but hates her job as a coder. She is thinking of abandoning her career in IT.

Among the 14 professionals who were highly satisfied with their jobs, 12 mentioned task variety or skill-set utilization as the major reasons for their satisfaction. In contrast to the previous participants, these participants talked enthusiastically about their jobs.

P14 is a male who reported high job satisfaction. When asked what he likes best about his job, he said, "dealing directly with the clients. Customer satisfaction is one thing that makes me happy."

P15 reported high job satisfaction and again mentioned direct contact with customers as a reason for his satisfaction: "Every software release or every major target, we are getting feedback from the customer as well as our managers."

P21 is a male working as software engineer. He stated:

> My job is completely fulfilling. The challenges they throw at me. The challenges I get in my job. The technology with which I am working is really good and you get so many challenges each day. I do get a lot of variety. Like I have to send the proposal document, talk to the clients, and I even have to do development and testing.

P25 is a female with high job satisfaction. She is a project manager in charge of development. She stated: "I'm very much happy with this job. The most interesting part is development part. We get a new module to be delivered to our various customers so, it's more interesting. We get opportunities to work on different platforms."

Thus, while compensation matters, the type of work was a more important component of job satisfaction. P11 typified the participants' views on job characteristics and compensation:

> The first part that makes me satisfied is the nature of the work. How challenging is it? The second part is: What new technologies can you learn from this project or particular company? Third comes the salary part. These are the three main parts, which I look for in a job.

2. Organizational commitment is a strange idea for many Indian IS professionals and was not a determinant of turnover intentions. In the US/Western organizational behavior literature, over 300 studies have used the construct organizational commitment since 1967. Within the US/Western IS turnover literature, organizational commitment has been studied 11 times.[27] The majority of these studies have found a strong negative relationship between organizational commitment and turnover intentions.[28] Although there are various definitions of organizational commitment, the most current and widely adopted definition of organizational commitment (affectual) comes from Meyer and Allen (1997).[29] They define affective commitment as the "individual's emotional attachment to the organization."

We hypothesized that organizational commitment is negatively related to turnover intentions for Indian IS professionals. The evidence did not support the hypothesis as evidenced by the two statistical tests.[30] One possible explanation is that the Indian IS professionals could not relate to the concept of being emotionally attached to an organization. Organizational commitment resulted in the highest number of uncodable responses (n = 6) during our initial seven interviews, when we only asked participants how they felt about the organization. Participants did not naturally reply to this question by expressing emotional attachment to an organization. Instead, the six expressed satisfaction or dissatisfaction with certain aspects of the organization. After P7, we added the specific question, "Do you feel emotionally attached to the organization?" Responses were interesting because many hesitated. Some even laughed at the notion that a human is bonded to an organization. Consider some of the following interview excerpts.

When we asked P13 how he felt about the organization, he said, "Company as such is great. It is a number two company in the world. If I see the company on the whole, definitely one of the best companies to have ever existed." The follow-up question, "Do you feel emotionally attached to your company?" resulted in, "No, no, no!"

For another example, consider the following dialog with P11:

Author: How do you feel about your company?
P11: General feeling is satisfactory, not good.
Author: Does the organization mean a lot to you?
P11: Yeah, as I have worked here all these years, I must be loyal.
Author: Do you feel emotionally attached to your company?
P11: No, not at all … My responsibility is my personal life.

P25 provides a third example of positive feelings about the organization, yet not feeling emotionally attached:

Author: How do you feel about your company? What is the general feeling that you have?
P25: In general it is a good company where we can learn a lot of knowledge in the semiconductor industry and we get lot of opportunities to grow. Good for growth also.
Author: Do you feel emotionally attached to your company?
P25: Emotionally, not so.

In some other interviews, individuals reported that they did not feel emotionally connected to the organization, but they did feel emotionally connected to their colleagues. When asked, "Do you feel emotionally attached to your company?" P10 said no, but clarified with: "But they are a very good group. We are very close. I think if I leave this company, I will miss those people." P23 had a similar response: "Not really. Not the company, but maybe with the people I work with."

Thus, among many Indian IS professionals, the concept of emotional attachments to organizations is a foreign concept.

3. Job stress/burnout among most Indian IS professionals was not a determinant of turnover intentions. Work exhaustion directly affects turnover intentions among US IS professionals in two important studies.[31] During the interviews, we asked participants "Do you experience a lot of stress and burnout in your job?" Among the 24 participants that discussed job stress/burnout, seven reported low levels, eight reported intermittent levels (stress only during certain deadlines), three reported moderate levels, and six reported high levels of job stress/burnout. Below is a sample of their perceptions on job stress/burnout:

P2 (low job stress/burnout): I'm not working to deadlines. We just maintain the deadlines. At the end of the day, we can close all the issues and go home happily.

P21 (low job stress/burnout): No [stress], see the company doesn't expect us to work in the nights, past regular hours or come on Saturdays.

P6 (intermittent job stress/burnout): Workload is okay. Workload tends to get stressful when there are new phases happening, when there are new bugs coming out, new projects happening.

P7 (intermittent job stress/burnout): When deadlines are there, there is a little stress.

P16 (moderate job stress/burnout): Usually some stress will be there.

P3 (high job stress/burnout): If you are working in IT, it's the stress level and the kind of work pressure you have that are too much.

P24 (high job stress/burnout): Work gets intense and takes over your life. That is what I experienced for six months when I joined S8 – very intense. If you get into work, then you really don't have time for anything else.

In the Indian context, we did not find evidence that job stress/burnout was a determinant of turnover intentions.[32] The Indian context might be different from US findings because of cultural differences or the high status associated with working in the Indian IS industry.

4. Social norms as the trump card: family pressure may be a determinant of turnover intentions among Indian IS professionals. One construct that was missing from the initial model but may be important is social norms. Ajzen and Fishbein (1980) define norms as "an individual's perceptions of the social pressures put on him to perform or not to perform the behavior in question."[33] Among our interviews, nine Indian IS professionals mentioned pressure to reside in the same city as the family. We did not ask this question directly, yet it became a prominent theme during these nine interviews. This frequently trumped all other reasons for intending to stay or leave an organization.   Four participants mentioned the importance of family/work life balance. Both types of family pressures are discussed below.

Family pressure to reside in the same city as the family. The participants did not claim that their family pressured them to remain or leave a particular *organization*, only to remain or leave a particular *location*. If the current organization was located near the family, the pressure was to remain. If the current organization was remotely located, the pressure was to relocate to the family. Below are some excerpts from the interviews to illustrate family location pressures:

- P2 (male) feels pressured to remain in Bangalore. While his family does not care which organization he works for, he states, "I am not willing to relocate to any other city. We generally live with our parents and it would be generally difficult to relocate to another part of the country."

- P3 (female, married) does not like living in Delhi, but she moved back to Delhi to be near her husband's family. "I have adjusted here but it was not my choice of place."
- P8 (male) said, "Since I'm married with a family, I won't prefer to switch over to a different city."
- P9 (male) said that he left his last job to come to this job. "This city [Pune] is very near to my hometown. That was the reason for me to switch my last job."
- P10 (male) said, "My parents are dependent upon me. So I can't go long distance because I have to go home every 15–20 days."
- P13 (male) said a change of cities would be very hard on his family, "It would require adjustments on my personal front. My family would have to adjust to a new place."
- P11 (male) feels pressure to move from Pune back to his hometown to be near his family. In this instance, social norms are strong for leaving the organization.
- P20 (male) is working in Bangalore. Despite his high organizational commitment and medium job satisfaction, he intends to leave his organization within six months to move back home to Belgaum. He stated, "On a personal front, I am not happy. I want to spend more time with my friends and family in Belgaum … The only reason I want to leave is to make sure I spend more time with my family."
- P25 (female) works in Bangalore. When asked if living in Bangalore offered any advantages, she replied, "Yes, because within India, family-wise, I do not want to move to any other city so, this city is more comfortable to me."

Family pressure to balance work and family life.   Four participants said that family pressures to better balance work and family life affected their turnover intentions.

- P22 (female, married) is pregnant. She wants to continue working after her child is born, but intends to leave her current organization because they do not allow employees to work from home. But she wants to find an organization that will let her work from home. She states, "I have never sat idle at home. I really want to work from home. But if it is work from home that I am looking at, then I am left with very few companies."

- P17 is a male. He is essentially happy with this job because there is "not too much work pressure in the sense that I mean that there should be work/life balance. We should be free on evenings and weekends."
- P20 is a male who was happier in his work/family balance in his previous job. In his current job, "The work load is much higher. Work/family gets affected." He has high intentions to leave his current employer even though he has moderate satisfaction with his job.
- P23 is a married female. She likes most aspects of her job, but the commute across Bangalore consumes too much time and she feels work/family conflict: "The days when your family needs you, I mean, lots of times, both [work and family] need you at the same time and it's difficult to balance the two – work life and professional life. You can't guarantee that you can leave work at 5:00. You could be late, it could extend for long hours."

We believe that the inclusion of social norms is important to our study of turnover intentions among Indian IS professionals for several reasons. First, research has shown that non-job factors such as transfer of spouse,[34] kinship responsibilities,[35] and family structure[36] affect organizational commitment and turnover intentions. As a specific example, Lee and Maurer (1999)[37] found that having children at home and a spouse were better predictors of turnover intentions than organizational commitment in a sample of US Navy officers.

Given the strong family orientation of Indian culture, we believe that an individual's turnover intention may be highly influenced by family preferences. In addition, anecdotal support comes from our prior work. We interviewed a CEO of an Indian supplier firm who indicated that the key to employee retention in India was family involvement: "The CEO learned that if spouses, parents, and children are actively involved in the company, then the family conspires to retain employees."[38]

For our proposed model of turnover intentions, social norms are defined as "The extent to which an employee believes that his/her family thinks that he/she should remain with their current employer."[39] And we believe social norms are negatively related to turnover intention.

5. Organizational satisfaction may be a determinant of turnover intentions. We highly suspect, based on the responses to the organizational commitment questions, that organizational satisfaction will better capture the sentiments of Indian IS professionals towards their organizations. Organizational satisfaction is the extent to which an employee is satisfied with their current organization. We found that when we initially asked participants how they felt about their organization, they frequently responded with the extent to which they were satisfied with their organization. They explained their organizational satisfaction in terms of organizational policies, management support, supervisor support, career development opportunities, organizational culture, and company reputation.

Organizational satisfaction is clearly different to organizational commitment (affectual). Indian IS professionals could be satisfied with their organization but not feel emotionally attached to it. In addition, organizational satisfaction is clearly a separate construct from job satisfaction, in that some participants were happy with their current jobs (job characteristics and compensation), yet dissatisfied with the overall organization. Conversely, a number of participants were dissatisfied with their current jobs, but were satisfied with their organizations. In these circumstances, the employees were seeking job changes within their organization.

Compared to the vast number of studies (over 300) on organizational commitment in the US/Western literature, little research has been done on organizational satisfaction. We only found 18 articles that even discussed this construct. One of the best articles we found was by Szamosi (2006).[40] Szamosi developed an 18-item measure of organizational satisfaction, which included many of the items mentioned by our participants. These items include:

- "the way company polices are put into practice"
- "advancement opportunities within the company"
- "working conditions"
- "openness of company management"
- "image of the company"

Within the small amount of literature on the subject, organizational satisfaction has been linked to turnover intention.[41] For example, Kittiruengcharn (1997)[42] administered a survey to 408 public sector engineers in Thailand and found a significant negative correlation between organizational satisfaction and turnover intention. Kittiruengcharn's path analysis of the survey data found that job satisfaction contributed to organizational satisfaction, and vice versa. However, the path was stronger from job satisfaction to organizational satisfaction than from organizational satisfaction to job satisfaction. The findings are consistent with the view that attitudes about jobs are formed quicker than attitudes about organizations.[43] We therefore have two hypotheses relating to organizational satisfaction. First, we believe that organizational satisfaction is negatively related to turnover intentions. Second, we believe that job satisfaction is positively related to organizational satisfaction.

Table 7.3 Determinants of organizational satisfaction

Construct	Spoke unfavorably	Spoke unfavorably & favorably	Spoke favorably	Total # of participants who mentioned this as a factor affecting their feelings towards the organization
Management support	3	3	14	20 (80%)
Organizational culture	4	1	13	18 (72%)
Career development	6	3	8	17 (68%)
Supervisor support	4	0	12	16 (64%)
Company policies	4	0	5	9 (36%)

When we asked participants how they felt about the organization, we noted they frequently expressed their level of satisfaction with the organization. They also justified the *reasons* for their feelings by discussing management support, supervisor support, career development opportunities, organizational culture, and company policies. Table 7.3 summaries the number of participants who mentioned these constructs as reasons for their feelings about the organization. We coded these responses as "participant spoke only unfavorably," "participant spoke unfavorably and favorably," and "participant spoke only favorably."

Management support. Twenty participants discussed management support as a justification for their feelings about the organization. Fourteen participants spoke favorably about their managers. Participants discussed that they could bring problems to their managers, ask for help, seek resources, and talk about career opportunities. Only three participants spoke unfavorably about management support. Below are representative quotes of the three classifications of management support:

P8 (favorably): Managers are very nice. They give enough time to the people who are not up to the work by trying to bring them up to the mark. It's a very good, friendly company.
P13 (favorably/unfavorably): Management is supportive of our endeavors but management does not have proper control of the people sitting in the US and Europe.
P11 (unfavorably): Management is not supportive.

Organizational culture. Eighteen participants discussed organizational culture as a justification for their feelings about the organization. Thirteen spoke only positively about the culture. Some examples of favorable. descriptions include:

P11 (favorably): The company culture is very good.

P21 (favorably): The work culture is good. Every individual shares his or her knowledge with everyone else in the company.

P24 (favorably): The work culture is among the best that I have seen. It's a great place to work in.

Only four participants spoke unfavorably about the organizational culture. For example, P13 did not like the relaxed culture in his company. He said: "What does not give you fulfillment is the kind of environment that we have in the business. People not applying proper processes, people not working in a structured format, that is disappointing with the organization."

Career development. Seventeen participants discussed career development as a justification for their feelings about the organization. Thirteen spoke favorably about career development. For example, P9 discussed the career paths as a clear "roadmap" at his company. Four participants spoke unfavorably about career development. For example, P1 believes management placates employees with the rhetoric of career development, but that in reality they assign employees where the company needs them. She stated: "To be very frank they talk a lot about career development. They call you and ask you what your career objectives are, but they want you to adjust according to their requirements. That's how it happens. They try to pacify you."

Supervisor support. Sixteen participants discussed supervisor support as a justification for their feelings about the organization. These responses were bipolar. Like management support, most participants spoke favorably about their direct supervisors:

P18 (favorably): My manager [direct supervisor] is like a guide to me. I go to him for guidance.

P7 (favorably): He is encouraging actually.

Only four spoke unfavorably about their direct supervisor. For example, P1 stated, "My manager [direct supervisor] is very bossy and sometimes I feel like quitting the job just because of him."

Company policies. Nine participants discussed company policies as a justification for their feelings about the organization. These responses were also bipolar. Five spoke only favorably about company policies such as the company's "open-door policy" and the policy at one supplier that allows employees to request a new position every 18 months. Four participants talked only unfavorably about company policies. P3, for example, was very frustrated with her company's HR recruiting policies. She felt that the company hired "freshers" and assigned them to projects without proper training. She said: "Sometimes we end up with really dumb recruits. They don't have any aptitude for the kind of job they have to do ... sometimes you end up doing their work."

To summarize, five constructs emerged from the interviews concerning participants' feelings about their organizations: management support, organizational culture, career development, supervisor support, and company policies. To further interpret some of the similarities and differences among Western and Indian IS professionals, we next consider some of these findings in the light of known cultural differences.

Cultural difference between India and Western countries

Some of our findings may be further understood by examining them from the perspective of cultural differences across countries. Two major studies have inspected the cultural dimensions of many countries. The most famous study is by Geert Hofstede (2001).[44] He surveyed hundreds of thousands of employees in 56 countries. He measured five cultural dimensions: power distance,[45] individualism,[46] masculinity,[47] uncertainty avoidance,[48] and long-term orientation.[49] Another good study of cultural differences was conducted by Aycan et al. (2000).[50] They measured cultural differences among 1,954 employees from businesses in ten countries. They measured power distance (same definition as Hofstede), paternalism,[51] loyalty towards community,[52] and fatalism. For our purposes, India's culture is compared to the cultures of the United States and three other countries representative of Western offshore outsourcing clients: Canada, Germany, and the United Kingdom. Table 7.4 contains the five cultural dimension scores from Hofstede's study for these countries. There is a clear pattern that India differs from the Western counties significantly on power distance, individualism, and long-term orientation. India is similar to these Western counties on the dimensions of masculinity and uncertainty avoidance.

Table 7.5 contains the four cultural dimension scores from the study by Aycan et al. (2000)53 for India, Canada, Germany, and the United States. (The United Kingdom was not measured.) Here again, the results show

Table 7.4 Cultural dimension scores from Hofstede (2001)

	Power distance: the extent to which individuals expect and agree that power is and should be unequally distributed in society	**Individualism:** the extent to which individuals are integrated into groups	**Masculinity:** the extent to which the distribution of roles is assigned to gender	**Uncertainty avoidance:** the extent to which individuals feel threatened by uncertainty	**Long-term orientation:** the extent to which individuals value thrift and perseverance
India	77	48	56	40	61
Canada	39	80	52	48	23
Germany	35	67	66	65	31
United Kingdom	35	89	66	35	25
United States	40	91	62	46	29
Country with highest score	Malaysia, Slovakia (both 104)	United States (91)	Slovakia (110)	Portugal (104)	China (118)
Country with lowest score	Austria (11)	Guatemala (6)	Sweden (5)	Singapore (8)	Czech Republic (13)

Table 7.5 Cultural dimension scores from Aycan et al. (2000)

	Power distance: the extent to which individuals expect and agree that power is and should be unequally distributed in society	**Paternalism:** the extent to which a supervisor or manager takes a personal interest in the employee	**Loyalty towards community:** the extent to which individuals feel loyal to their communities	**Fatalism:** the extent to which an individual feels they can control outcomes
India	123	137	127	95
Canada	96	97	105	62
Germany	99	79	117	45
United States	110	112	111	52
Country with highest score	India	India	Russia (132)	India
Country with lowest score	Israel (70)	Israel (66)	Israel (86)	Germany

that India scored higher than these Western countries on all four dimensions. So what do these differences suggest?

First, the cultural differences in terms of individualism and loyalty towards community may explain why family preferences (social norms) emerged as a determinant of turnover intentions among Indian IS professionals. India's significantly lower score on individualism and higher score on loyalty towards community suggests that their social ties to extended family and community are stronger than in Western societies. Therefore, it may not be surprising that family preferences have not been prevalent in the US/Western IS turnover literature.[54] Instead, the US/Western IS literature has focused more on job stress as defined by work overload, role ambiguity, role complexity, and work exhaustion.

Second, the cultural differences in long-term orientation and power distance may also explain some of the experiences our US clients had with offshore suppliers concerning the unwillingness to deliver bad news or provide accurate status reports. In Chapter 2, for example, clients consistently complained that the Indian suppliers could not be trusted to speak up when deadlines slipped or when they did not understand requirements or processes. In countries with high power distance scores, status reports would only be given up through the hierarchy. Lower-level supplier employees may not feel it is his/her place to inform the client, even when directly asked. The longer-term orientation of India compared to the US may also explain some of the difference on the perceptions of time deadlines. In the United States, deadlines are firm, as consistent with our short-term orientation. One Indian said: "When an Indian says 'The project will be finished tomorrow,' he is really only saying, 'The project will not be completed today.'"[55]

Third, the cultural difference in terms of paternalism may explain why supervisor support and manager support were prevalent themes among Indian IS professionals. In the US, top management support is a well-used determinant for achieving organizational change, such as a technology adoption. However, management support has not been prevalent in the literature concerning IS job satisfaction and turnover.[56] This is not to claim that paternalism is not important to Western IS employees, merely that it is less important, as indicated by Table 7.5.

Fourth, the cultural similarities in terms of masculinity and uncertainty avoidance suggest that India is compatible with Western clients in terms of integrating women in the IS workforce and dealing with uncertainty. Concerning gender, compatibility does not mean that the cultures have achieved equal status of women and men in IS, merely that they have similar gender patterns. Women in IS in the United States, for example, are underrepresented in middle- and senior-level IS management.[57] This is likely true in India as well. Concerning uncertainty avoidance, the Indian culture is actually closer to the US, Canada, and United Kingdom than these three Western countries are to Germany. This suggests that Indians, Canadians, Britons, and Americans are generally able to cope with ambiguity and feel comfortable with fewer rules and laws than Germans. The historical linkage to British rule may explain these similarities.

Thus far we have focused on the similarities and differences of Indian and US/Western IS professionals in terms of determinants of turnover intentions and how these similarities and differences may be explained by cultural dimensions. Next we discuss implications for practice.

Implications for practice

What does all this prior literature and our participants' 25 voices suggest for offshore outsourcing? If our proposed model is predictive, then clients and suppliers need to consider practices that impact three main determinants of turnover intentions among Indian IS professionals: job satisfaction, organizational satisfaction, and social norms.

1. To increase job satisfaction and reduce turnover, offer Indian IS professionals interesting work. Concerning job satisfaction, interesting work, combined with good compensation, was found to be the main component of job satisfaction that directly affected turnover intentions. Indian IS professionals preferred client-facing activities, design, and development work to application maintenance and support. This finding is troubling because many US clients justify offshore outsourcing by arguing that their internal IS staff should do more challenging work while offshore supplier employees can do more routine work. Clients might experience higher supplier turnover if they only offshore routine tasks such as monitoring and maintenance of existing systems or just outsource the coding or testing of new development.

2. Rotate Indian IS professionals from routine jobs within 18 months. What can suppliers do if routine tasks are the bulk of their clients' work? Most of our Indian respondents were willing to tolerate routine work provided the supplier had a *reliable* career path that promised more interesting work in the future. We stress *reliable* because some respondents indicated that their managers made false promises about career opportunities. In contrast, employees from one major global supplier were very happy with an HR policy that allowed employees to get a job transfer every 18 months. They were more willing to execute routine tasks because they knew it was a stepping stone to more challenging jobs. Clients might also investigate suppliers' HR policies to determine the extent to which a supplier can motivate and retain their IS staff.

3. Caring HR policies can increase job satisfaction and decrease turnover among Indian IS professionals. Concerning organizational satisfaction, while Indian IS professionals did not feel emotionally attached to their organizations, the extent to which they were satisfied with their organizations determined their turnover intentions. The good news is that suppliers have much control over the practices that affect employee turnover intentions. Indian IS employees want to remain with organizations that have supportive senior managers, supportive direct supervisors, fun and open cultures, and company policies such as flextime and the ability to occasionally work from home. This latter policy was particularly stressed by six participants who suffered long work commutes.

Within the US IS literature, there are two important studies that suggest that *collections* of HR IS practices influence IS employee turnover.[58] Offshore suppliers may be interested in the following findings. Ang and Slaughter (2004)[59] conducted 41 case studies and found that turnover varies by IS job categories. The managerial IS jobs such as CIO, application manager, and infrastructure manager had lower turnover rates than project leaders, analysts, programmers, network specialists, and systems programmers. Furthermore, the differences in turnover for job categories were explained by differences in HR policies for different IS job categories, such as hiring and promotion criteria, job ladders, wage systems, and training.

Two studies[60] identified five different IS HR configurations and found that the "Human Capital Focused Profile" was associated with the lowest turnover rates (10.3 percent) and that the "Incented Technician Profile" was associated with the highest IS turnover rates (19.9 percent). Organizations with a Human Capital Focused Profile implemented the most number of HR practices for work environment, career development, community-building initiatives, monetary incentives, and employment incentives.[61]

Within the US practitioner literature, *Computerworld* magazine regularly rates the 100 best places to work in IS based on total number of IS employees, IS employee turnover, IS employment promotions, and paid training days. In 2005, they found that the top-ranked retention practices for US firms were (1) competitive salaries, (2) competitive benefits, (3) flexible work hours, (4) work/life balance, (5) tuition reimbursement, (6) bonuses, and (7) telecommuting.[62]

4. Involve the family. Concerning social norms, what emerged from these interviews was a strong sense of family obligations. Primarily, Indian IS employees are obliged to live near their parents. This may suggest that suppliers are better off recruiting talent locally or relocating entire families for exceptional talent that currently resides afar. One small supplier moves entire families to his corporate campus in Hyderabad. While this practice is costly, the CEO said that family pressure to remain ·at his company is so strong, he can offer lower than market salaries and still retain most of his employees.

Within the US literature, there has been some evidence that "family-friendly HR policies" reduce turnover.[63] Although these HR practices have not been tested in the Indian context, they might be of interest. These 21 practices are: sick-child days off, part-time work, family leaves, flexible benefits, flexible time, flexible spending account, compensatory time, family picnic, family resource center, childcare subsidy, sick/emergency childcare, flexible work place, compressed work week, work/family seminars, job sharing, on-site childcare, work/family support group, caregiver fair, after-school program, summer camp, and adoption assistance.[64]

5. For clients, it is important to understand the supplier's culture. In work cultures with formalized hierarchies (high power distance), clients may not effectively communicate directly with the supplier's staff employees. Staff employees are not empowered to relay status information or may fear contradicting their superiors. In other work cultures where task autonomy was high and power distance was low, supplier staff employees really enjoyed direct relationships with clients.

Although we are naturally cautious to extrapolate too much based on 25 interviews or to prescribe HR practices based on Western research, we believe we have identified a good tentative model of turnover intentions for Indian IS professionals. Our next ambition is to test our model with a large sample survey and to assess the effectiveness of HR policies within offshore supplier firms. Our ultimate goal is to help clients and suppliers find innovative ways to reduce supplier turnover or to at least mitigate the losses it causes.

Notes

1. Joseph, D., Ng, K., Koh, C., and Ang, S., "Turnover of IT Professionals: A Narrative Review, Meta-Analytic Structural Equation Modeling, and Model Development," *MIS Quarterly*, Vol. 31, No. 3, 2007, pp. 1–31.

2. Ruby, A., "Internal Teacher Turnover in Urban Middle School Reform," *Journal of Education for Students Placed at Risk,* Vol. 7, No. 4, 2002, pp. 379–406.
3. Gupta, P., "Growth Scenario of IT Industries in India," *Communications of the ACM*, Vol. 44, No. 7, July 2001, pp. 40–1.
4. Mitchell, A., "India Maintains Outsourcing Advantage," *E-commerce Times*, 3 May 2005, available at: http://crmbuyer.com/story/42781.html; Mitchell, A., "Pakistan Now a Hot Spot for IT Outsourcing," *Medialinkers*, 2007, available at: http://www.medialinkers.com/itoutsourcingpakistan.html
5. McCue, A., "High Staff Turnover Hits India Offshore Firms," Silicon Research, January 2005, available at: http://www.silicon.com/research/specialreports/offshoring/0,3800003026,39127243,00.htm/
6. Mitchell, A., "Offshore Labor Markets Impact IT Outsourcing," *Technewsworld*, 28 September 2004, available at: http://www.technewsworld.com/story/36949.html
7. Jiang, J. and Klein, G., "A Discrepancy Model of Information Systems Personnel Turnover," *Journal of Management Information Systems*, Vol. 19, No. 2, Fall 2002, pp. 249–72.
8. Mitchell, "Offshore Labor Markets Impact IT Outsourcing."
9. McCue, "High Staff Turnover Hits India Offshore Firms."
10. Special Correspondent, "75 per cent of Engineering Graduates are Unemployable," *The Hindu*, Wednesday, 4 January 2006, available at: http://www.thehindu.com/2006/01/04/stories/2006010407060400.htm
11. Sujdak, E., "An Investigation of the Correlation of Job Satisfaction, Organizational Commitment, Perceived Job Opportunity, Organizational Communications, Job Search Behavior, and the Intent to Turnover in IT Professionals," unpublished PhD thesis, Wayne Huizenga School of Business and Entrepreneurship, Nova Southeastern University, 2002.
12. Baroudi, J., "The Impact of Role Variables on IS Personnel Work Attitudes and Intentions, *MIS Quarterly*, Vol. 9, No. 4, December 1985, pp. 341–56.
13. Igbaria, M., and Greenhaus, J., "Determinants of MIS Employees' Turnover Intentions: A Structural Equation Model," *Communications of the ACM*, Vol. 35, No. 2, 1992, pp. 34–49.
14. Ahuja, M., Chudoba, K., Kacmar, C., McKnight, D., and George, J., "IT Road Warriors: Balancing Work-Family Conflict, Job Autonomy, and Work Overload to Mitigate Turnover Intentions," *MIS Quarterly*, March 2007, Vol. 31, No. 1, pp. 1–17.

15. Moore, J.E., "One Road to Turnover: An Examination of Work Exhaustion in Technology Professionals," *MIS Quarterly*, Vol. 24, No. 1, 2000, pp. 141–8.
16. Ahuja *et al.*, "IT Road Warriors."
17. Gallivan, M., "Examining IT Professionals' Adaptation to Technological Change: The Influence of Gender and Personal Attributes," *Database for Advances in Information Systems*, Vol. 35, No. 3, Summer 2004, pp. 28–49.
18. Sethi, V., Barrier, T., and King, R., "An Examination of the Correlates of Burnout in IS Professionals," *Information Resources Management Journal,* Vol 12, No. 3, July–September 1999, pp. 5–13.
19. Tett, R., and Meyer, J., "Job Satisfaction, Organizational Commitment, Turnover Intention, and Turnover: Path Analyses Based on meta Analytic Findings," *Personnel Psychology,* Vol. 46, No. 2, Summer 1993, pp. 259–93.
20. Lacity, M., Iyer, V., and Rudramuniyaiah, P., "Modeling Turnover Intentions of Indian IS Professionals," *Third International Conference on Outsourcing of Information Systems*, Hiedelberg, 2007.
21. Rogers, E.M., *Diffusion of Innovations*, Free Press, 2006.
22. Lacity, Iyer, and Rudramuniyaiah, "Modeling Turnover Intentions of Indian IS Professionals."
23. Carsten, J., and Spector, P., "Unemployment, Job Satisfaction, and Employee Turnover: A Meta-analytic Test of the Munchinsky Model," *Journal of Applied Psychology,*" Vol. 73, No. 3, 1987, pp. 374–81; Spector, P., *Industrial and Organizational Psychology: Research and Practice*, Wiley, 1996.
24. Several meta-analyses have found that job satisfaction is negatively related to turnover intentions. A meta-analysis of 126 studies concluded that job satisfaction was to be a reliable correlate with turnover. See Cotton, J., and Tuttle, J., "Employee Turnover: A Meta-analysis and Review with Implications for Research," *The Academy of Management Review*, Vol. 11, No. 1, 1986, pp. 55–70. A meta-analysis of 17 studies comprising 5,013 employees found a significant negative relationship between job satisfaction and quit intentions. See Hom, P., Caranikas-Walker, F., and Prussia, G., "A Meta-Analytical Structural Equations Analysis of a Model of Employee Turnover," *Journal of Applied Psychology*, Vol. 77, No. 6, 1992, pp. 890–909. A meta-analysis of 1,424 accounting professionals found a significant negative relationship between job satisfaction and turnover intentions. See Dole, C., and Schroeder, R., "The Impact of Various Factors on the Personality, Job Satisfaction, and Turnover Intentions of Professional

Accountants," *Managerial Auditing Journal,* Vol. 16, No. 4, 2001, pp. 234–45. A meta-analysis of 178 independent samples showed that job satisfaction predicted turnover intentions and, furthermore, that organizational commitment and job satisfaction contribute independently to turnover intentions. See: *Tett and Meyer, "Job Satisfaction, Organizational Commitment, Turnover Intention, and Turnover."*

25. Because the data is ordinal, with small and opportunistic sample, we ran two non-parametric tests. Kendall's tau-c is a symmetrical test of association between X and Y. Somers's d is asymmetrical, testing the directional association of X on Y. Both tests generate values ranging from -1 for a perfectly negative relationship to +1 for a perfectly positive relationship. For the six tests, we applied p<.01 as the required level of significance. In cross-tabulating job satisfaction and turnover intentions, we found a significant relationship as evidenced by Kendall's tau-c = $-.634$ (significance = .000) and Somers's d: = $-.717$ (significance = .000).

26. Farrell, D., and Rusbult, C., "Exchange Variables as Predictors of Job Satisfaction, Job Commitment, and Turnover: The Impact of Rewards, Costs, Alternatives, and Investments," *Organizational Behavior and Human Performance,* Vol. 28, No. 1, August 1981, pp. 78–96; Rusbult, C, and Farrell, D., "A Longitudinal Test of the Investment Model: The Impact on Job Satisfaction, Job Commitment, and Turnover Variations in Rewards, Costs, Alternatives, and Investments," *Journal of Applied Psychology,* Vol. 68, No. 3, 1983, pp. 429–38; *Van Dam, K.,* "Employee Attitudes Toward Job Changes: An Application and Extension of Rusbult and Farrell's Investment Model," *Journal of Occupational and Organizational Psychology*, Vol. 78, No. 2, June 2005, pp. 253–73.

27. Joseph *et al.*, "Turnover of IT Professionals."

28. Within the organizational behavior literature, several researchers have conducted meta-analyses on the relationship between organizational commitment and turnover/turnover intentions. For example, a meta-analysis of 36 empirical studies capturing 14,080 individuals' perceptions of organizational commitment and intentions to leave found consistent evidence that high organizational commitment was negatively related to intentions to leave. See Mathieu, J., and Zajac, D., "A Review and Meta-analysis of Antecedents, Correlates, and Consequences of Organizational Commitment," *Psychological Bulletin*, Vol. 108, No. 2, 1990, pp. 171–94. A meta-analysis of 126 studies concluded that organizational commitment was negatively related to turnover. See Cotton and Tuttle, "Employee Turnover." A meta-analysis of 178 independent samples showed that organizational

commitment predicted turnover intentions. See Tett and Meyer, "Job Satisfaction, Organizational Commitment, Turnover Intention, and Turnover." Within the IS literature, Gallivan, "Examining IT Professionals' Adaptation to Technological Change," summarized 20 years of empirical research on IS professionals and also found that organizational commitment is negatively related to turnover intentions.

29. Meyer, J., and Allen, N. *Commitment in the Workplace: Theory, Research, and Application*, Sage, 1997.
30. In cross-tabulating organizational commitment and turnover intentions, Kendall's tau-c = −.066 (significance = .742) and Somers's d: = −.067 (significance = .742).
31. Moore, "One Road to Turnover: An Examination of Work Exhaustion in Technology Professionals," and Ahuja *et al.*, "IT Road Warriors."
32. We did two analyses for job stress/burnout, both of which found that job stress/burnout is not a determinant of turnover intentions. One analysis used four levels of job stress/burnout (low, intermittent, moderate, high). In cross-tabulating job stress/burnout and turnover intentions with four categories of job stress/burnout, Kendall's tau-c = −.01 (significance = .995) and Somers's d: = −.01 (significance = .995). The second analysis combined moderate and intermittent categories. In cross-tabulating job stress/burnout and turnover intentions with three categories of job stress/burnout, Kendall's tau-c = −.135 (significance = .408) and Somers's d: = −.141 (significance = .408).
33. Ajzen, I. and Fishbein, M., *Understanding Attitudes and Predicting Social Behavior*, Prentice-Hall, 1980.
34. Mobley, W., "The Intermediate Linkages in the Relationship Between Job Satisfaction and Employee Turnover," *Journal of Applied Psychology*, Vol. 62, 1977, pp. 237–40.
35. Price, J., and Mueller, C., *Absenteeism and Turnover of Hospital Employees*, JAI Press, 1986.
36. Stroh, L., Brett, J., and Reilly, A., "Family Structure, Glass Ceiling, and Traditional Explanations for the Differential Rate of Turnover of Female and Male Managers," *Journal of Vocational Behavior*, Vol. 49, 1996, pp. 99–118.
37. Lee, T., and Maurer, S., "The Effects of Family Structure on Organizational Commitment, Intention to Leave, and Voluntary Turnover," *Journal of Managerial Issues*, Vol. 11, 1999, pp. 493–513.
38. Willcocks, L., and Lacity, M., *Global Sourcing of Business and IT Services*, Palgrave, 2006, p. 104.
39. Although some might argue that our definition of social norms is equivalent to Allen and Meyer's definition of normative commitment,

it is not. See Allen, N., and Meyer, J., "The Measurement and Antecedents of Affective, Continuance, and Normative Commitment to the Organization," *Journal of Occupational Psychology,* Vol. 63, 1990, pp. 1–18. When measuring normative commitment, Allen and Myer focus on the individual's beliefs, such as "I think that people these days move from company to company too often" and "Things were better in the days when people stayed with one organization for most of their careers." We want to capture the individual's perceptions of what their family and peers think.

40. Szamosi, L., "Just What are Tomorrow's SME Employees Looking for?" *Education & Training,* Vol. 48, No. 8/9, 2006, pp. 654–65.

41. Kittiruengcharn, N., "Impacts of Job and Organizational Satisfaction, and Organizational Commitment on Turnover Intentions in Thai Public Sector Engineers," PhD thesis, Concordia University, Quebec, 1997; Shore, L., and Tetrick, L., "A Construct Validity Study of the Survey of Perceived Organizational Support," *Journal of Applied Psychology,* Vol. 76, 1991, pp. 637–43.

42. *Ibid.*

43. Tett and Meyer, "Job Satisfaction, Organizational Commitment, Turnover Intention, and Turnover."

44. Hofstede, G., Cultural Consequences: Comparing Values, Behaviors, Institutions, and Organizations Across Nations, 2nd edn, Sage, 2001.

45. Power distance is the extent to which individuals expect and agree that power is and should be unequally distributed in society. Hofstede calls this the "view from below" because it suggests that a society's level of inequality is endorsed by the followers as much as by the leaders. High scores on this dimension suggest cultures that strongly accept inequality in power.

46. Individualism is the extent to which individuals are integrated into groups. High scores suggest cultures in which individuals are not highly integrated into groups, but rather are expected to look after themselves. Low scores suggest collectivist cultures. According to Hofstede's website, "collective" refers to societies in which "people from birth onwards are integrated into strong, cohesive in-groups, often extended families (with uncles, aunts and grandparents) which continue protecting them in exchange for unquestioning loyalty. The word 'collectivism' in this sense has no political meaning: it refers to the group, not to the state."

47. Masculinity is the extent to which the distribution of roles is assigned to gender. In masculine cultures, men are more dominant, hold more power, are more assertive and are more competitive than women.

Women are controlled by male domination and are more modest and caring than men. In feminine cultures, gender differences are less.

48. Uncertainty avoidance is the extent to which individuals feel threatened by uncertainty and try to avoid uncertain situations. Hofstede says that this dimension "ultimately refers to man's search for Truth. It indicates to what extent a culture programs its members to feel either uncomfortable or comfortable in unstructured situations." High scores on this dimension are associated with cultures that avoid uncertainty by enforcing strict laws and rules, safety and security measures, and have absolute philosophical and religious beliefs, i.e. one version of truth. Low scores on this dimension are associated with cultures that tolerate different opinions, limit rules and laws, and have relativist philosophical and religious beliefs.

49. Long-term orientation vs short-term orientation. This dimension actually deals with a society's virtues. Cultures with long-term orientation value thrift and perseverance. Cultures with short-term orientations value tradition, fulfilling social obligations and protecting one's "face." As this scale might relate to IT, one important aspect of the dimension is the immediacy of results: "A short-term orientation occurs when we know what result we want, thus we are willing to play with the truth to get it. A long-term view of results means that we will get it when we get it – it is more important to find the greatness in our results than to find the result that we want." Among the five constructs, this has been the least examined.

50. Aycan, Z., Kanungo, R., Mendonca, M., Yu, K., Deller, J., Stahl, G., and Krshid, A., "Impact of Culture on Human Resource Management Practices: A 10 Country Comparison," *Applied Psychology: An International Review*, Vol. 49, No. 1, 2000, pp. 192–221.

51. Paternalism is the extent to which a supervisor or manager takes a personal interest in the employee by providing guidance, protection, nurturance and care to the subordinate. See Pellegrini, E., and Scandura, T., "Leader-Member Exchange (LMX), Paternalism, and Delegation in Turkish Business Culture: An Empirical Investigation," *Journal of International Business Studies*, Vol. 37, 2006, pp. 264–79. In turn, the subordinate is loyal and deferent to the superior. This construct differs from power distance in that paternalism can be high even in cultures with low power distance. Paternalism is valued in Eastern cultures but viewed negatively in Western cultures. See Aycan *et al.*, "Impact of Culture on Human Resource Management Practices."

52. Loyalty towards community is the extent to which individuals feel loyal to their communities and feel compelled to fulfill

obligations to relatives, clans, and organizations, even when it is highly inconvenient.

53. Aycan *et al.*, "Impact of Culture on Human Resource Management Practices."

54. One exception was a study that found work/family conflict as a determinant of work exhaustion and work exhaustion as a determinant of turnover intention. See Ahuja *et al.*, "IT Road Warriors."

55. Carmel, E., and Tjia, P., *Offshoring Information Technology: Sourcing and Outsourcing to a Global Workforce*, Cambridge University Press, 2005.

56. One exception is a study of 101 entry-level IS employees that found a link between supervisor support and career satisfaction. See Jiang and Klein, "A Discrepancy Model of Information Systems Personnel Turnover."

57. Armstrong, D., Riemenschneider, C., Allen, M., and Reid, M., "Advancement, Voluntary Turnover and Women in IT: A Cognitive Study of Work-Family Conflict," *Information & Management*, Vol. 44, No. 2, March 2007, pp. 142–53. Arnold, D., and Niederman, F., "The Global IT Workforce," *Communications of the ACM*, Vol. 44, 2001, pp. 30–4; Igbaria, M. and Parasuraman, S., "Status Report on Women and Men in the IT Workforce," *Journal of Information Systems Management*, Vol. 14, No. 3, Summer 1997, pp. 44–54.

58. Ang, S., and Slaughter, S., "Turnover of IT Professionals: The Effects of Internal Labor Market Strategies," *Database for Advances in Information Systems,* Summer 2004, Vol. 35, No. 3, pp. 11–27; Ferratt, T., Agarwal, R., Brown, C., and Moore, J.E., "IT Human Resource Management Configurations and IT Turnover: Theoretical Synthesis and Empirical Analysis," *Information Systems Research*, Vol. 16, No. 3, September 2005, pp. 237–55; Agarwal, R., Brown, C., Ferratt, T., and Moore, J.E., "Five Mindsets for Retaining IT Staff," *MIS Quarterly Executive*, Vol. 5, No. 3, September 2006, pp. 137–50. Agarwal, R., Ferratt, T., and De, P., "An Experimental Investigation of Turnover Intentions Among New Entrants in IT," *Database for Advances in Information Systems,* February 2007, pp. 8–28. Igbaria, M., Parasuraman, S., and Bawawy, M., "Work Experiences, Job Involvement, and Quality of Work Life among IS Personnel," *MIS Quarterly*, Vol. 18, No. 2, 1994, pp. 175–201.

59. Ang and Slaughter, "Turnover of IT Professionals."

60. Ferratt *et al.*, "IT Human Resource Management Configurations and IT Turnover," and Agarwal *et al.*, "Five Mindsets for Retaining IT Staff."

61. *Ibid.*

62. Keefe, M., and Fanning, E., "Computerworld 100 Best Places to Work in IT," *Computerworld*, Vol. 39, No. 26, June 27, 2005, pp. 44–53.
63. Kopelman, R., Prottas, D., Thompsom, C., and White Jahn, E., "A Multi-level Examination of Work-Life Practices: Is More Always Better?" *Journal of Managerial Issues*, Vol. 18, Summer 2006, pp. 232–54.
64. Mesmer-Magnus, J., and Viswesvaran, C., "How Family-Friendly Work Environments Affect Family/Work Conflict: A Meta-Analytical Examination," *Journal of Labor Research*, Vol. 28, No. 4, Fall 2006, pp. 555–74.

References

Ahuja, M., Chudoba, K., Kacmar, C., McKnight, D., and George, J., "IT Road Warriors: Balancing Work-Family Conflict, Job Autonomy, and Work Overload to Mitigate Turnover Intentions," *MIS Quarterly*, March 2007, Vol. 31, No. 1, pp. 1–17.

Ajzen, I. and Fishbein, M., *Understanding Attitudes and Predicting Social Behavior*, Prentice-Hall, 1980.

Allen, N., and Meyer, J., "The Measurement and Antecedents of Affective, Continuance, and Normative Commitment to the Organization," *Journal of Occupational Psychology*, Vol. 63, 1990, pp. 1–18.

Ang, S., and Slaughter, S., "Turnover of IT Professionals: The Effects of Internal Labor Market Strategies," *Database for Advances in Information Systems,* Summer 2004, Vol. 35, No. 3, pp. 11–27.

Agarwal, R., Brown, C., Ferratt, T., and Moore, J.E., "Five Mindsets for Retaining IT Staff," *MIS Quarterly Executive*, Vol. 5, No. 3, September 2006, pp. 137–50.

Agarwal, R., Ferratt, T., and De, P., "An Experimental Investigation of Turnover Intentions Among New Entrants in IT," *Database for Advances in Information Systems*, February 2007, pp. 8–28.

Armstrong, D., Riemenschneider, C., Allen, M., and Reid, M., "Advancement, Voluntary Turnover and Women in IT: A Cognitive Study of Work-Family Conflict," *Information & Management*, Vol. 44, No. 2, March 2007, pp. 142–53.

Arnold, D., and Niederman, F., "The Global IT Workforce," *Communications of the ACM*, Vol. 44, 2001, pp. 30–4.

Aycan, Z., Kanungo, R., Mendonca, M., Yu, K., Deller, J., Stahl, G., and Krshid, A., "Impact of Culture on Human Resource Management

Practices: A 10 Country Comparison," *Applied Psychology: An International Review*, Vol. 49, No. 1, 2000, pp. 192—221.

Baroudi, J., "The Impact of Role Variables on IS Personnel Work Attitudes and Intentions, *MIS Quarterly*, Vol. 9, No. 4, December 1985, pp. 341–56.

Carmel, E., and Tjia, P., Offshoring Information Technology: Sourcing and Outsourcing to a Global Workforce, Cambridge University Press, 2005.

Carsten, J., and Spector, P., "Unemployment, Job Satisfaction, and Employee Turnover: A Meta-analytic Test of the Munchinsky Model," *Journal of Applied Psychology*," Vol. 73, No. 3, 1987, pp. 374–81.

Cotton, J., and Tuttle, J., "Employee Turnover: A Meta-analysis and Review with Implications for Research," *The Academy of Management Review*, Vol. 11, No. 1, 1986, pp. 55–70.

Dole, C., and Schroeder, R., "The Impact of Various Factors on the Personality, Job Satisfaction, and Turnover Intentions of Professional Accountants," *Managerial Auditing Journal*, Vol. 16, No. 4, 2001, pp. 234–45.

Farrell, D., and Rusbult, C., "Exchange Variables as Predictors of Job Satisfaction, Job Commitment, and Turnover: The Impact of Rewards, Costs, Alternatives, and Investments," *Organizational Behavior and Human Performance*, Vol. 28, No. 1, August 1981, pp. 78–96.

Ferratt, T., Agarwal, R., Brown, C., and Moore, J.E., "IT Human Resource Management Configurations and IT Turnover: Theoretical Synthesis and Empirical Analysis," *Information Systems Research*, Vol. 16, No. 3, September 2005, pp. 237–55.

Gallivan, M., "Examining IT Professionals' Adaptation to Technological Change: The Influence of Gender and Personal Attributes," *Database for Advances in Information Systems*, Vol. 35, No. 3, Summer 2004, pp. 28–49.

Gupta, P., "Growth Scenario of IT Industries in India," *Communications of the ACM*, Vol. 44, No. 7, July 2001, pp. 40–1.

Hofstede, G., Cultural Consequences: Comparing Values, Behaviors, Institutions, and Organizations Across Nations, 2nd edn, Sage, 2001.

Hom, P., Caranikas-Walker, F., and Prussia, G., "A Meta-Analytical Structural Equations Analysis of a Model of Employee Turnover," *Journal of Applied Psychology*, Vol. 77, No. 6, 1992, pp. 890–909.

Igbaria, M., and Greenhaus, J., "Determinants of MIS Employees' Turnover Intentions: A Structural Equation Model," *Communications of the ACM*, Vol. 35, No. 2, 1992, pp. 34–49.

Igbaria, M., and Parasuraman, S., "Status Report on Women and Men in the IT Workforce," *Journal of Information Systems Management*, Vol. 14, No. 3, Summer 1997, pp. 44–54.

Igbaria, M., Parasuraman, S., and Bawawy, M., "Work Experiences, Job Involvement, and Quality of Work Life among IS Personnel," *MIS Quarterly*, Vol. 18, No. 2, 1994, pp. 175–201.

Jiang, J. and Klein, G., "A Discrepancy Model of Information Systems Personnel Turnover," *Journal of Management Information Systems*, Vol. 19, No. 2, Fall 2002, pp. 249–72.

Joseph, D., Ng, K., Koh, C., and Ang, S., "Turnover of IT Professionals: A Narrative Review, Meta-Analytic Structural Equation Modeling, and Model Development," *MIS Quarterly*, Vol. 31, No. 3, 2007, pp. 1–31.

Keefe, M., and Fanning, E., "Computerworld 100 Best Places to Work in IT," *Computerworld*, Vol. 39, No. 26, June 27, 2005, pp. 44–53.

Kittiruengcharn, N., "Impacts of Job and Organizational Satisfaction, and Organizational Commitment on Turnover Intentions in Thai Public Sector Engineers," PhD thesis, Concordia University, Quebec, 1997.

Kopelman, R., Prottas, D., Thompsom, C., and White Jahn, E., "A Multi-level Examination of Work-Life Practices: Is More Always Better?" *Journal of Managerial Issues*, Vol. 18, Summer 2006, pp. 232–54.

Lacity, M., Iyer, V., and Rudramuniyaiah, P., "Modeling Turnover Intentions of Indian IS Professionals," *Third International Conference on Outsourcing of Information Systems*, Hiedelberg, 2007.

Lee, T., and Maurer, S., "The Effects of Family Structure on Organizational Commitment, Intention to Leave, and Voluntary Turnover," *Journal of Managerial Issues,* Vol. 11, 1999, pp. 493–513.

Mathieu, J., and Zajac, D., "A Review and Meta-analysis of Antecedents, Correlates, and Consequences of Organizational Commitment," *Psychological Bulletin*, Vol. 108, No. 2, 1990, pp. 171–94.

McCue, A., "High Staff Turnover Hits India Offshore Firms," Silicon Research, January 2005, available at: http://www.silicon.com/research/specialreports/offshoring/0,3800003026,3 9127243,00.htm/

Mesmer-Magnus, J., and Viswesvaran, C., "How Family-Friendly Work Environments Affect Family/Work Conflict: A Meta-Analytical Examination," *Journal of Labor Research*, Vol. 28, No. 4, Fall 2006, pp. 555–74.

Meyer, J., and Allen, N., Commitment in the Workplace: Theory, Research, and Application, Sage, 1997.

Mitchell, A., "Offshore Labor Markets Impact IT Outsourcing," *Technewsworld*, 28 September 2004, available at: http://www.tech-newsworld.com/story/36949.html

Mitchell, A., "India Maintains Outsourcing Advantage," *E-commerce Times*, 3 May 2005, available at: http://crmbuyer.com/story/42781.html

Mitchell, A., "Pakistan Now a Hot Spot for IT Outsourcing," *Medialinkers*, 2007, available at: http://www.medialinkers.com/itoutsourcingpakistan.html

Mobley, W., "The Intermediate Linkages in the Relationship Between Job Satisfaction and Employee Turnover," *Journal of Applied Psychology*, Vol. 62, 1977, pp. 237–40.

Moore, J.E., "One Road to Turnover: An Examination of Work Exhaustion in Technology Professionals," *MIS Quarterly*, Vol. 24, No. 1, 2000, pp. 141–8.

Pellegrini, E., and Scandura, T., "Leader-Member Exchange (LMX), Paternalism, and Delegation in Turkish Business Culture: An Empirical Investigation," *Journal of International Business Studies*, Vol. 37, 2006, pp. 264–79.

Price, J., and Mueller, C., *Absenteeism and Turnover of Hospital Employees*, JAI Press, 1986.

Rogers, E.M., *Diffusion of Innovations*, Free Press, 2006.

Ruby, A., "Internal Teacher Turnover in Urban Middle School Reform," *Journal of Education for Students Placed at Risk,* Vol. 7, No. 4, 2002, pp. 379–406.

Rusbult, C, and Farrell, D., "A Longitudinal Test of the Investment Model: The Impact on Job Satisfaction, Job Commitment, and Turnover Variations in Rewards, Costs, Alternatives, and Investments," *Journal of Applied Psychology,* Vol. 68, No. 3, 1983, pp. 429–38.

Sethi, V., Barrier, T., and King, R., "An Examination of the Correlates of Burnout in IS Professionals," *Information Resources Management Journal,* Vol 12, No. 3, July–September 1999, pp. 5–13.

Shore, L., and Tetrick, L., "A Construct Validity Study of the Survey of Perceived Organizational Support," *Journal of Applied Psychology,* Vol. 76, 1991, pp. 637–43.

Special Correspondent, "75 per cent of Engineering Graduates are Unemployable," *The Hindu*, Wednesday, 4 January 2006, available at: http://www.thehindu.com/2006/01/04/stories/2006010407060400.htm

Spector, P., *Industrial and Organizational Psychology: Research and Practice*, Wiley, 1996.

Stroh, L., Brett, J., and Reilly, A., "Family Structure, Glass Ceiling, and Traditional Explanations for the Differential Rate of Turnover of Female and Male Managers," *Journal of Vocational Behavior*, Vol. 49, 1996, pp. 99–118.

Sujdak, E., "An Investigation of the Correlation of Job Satisfaction, Organizational Commitment, Perceived Job Opportunity, Organizational Communications, Job Search Behavior, and the Intent to Turnover in

IT Professionals," unpublished PhD thesis, Wayne Huizenga School of Business and Entrepreneurship, Nova Southeastern University, 2002.

Szamosi, L., "Just What are Tomorrow's SME Employees Looking for?" *Education & Training,* Vol. 48, No. 8/9, 2006, pp. 654–65.

Tett, R., and Meyer, J., "Job Satisfaction, Organizational Commitment, Turnover Intention, and Turnover: Path Analyses Based on meta Analytic Findings," *Personnel Psychology,* Vol. 46, No. 2, Summer 1993, pp. 259–93.

Van Dam, K., "Employee Attitudes Toward Job Changes: An Application and Extension of Rusbult and Farrell's Investment Model," *Journal of Occupational and Organizational Psychology*, Vol. 78, No. 2, June 2005, pp.253–73.

Willcocks, L., and Lacity, M., *Global Sourcing of Business and IT Services*, Palgrave, 2006.

CHAPTER 8

Emerging trends
Mary Lacity and Joseph Rottman

Introduction

In this final chapter, we look at 13 emerging trends in global spend on information and communication technologies (ICT), information technology outsourcing (ITO), and business process outsourcing (BPO). These trends are evident from our own case studies, government reports, and industry analysts. The overall trends indicate growth in all three markets (ICT, ITO, and BPO). Furthermore, countries from all six continents will actively participate in these markets as both clients and providers. We also predict growth in niche markets such as rural sourcing, nearshoring, knowledge process outsourcing, and freelance outsourcing.

1. The US, while still the number one ICT spender, is spending proportionally less of the total global ICT spend. Global spend on ICT, which includes both ICT goods and services, has increased every year during the past 40 years. Worldwide in 2007, the total spend on ICT exceeded $3 trillion. In 2007, the US portion of global spend in ICT represented a staggering 38.5 percent.[1] However, the US portion of global IT spend was 41.5 percent in 2001 and has declined each year since then.[2] Although the US remains the top overall spender, other countries are spending money on IT at a faster rate.

In 2005, the top spenders were the United States, Japan, Germany, United Kingdom, France, China, Italy, Canada, Brazil, and Korea. By 2007, India replaced Korea as a member of the top ten list of IT spenders, with $65.5 billion. By 2009, China will be the third-largest ICT spending country after the US and Japan.[3] Thus, despite Nicolas Carr's argument that, "as for IT-spurred industry transformations, most of the ones that are going to happen have already happened," the world continues to invest heavily in ICT.[4]

2. The ITO market will continue to grow through multi-sourcing. While most of the enormous ICT spend is consumed internally by organizations (such as paying for IT salaries, hardware leases, software licenses), the global ITO market has increased each year since we've been tracking it. Back in 1989, global ITO was only a $9–12 billion market.[5] In 2007, the global ITO market is estimated to be between a $200 and $250 billion market.[6]

Although the overall ITO spend has increased, the size of individual contracts and the duration of contracts have decreased between 1998 and 2005. For example, the Everest Group found that among the ITO contracts signed in 1998, 24 percent of contracts were worth more than $400 million and 33 percent of contracts were worth between $50 and $100 million. In 2005, only 11 percent of contracts were worth more than $400 million and 57 percent of contracts were worth between $50 and $100 million. Concerning contract duration, the Everest Group found that 37 percent of contracts signed in 1998 were more than nine years in duration compared to 18 percent in 2005.[7]

How can we reconcile smaller, shorter deals with an overall increase in the ITO market? All these figures suggest that client organizations are actively pursuing more multi-sourcing. The overall growth in ITO is driven by client organizations signing *more* ITO contracts with *more* ITO suppliers. While multi-sourcing helps clients access best-of-breed suppliers and mitigates the risks of reliance on a single supplier, it also means increased transaction costs as clients manage more suppliers. Multi-sourcing also means that suppliers incur more transaction costs. Suppliers must bid more frequently because contracts are shorter. Suppliers face more competition because smaller deals mean more suppliers will qualify to bid. Suppliers need to attract more customers in order to meet growth targets.

3. Developed countries actually export more ICT services than they import. Overall, the G7 countries (Canada, France, Germany, Italy, Japan, United Kingdom, and United States) had an ICT services surplus in 2005. According to the Organization for Economic Cooperation and Development (OECD), these seven countries imported $29 billion-worth of ICT services and exported $33.8 billion in 2005. However, the percentage change between imports and exports between 2000 and 2005 shows that imports grew by 12.3 percent annually whereas exports grew 10.9 percent annually.[8] (As of July 2007, the OECD had not posted 2006 data.)

Table 8.1 shows the ICT services trade exports, imports, and net (exports minus imports) for nine countries as extracted from the OECD database.[9] This database tracks ICT spend for 33 countries. We included the data on the G7 countries, plus Ireland and Australia. According to the OECD, the United States had an ICT services deficit of $730 million (exports of $8.239 billion compared to imports of $8.969 billion) in 2005. This was the only year a deficit was recorded between 1991 and 2005. Between 1991 and 2005, the United Kingdom had ICT services surpluses each year. In 2005, the United Kingdom

Table 8.1 Trade in ICT services in $US million

		2004	**2005**
Australia	Net	$155.2	$83.2
	Exports	$937.7	$885.9
	Imports	$782.5	$802.6
Canada	Net	$1,281.3	$1,319.1
	Exports	$3,139.8	$3,417.3
	Imports	$1,858.5	$2,097.8
France	Net	$41.0	$–79.6
	Exports	$1,478.8	$1,681.3
	Imports	$1,437.9	$1,760.9
Germany	Net	$–54.4	$–304.7
	Exports	$8,017.5	$8,158.0
	Imports	$8,070.9	$8,462.7
Ireland	Net	$18,368.1	$18,254.7
	Exports	$18,749.3	$18,672.6
	Imports	$381.2	$417.8
Italy	Net	$–637.0	$–902.9
	Exports	$562.5	$595.7
	Imports	$1,199.5	$1,498.5
Japan	Net	$–1.146.1	$–1,315.6
	Exports	$1,042.6	$1,126.9
	Imports	$2,188.7	$2,442.4
United Kingdom	Net	$7,984.5	$6,767.3
	Exports	$11,668.3	$10,603.6
	Imports	$3,683.8	$3,836.4
United States	Net	$2,256.0	$–730.0
	Exports	$8,939.0	$8,239.0
	Imports	$6,683.0	$ 8,969.0

Source: OECD

exported $10.6 billion in ICT services and imported $3.8 billion, generating a surplus of $6.8 billion. The 2005 surplus was slightly lower than the 2004 surplus of $7.98 billion. Ireland provides one example of a developed country with a significant ICT services surplus. In 2005, Ireland exported $18.672 billion in ICT services and imported $418 million, thus generating a surplus of $18.254 billion. Ireland's export of ICT and business services was 20 percent of its country's total exports in 2004.[10]

One must be cautious in interpreting figures, however. Some sources report very different numbers. Discrepancies in numbers are attributable to different definitions of ICT (goods and services vs just services or just goods) and different estimating techniques. Consider the case of Australia. According to an article in *Information Age*, Australia exported ICT *goods and services* worth $5.3 billion and imported $25 billion in 2005. Thus, according to this source, Australia's ICT trade deficit reached $19.7 billion during 2005. In 2006, the trade deficit reached $21 billion.[11] The OECD, however, reports that Australia experienced ICT *services* trade surpluses in 2004 and 2005. According to that data, Australia's ICT service exports were $885.9 million and imports were $802.6 million, generating a net surplus of $83.2 million. A third source – the United Nations Conference on Trade and Development (UNCTAD) – reports that Australia's ICT services exports were $720 million in 2003, whereas the OECD reports it to have been $762 million.[12]

4. Domestic demand for IT talent will be outpace domestic supply of IT talent within developed countries. One of the unfortunate negative consequences of the offshore outsourcing press coverage has been the false impression that developed countries will no longer have vibrant career opportunities for domestic IT workers. This message became prominent during the 2004 US presidential and congressional elections. Front-page headlines questioned, "Software: Will Outsourcing Hurt America's Supremacy?" and claimed offshore sourcing was stealing American IT jobs and dragging down US IT bonus pay.[13] US companies that offshore outsourced were blacklisted on television shows such as CNN's *Tonight with Lou Dobbs*. This frightened many young college students from pursuing IT careers as evidenced by the 45 percent decline in Information Systems and Computer Science majors at many large US universities.

However, nearly every research report suggests that the US, United Kingdom, and likely other developed countries, will suffer a shortage of domestic IT workers within the next five to ten years. In the United Kingdom, for example, some research has found that the UK will experience a shortage of 714,000 IT workers by 2010.[14] The shortages in developed countries will be caused by the gap between a strong demand for domestic IT workers and a dwindling supply of domestic IT workers due to the lingering effects of declining enrollments today and future effects of "baby boomers" retiring from IT.

One example of research that found a strong US domestic demand for domestic IT workers was published by Zwieg *et al.* (2006).[15] The research was sponsored by the Society for Information Management Advocacy program. We participated on that 20-person research team. Our team interviewed senior executives in 77 IT departments about their current and future workforce trends and skill requirements. We found that more organizations were increasing their in-house IT staffs than were decreasing them. IT executives said it was critical to own business and project management skills. IT executives still planned to hire entry-level positions for technical IT skills, partly because technical skills provide the breeding ground for more advanced IT work, such as business systems analysts and project managers.

Beyond our study, the Cato Institute argues that by offshoring low-paying IT jobs, newer and more high-paying IT jobs will be created in the US over the next eight years.[16] Indeed, the US Department of Labor (Bureau of Labor Statistics) predicts that seven of the 30 fastest-growing jobs between 2002 and 2012 are in IT. These seven jobs are:

1. Network systems and data communication analysts
2. Computer software engineers/applications
3. Computer software engineers/systems software
4. Database administrators
5. Computer systems analysts
6. Network and computer system administrators
7. Computer and information systems managers

Considering the unexpected increases in domestic IT demand caused by the PC in the 1980s or by ERP, the Internet, and Y2K in the 1990s, it is very likely that the future will bring even stronger demand for domestic IT workers that we cannot fully grasp today. All we can confidently declare is that new IT careers will be prompted by new inventions, new innovations, or new uses of existing technologies.

Given the likely shortages in domestic supply of IT talent in developed countries, organizations based in developed countries will increasingly search for IT talent globally.

5. India will still dominate the offshore outsourcing market but will increasingly compete based on value-added rather than lower costs. Most ITO contracts are domestic (client and supplier based in the same country), but the offshore outsourcing portion of the ITO market is growing. The offshore ITO market (primarily India) will conservatively represent about 25 percent of the global ITO market, at $56 billion by 2008, according to financial services firm WR Hambrecht.[17] The United States spends the most money on IT offshoring, estimated to be $11 billion in 2004. The next-largest spenders on IT offshoring are the United Kingdom and Ireland. These two countries represented 72 percent of Western Europe's $2.5 billion spend on IT offshoring in 2004.[18]

Concerning the suppliers of offshore ITO, India is still leading. Forrester, McKinsey, and NASSCOM predict that India alone could grab $142 billion of the ITO market by 2009.[19] Although there have been recent reports that India is struggling with high turnover, wage increases, and infrastructure issues associated with rapid growth,[20] evidence suggests that India will continue to be a dominant player in the global ITO market,[21] with China emerging as the next-biggest rival.[22]

The 3 July 2006 issue of *Business Week*, for example, listed India's Tata Consultancy Services, Infosys, Satyam, and Wipro among the Global Information Technology 100. Their prospects for continued growth in the world market are strong.[23]

By all indications, offshore clients will stop viewing India primarily as a destination to lower costs, but rather as a destination for IT excellence. Within our case studies, we saw considerable evidence that US clients initially engaged Indian suppliers to provide technical services such as programming and platform upgrades. But, as these relationships matured, US clients assigned more challenging work to Indian suppliers. At Retail (Chapter 3), the US client first engaged their Indian supplier to help with Y2K compliance and CICS upgrades. As the relationship matured, Retail assigned development and support tasks for critical business applications to the supplier. At US Manufacturing (Chapter 4), the US client initially assigned technical tasks to their Indian suppliers. As the US–Indian partnerships continued to invest in social capital and knowledge transfer, the US client assigned embedded software development tasks for core products to their three Indian partners. From the US client perspective, the general finding across our cases was, "We went to India for lower costs, but we stayed for quality."

From the supplier perspective, the interviews we conducted with young Indian IT professionals found that the main determinant of their job satisfaction was interesting work (see Chapter 7). Our participants were eager to develop new software for clients, to learn new skill sets, to work on emerging technologies, and to manage other people. They complained about performing monotonous maintenance on a client's existing applications and merely coding and testing programs from predefined specifications. Moreover, the extent to which the Indian IT professionals were satisfied with their jobs determined their intentions to remain with their current employer.

Interviews with more senior supplier managers also found that suppliers are positioning themselves as higher-valued partners. Executives we interviewed from three of the large Indian suppliers all mentioned their desire to assume higher-value tasks for their clients, like research and development. According to the vice president at the Indian supplier firm for Retail (Chapter 3): "Our customers are beginning to come to us for entire turnkey solutions and research. I think Indian firms have had the long-standing reputation as being able to 'automate, not innovate'. Our relationships are moving towards more partnerships and away from strictly staff augmentation."

6. China: the world is watching. In 2006, China was second only to the United States in terms of the size of economy (measured on a purchasing power parity (PPP) basis).[24] Because of its sheer size, the world is watching China.

Within China's ITO and BPO markets, China invested $142.3 billion in ICT in 2006.[25] China's huge investment in IT is expected to pay off in terms of its ability to complete globally in the offshore services market. Although every research report and the second author's own trip to China confirm the market is currently immature, China's long-term ITO/BPO future is strong. For example, the Everest Group estimated that the Chinese offshore services market was only $2 billion in 2006, but it predicts that China's market will grow 38 percent annually to reach $7 billion by 2010.[26]

So far, the main ITO/BPO suppliers in China are either large US-based suppliers like Accenture, Cap Gemini, Dell, EDS, HP and IBM, or large Indian-based suppliers like Genpact, Infosys, Satyam, and TCS. Among our case studies, we have only four companies establishing IT captive centers in China: the financial information services firm highlighted in Chapter 5, a financial services firm, Oracle, and a staff-augmentation firm. However, some homegrown Chinese firms, like Neusoft, are expected to succeed as well (see Chapter 6).

About 80 percent of China's current offshore IT services customers are Japanese.[27] Dalian, China, in particular is a good destination for Japanese firms because the people of Dalian are fluent in Japanese and understand the Japanese culture. The city's close proximity to Japan is also a favorable factor.

Beyond Japan, the developed world is attracted to China because of its large workforce, low wages, and good transport and communications infrastructures. However, language barriers, cultural barriers, and fears over losing intellectual property remain significant obstacles for offshore clients in North America and Western Europe. The Chinese government and Chinese business sectors are well aware of these barriers and are actively seeking to address them. For example, the Chinese government is investing $5 billion in English-language training to target the ITO/BPO markets.[28]

As we have previously stated, senior executives are advised to select offshore destinations based on strategic business reasons rather than IT cost reasons alone. Whereas IT cost structures can rapidly shift due to exchange rates, inflation, and market prices, strategic reasons for selecting an offshore destination are more enduring. The real value in selecting China as an offshore destination for ITO or BPO may be to establish a presence in China and to learn about Chinese culture. What better way to eventually access the purchasing power of China's growing middle class? In 2003, about 19 percent of China's population was considered middle class (about 275 million people out of 1.3 billion people). The Chinese middle class is expected to reach 40 percent in 2020.[29]

Another reason firms are looking to China is geopolitical risk diversification. Firms we interviewed mentioned the recent difficulties between India and Pakistan as specific examples of the risk associated with an "Indian only" sourcing strategy. While India's political situation with Pakistan has stabilized, firms want to set up parallel development centers in China to assure business continuity.

As detailed in Chapter 6, China has a *national* plan for migrating their economy from a manufacturing force to a service force. While still lacking a common face similar to India's NASSCOM to coordinate brand image, marketing, and value propositions, China's national momentum, government initiatives, and strong workforce make it a "must watch" for companies structuring a global sourcing strategy.

Like Indian suppliers, many Chinese suppliers do not want to compete solely on programming skills. China is also trying to show it can fill the needs for product development, systems design and consulting services. According to the CTO of Neusoft,

> China has become the leading offshore destination for product development, with 41% of the Chinese offshore work being done in product research and development. The $2.5 billion investment by Intel in a chip manufacturing plant in Dalian, also signals that China may be moving up in the value chain for engineering services.

7. All six continents will develop centers of IT excellence. In addition to India and China, most IT research firms predict that many other countries around the world will develop significant IT centers of excellence. For example, the 2007 report *The Globalization of White-Collar Work* (Couto *et al.*), commissioned by Booz, Allen, and Hamilton, found that "labor arbitrage is giving way to accessing talent as the primary driver of next generation offshoring." Their report, based on a survey of 537 US and European client firms, found that the top offshore destinations for IT services were India, the Philippines, China, Latin America, Eastern Europe, Mexico, and Canada.[30] Each of these countries – representing four continents – have the government policies, infrastructure, talent, and other enabling factors to provide centers of IT excellence. A fifth continent, Australia, obviously has a well-developed IT sector. But what may surprise some is that even African countries are committed to joining the global IT services market.

For example, a 2006 report by Chillibreeze placed South Africa as the eighth emerging country.[31] The 2007 *Black Book of Outsourcing*[32] found that South Africa was the number one "country of interest as option to India" among a sample of 18,272 buyers. South Africa appeals primarily to UK-based clients because of the similar time zone, cultural similarities, English-speaking capabilities, and good infrastructure. But juxtaposed to the *interest* in South Africa, the same survey found that South Africa was not in the top ten list of current offshore destinations.

North Africa is also exporting IT services to Europe. One interesting study examined five Moroccan IT suppliers that provide services to clients in France.[33] Again, the common language, similar time zone, and cultural capability make Morocco an attractive destination for French organizations. In-between North Africa and South Africa, even some sub-Saharan countries are building their future economies on IT. Below we profile one such country – Rwanda. Can a country plagued by a past of civil wars, corruption, and disease compete in the global IT market?

Rwanda

Three of our University of Missouri, St. Louis, MBA students – Samantha Cagle, Mark Reinsch, Xilu Zhang – investigated the Rwandan government's plans to build their new economy on ICT.[34] While the challenges of building an economy on ICT in sub-Sahara Africa are daunting, the Rwandan government, under the leadership of President Paul Kagame, had an opportunity to completely rebuild the country after the genocide. The government, for example, ratified a new constitution that includes freedom of the press and requires that one-third of the parliamentary representatives be female.[35] The first draft of Rwanda's economic development plan was released in October 1999 with the aid of the United Nations Economic Commission for Africa (UNECA). The plan is called "An Integrated Socio-economic and ICT Policy and Strategies for Accelerated Development".[36] After almost one year of consultation with governmental entities and stakeholders, the Rwandan government decided to adopt the plan. The 20-year development policy is segmented into four five-year plans. Since the plan's ratification, a number of ICT investments have been made:

- In 2000, there was only one school with a computer. As of August 2006, more than half of the 2,300 primary schools had at least one computer.

- In 2000, fewer than 100,000 people had a telephone (mobile or land). By 2006, 300,000 people had cellular phones.
- By 2006, the large cities hosted 30 Internet cafés with plans to erect 30 more in rural areas.
- By 2006, hundreds of miles of fiber-optic cables were laid underground.
- Rwanda has had wireless Internet access via radio-waves since February 2005.[37]
- The government sets an example of ICT use with "paperless cabinet meetings" in which every minister uses a laptop.[38]

Mwangi (2006)[39] interviewed 21 Rwandans representing the government, business, academia, and voluntary not-for-profit organizations. He concluded that the *convergence* of four factors unique to Rwanda drove ICT development quicker than the other sub-Saharan African countries: (1) educated emigrants and refugee returnees, (2) networking with communities, (3) political leadership, and (4) an under-contested political environment. Rwanda may indeed provide a bellwether for other sub-Saharan African countries' ICT capabilities.

8. Nearshoring becomes an increasingly attractive complement to India. We define "nearshoring" as outsourcing work to a supplier located in an adjacent country. Compared to offshore outsourcing, the benefits of nearshoring include fewer travel costs, fewer time-zone differences, and closer cultural compatibility. Canada, for example, is a significant nearshore destination for US clients. US clients are attracted to Canada because of excellent IT skills, proven data security, 35 percent lower labor costs than the US, low turnover, and great infrastructure. Some analysts argue that US clients can have lower total costs with nearshoring to Canada than with offshoring to India. For example, Ramanujam (2005) took a typical six-month project – a web-based intranet application – and argued that the total cost of the project would cost $326,000 in Canada compared to $386,000 in India.[40]

The Czech Republic, Poland, and Hungary are significant nearshore destinations for Western Europe. According to a report by Deutsche Bank Research,[41] imports of IT-based services from Central and Eastern Europe to Western Europe rose an average of 13 percent per year between 1992 and 2004. This growth rate is nearly comparable to the import of IT services from India, which averaged 14 percent per year over the same time period. Clients in Western Europe are attracted to Central and Eastern European suppliers for many of the same reasons that the US is attracted to Canadian suppliers: common language, cultural understanding, minimal time-zone differences, and low labor costs. However, Central and Eastern Europe may be more attractive for BPO than ITO because these countries provide excellent general education, but have not graduated IT students at anywhere near the pace of India. For that reason, IDC predicts that Western Europe's growth in BPO will increased annually by 14.6 percent compared to 7.2 percent for ITO.

Of course, many suppliers offer blended, global models that combine onshore, nearshore, and offshore delivery for clients. CGI, the largest IT firm in Canada and the fifth largest in North America, provides one example. We interviewed 14 people from one of CGI's US clients. This client has an engagement with CGI worth $167 million over ten years. Participants were interviewed in Dallas, Toronto, and Mumbai. The client partly chose CGI because of its ability to distribute work among global development centers in Toronto, Montreal, Nova Scotia, Bangalore, and Mumbai. CGI uses nearshore development when the client requires significant and direct contact between developers and business units. CGI uses offshore for delivery of more standardized work. This way, issues of accent, culture, and time zones are CGI's responsibility to over-come, not their client's responsibility. According to the CIO of CGI's US client: "CGI has been great! Having two very different options, each with its own strengths and weaknesses, makes our partnership work. CGI knows when we need high-touch and when we need low cost."

9. Within the US, rural sourcing will meet a niche market. Rural sour-cing is a niche sourcing strategy that combines the high-touch value of domestic outsourcers with the lower costs offered by offshore outsourcing. With rural sourcing, suppliers locate development centers in remote areas that have significantly lower cost of living than urban areas. Lower cost of living enables suppliers to pay lower salaries for IT employees without compromising on their employees' quality of life. Lower salaries are passed on to the customer in terms of lower prices. Rural sourcing offers prices that are 30–50 percent less expensive per hour than urban rates.

Within the United States, about 60 million people (20 percent of Americans) live in 80 percent of America's landmass, classified as "rural".[42] We talked to two suppliers that offer rural sourcing – CrossUSA, based in Minnesota, and Rural Sourcing, based in Arkansas. Their models are very different, but both companies offer US clients lower prices and good-quality services.

CrossUSA

CrossUSA was founded by Nick Debronsky in 1998. By 2007, the company employed over 85 people. The corporate office is located in Burnsville,

Minnesota, and the three rural development centers are located in Sebeka (Minnesota), Eveleth (Minnesota), and Watford City (North Dakota). Each development center is located in a secure building to protect IT systems, and provides office space for IT employees. Although IT work could theoretically be done from home, CrossUSA believes in providing team-based work to ensure collaborative, high-quality outputs. For clients, the two distinguishing features of this company are the lower prices and the stable, highly motivated workforce.

In terms of costs, CrossUSA's hourly billing rates in 2007 were between $40 and $60, which is significantly lower than the $80–100 range in urban areas. While this rate is still higher than the $30 rate of Indian suppliers, CrossUSA argues that total cost of rural sourcing and offshore outsourcing are comparable. With rural sourcing, on-site/off-site ratios can be as low as 1:10, whereas the ratios are closer to 1:4 with offshore outsourcing. With offshore outsourcing, the supplier needs to maintain more of a presence to coordinate offshore work that occurs during a different time zone and within a different culture. The supplier's on-site engagement manager may cost as much as $125 per hour and is needed to stabilize the relationship, particularly when offshore turnover is high. Because offshore suppliers are paid on-site rates, the blended rates for offshoring are nearer to the $40–60 range, which is equivalent to the per hour costs of the rural model. In addition, rural sourcing has lower transaction costs associated with travel to client sites, providing on-site office space, and lodging (because trips can be shorter in duration). Thus, in comparison to domestic outsourcing in urban areas, rural rates are cheaper and, in comparison to offshore outsourcing, total costs may be comparable.

Besides the rural location and lower on-site/off-site ratio, CrossUSA also keeps costs low by not having a "bench." (A "bench" is IT vernacular for the practice of paying IT professionals when they are not working on an active client account.) Client teams are custom built for specific clients with a long-term staffing strategy in mind. One obvious question is: How can CrossUSA afford the risk of hiring and relocating a full-time employee when the client may only sign a six-to 12-month contract? According to Ross Graba, Vice President of Business Development for CrossUSA, the risk has been minimal because most relationships with clients end up being long term. Clients and CrossUSA co-develop a new employee by sharing in joint training. Because clients invest in the employees, they are highly motivated to maintain a good relationship with CrossUSA, thereby getting a longer-term return on the initial training investment. This joint investment benefits both client and supplier because it facilitates knowledge transfer. The CrossUSA employee works directly with the client to learn their domain-specific knowledge, work processes, and, most importantly, to develop relationships with client counterparts. Finally, even when contracts will not be renewed – for example, because CrossUSA was hired to assist with retiring a sunset application – there is enough notice to assign employees to other accounts.

In terms of the highly motivated workforce, CrossUSA boasts a company-wide turnover rate of less than 10 percent, compared to the 30–100 percent turnover rates of Indian suppliers. The key to the low turnover is that CrossUSA seeks employees from all over the country who are looking for a rural lifestyle. The workforce is generally seeking a lifestyle focused on family, good education, and tight-knit, small communities, where crime and large-city headaches are absent. In an ABC news special report that aired on 26 August 2005, the news correspondent Barbara Pinto asked Nick Debronsky, CEO of CrossUSA, how he knows his staff will remain with the company. The CEO responded, "because there is not other work within 200 miles." This broadcast featured one CrossUSA employee who left Chicago to move to Sebeka, Minnesota, with a population of less than 1,000. He was thrilled that he could buy a seven-acre farm for less money than he sold his home for in Chicago. The mayor of Sebeka is also a CrossUSA employee. Low turnover translates into stable, long-term relationships with clients. According to Ross Graba, once the relationship is established, the clients feel 100 percent comfortable and confident to work directly with CrossUSA's employees:

> This minimizes the overhead needed to service clients effectively. An added benefit to the rural model is that CrossUSA is keeping jobs here in the US. CrossUSA's development centers bring hundreds of thousands of payroll dollars to small towns and communities. These employees, and now residents, help stimulate economic development in places that would otherwise be economically depressed.

As of 2007, CrossUSA has 12 active clients, ranging from Fortune 100 to Fortune 1000 in size, and in various industries such as insurance, retail, banking, and manufacturing.

Rural Sourcing, Inc.

Rural Sourcing, Inc., is another US-based company offering the advantages of rural sourcing. The company was founded in 2003 by CEO of the company, Dr. Kathy Brittain White. The business model relies on locating in rural communities near a university with a robust IT program. This allows recent graduates to remain in their communities but still work in their preferred profession. Rural Sourcing specializes in current technologies including Internet technologies (HTML, XML, ASP, JSP, PHP, Perl), SAP, Java, .Net (VB, ASP, C), ColdFusion, Windows, Unix, Linux, Database Services (Oracle, SQL Server), and Enterprise Applications. Graduates go through a rigorous training program to supplement their technical skills. So far, Rural Sourcing has development centers in rural Arkansas, New Mexico, and North Carolina.

10. Knowledge process outsourcing will increase. Knowledge process outsourcing (KPO) is the outsourcing of business, market, and/or industry research that requires a significant amount of domain knowledge and analytical skills. KPO suppliers design surveys, collect new data, mine existing data, statistically analyze data, and/or write reports. According to Evalueserve, the term KPO was first coined by Ashish Gupta, COO of Evalueserve, in September 2003. Although the KPO market is currently small, industry analysts expect a huge growth in this sector over the next five years. For example, the Everest Group evaluated the current offerings of the top 11 Indian suppliers and found that KPO is currently only 4 percent of their revenues. However, this advisory firm predicts a rapid growth in KPO as suppliers cannibalize some of the onshore work and actively create demand for these services.[43] Evalueserve estimated that the KPO market in 2007 was $3.05 billion and will grow annually by 39 percent. They expect the KPO market to be $16 billion by 2010 or 2011 and that it will employ approximately 350,000 professionals globally.[44]

The increase in KPO is directly related to the previous observation that offshore suppliers are moving up the value chain. As client/supplier relationships mature, the suppliers have gained an enormous amount of knowledge about the client's business domain as well as the IT expertise to find, analyze, and report on domain knowledge. US, Canadian, and UK clients value this deep knowledge and will pay Indian suppliers $20–100 per hour for KPO services, compared to onshore rates of $80–500 per hour.[45] Offshore suppliers are struggling to find enough workers with advanced degrees to fill the demand. But once hired, we anticipate that supplier-employee turnover in this space will be lower because professionals finally have the client-facing and intellectually challenging work they did not find in programming. This prediction is based on our research that found that interesting work – not pay – was the main determinant of an Indian employee's intentions to remain with their current employee.

11. Freelance offshoring will increase. The research for this book was based on interviews with US client and offshore supplier *organizations*.

While organizations will continue to be the predominant consumers and suppliers of global IT talent, there is an interesting trend in the use of freelance offshoring. ***With freelance offshoring, individuals offer their talents globally, primarily through freelance Internet sites.*** Internet portals that already have a significant number of registered freelancers and buyers include elance.com, guru.com, and rentacoder.com.[46] Rentacoder.com, for example, had nearly 80,000 registered buyers and 200,000 registered coders in July 2007. The company had nearly 2,500 open bids on 11 July 2007. On that same date, Guru.com boasted over 700,000 registered gurus and 80,000 registered buyers. More than 60 percent of the "gurus" are from low-wage countries. Research by Evalueserve estimates that this market was worth $250 million in 2007, but will grow at least 25 percent annually to reach over $2 billion by 2015.[47]

12. More companies will sell their IT captive centers or create virtual captive centers. This trend might be called the "GE effect." General Electric may not have been the first US footprint in India, but certainly Jack Welch's enthusiasm for India made it acceptable for other CEO/CIOs to locate IT in India. (Read a great anecdote by Vivek Paul on the GE executives' initial visits to India in Friedman, 2005.)[48] GE established GECIS (GE Capital International Services) as a captive center in India in 1997. In the winter of 2004, GE sold off 60 percent of GECIS to two equity companies, Oak Hill Capital Partners and General Atlantic Partners. A year later, the name was changed to Genpact, which is now one of the top ten BPO/ITO suppliers in India. Some have called GE's approach the "virtual captive center" because GE still maintains primary equity holding.[49] With a virtual captive center, the company owns the physical operations, but the staff is employed by a third-party supplier.[50] Presumably the virtual captive center offers the best of both worlds – the client investor still maintains strategic control but the supplier is better equipped to attract, develop, and retain local IT talent.

Within our own sample of US clients, we also have examples of US organizations selling their captive centers. One financial services firm, for example, set up a joint venture with an Indian supplier in 2002 in Chennai, India. The client investor was the only "customer." The financial services company used this model for security reasons: "One of the key issues with the joint venture was to be able to leverage offshore resources in a secure model. We can't just farm out work to anybody because of data sensitivity" (Director of Technologies, Financial Services).

By 2004, the captive center had 250 IT workers providing services to the US client investor. The business case was that the financial services company would save $1 million for every 15 IT jobs based in India. The savings are calculated by comparing the higher costs of domestic contractor workers to labor in India. But costs were not the only driver:

> Our take on cost savings with offshore, even if it's a wash on cost savings, I'd have a hard time finding and bringing in 250 employees here at headquarters. So there's a physical limitation issue. Also, if I can get the processes in place, we can do sunrise-to-sunrise development, which will give me a speed and agility factor. I couldn't get that by having them here in the States. We are currently at 18–20 hours of development time a day, which is pretty good. (Director of Technologies, financial services)

In late 2005, the US client sold the captive center to a large Indian supplier. The US client thought the large Indian supplier would be better equipped to deal with the high turnover of Indian staff and would be better able to provide critical skill shortages in Java, Pearl, and web-based development. Also, the US client was confident the supplier was well equipped to ensure data security, which was the impetus for erecting the captive center in the first place.

Beyond the anecdotes of GE and the US Financial Services firm, the 2007 *Black Book of Outsourcing*[51] survey of 18,272 buyers found that selling captive centers may indeed be a significant trend. Among the survey respondents were 487 companies with captive centers in India and the Philippines. The survey found that 29 percent of these companies were actively seeking to sell out or already had an exist strategy in place. Respondents from large organizations were more likely to investigate a sell-out than mid-sized businesses. The main reasons for selling captive centers were:

1. Captive center was built to protect data and intellectual property, which is no longer viewed as a threat if provided by a third-party supplier.
2. Senior executives are no longer committed to captive centers.
3. No longer necessary to keep decision-making authority in-house.
4. Third parties are now able to handle complex processes.

There is a difference between the ITO and BPO captive centers: Companies are much more likely to erect a captive center for BPO than ITO. For example, the Everest Group tracked 150 captive centers in India. In the BPO space, about half of Indian offshore services were provided through captive centers in 2006, compared to less than 25 percent in the

ITO space.[52] We reason that the differences are attributed to higher maturity of Indian IT services compared to BPO, as well as the client view that BPO services are more critical to operations.

13. US client organizations will no longer hide their offshore outsourcing initiatives. We don't know if this is so much a *trend* as it is a *plea*. Back in 1989, when the first author began her dissertation and wrote her first book with Rudy Hirschheim on domestic ITO, every client organization requested anonymity.[53] At that time, CIOs were legitimately afraid of being criticized for outsourcing IT to domestic suppliers. The popular press at the time accused CIOs of "selling their crown jewels" or "selling their birthright" and they accused suppliers of "outsourcery." It wasn't until the practice matured in the mid-1990s, that CIOs became vocal about their sourcing strategies, and allowed us to name their companies in our subsequent books. (Thank you, DuPont and British Aerospace (now BAE Systems), for being among our first named cases.[54])

Since we began our research on offshore outsourcing in 2004, every client company requested anonymity. During our interviews, many client IT leaders are clearly proud of their accomplishments and partnerships with offshore suppliers, yet the public perception against offshoring still weighs on their minds. They have a legitimate concern that the popular press[55] will view any offshoring of IT work negatively. It is our hope that academics can help educate the public about global IT sourcing so that it becomes an accepted business practice, just as domestic IT outsourcing became accepted business practice more than a decade ago. We live in a global economy, and can longer afford to think in terms of protectionism, national boundaries, and local interests. We all consume and produce products and services worldwide. In the words of our favorite contemporary philosopher, John Searle, "We live in exactly one world, not two or three or seventeen ..."[56]

Notes

1. Digital Planet/Global Insight, available at: www.itaa.org
2. *Ibid.*
3. *Ibid.*
4. Carr, N., "IT Doesn't Matter," *Harvard Business Review*, Vol. 81, No. 5, May 2003, pp. 41–9.
5. Krass, P., "The Dollars and Sense of Outsourcing," *Information Week*, No. 259, 26 February 1990, pp. 26–31; Rothfederand Coy, P., "Outsourcing: More Companies are Letting George Do It," *BusinessWeek*, No. 3181, 8 October 1990, p. 148.

6. Willcocks, L., and Lacity, M., *Global Sourcing of Business and IT Services*, Palgrave, 2006; Blackmore, D., De Souza, R., Young, A., Goodness, E., and Silliman, R., "Forecast: IT Outsourcing, Worldwide, 2002–2008 (Update)," *Gartner Report*, March 2005.

7. R. Tisnovsky, "IT Outsourcing in SME Businesses," an Everest Research Institute white paper, 2006. See www.everestresearchins titute.com

8. To access this database, see: http://stats.oecd.org/wbos/

9. *Ibid.*

10. T. Meyer, *Nearshoring to Central and Eastern Europe*, Deutsche Bank Research white paper, August 2006.

11. J. Houghton, "ICT Adds 21bn to our Trade Deficit," *Information Age*, June 2007, available at: http://infoage.idg.com.au/index.php/ id;673784999;fp;16;fpid;0

12. http://new.unctad.org/upload/Data/Exports %20of %t20computer %20and %20information %20services %20by %20country.PDF

13. R. Hof and J. Kerttetter, "Software: Will Outsourcing Hurt America's Supremacy?" *Business Week*, 1 March 2004, pp. 84–95. M. McGee, "Offshore Outsourcing Drags Down US Bonus Pay," *InformationWeek*, 25 August 2003.

14. A. Aggarwal and A. Pandey, *Offshoring of IT Services – Present and Future*, Evaluserve, 2004.

15. P. Zwieg, K.M. Kaiser, C. Beath, C. Bullen, K. Gallagher, T. Goles, J. Howland, J. Simon, P. Abbott, T. Abraham, E. Carmel, R. Evaristo, S. Hawk, M. Lacity, M. Gallivan, S. Kelly, J. Mooney, C. Ranganathan, J. Rottman, T. Ryan, and R. Wion, "The Information Technology Workforce Trends and Implications 2005–2008," *MIS Quarterly Executive*, Vol. 5, No. 2, 2006, pp. 47–54.

16. B. Lindsey, "Job Losses and Trade: A Reality Check," *Cato Institute Trade Briefing*, No. 19, 17 March 2004.

17. E-business Strategies, "Offshoring Statistics: Dollar Size, Job Loss, and Market Potential," http://www.ebstrategy.com/Outsourcing/trends/ statistics.htm, last accessed on 7 December 2007.

18. Meyer, Nearshoring to Central and Eastern Europe.

19. C. Ross, "Services Market Sizing Update: 2003 to 2008," Forrester Research Report, 27 April 2004.

20. A. McCue, "Outsourcing Flops Blamed on Tunnel Vision," Silicon. com, published on ZDNet News: 22 June 2005, available at: http:// news.zdnet.com/2100-9589_22-5757832.html; S. Srivastava, "Could Rising Wages Diminish India's Outsourcing Edge?" News Report, *Siliconeer*, 21 January 2005, available at: http://news.pacificnews.org/

news/view_article.html?article_id=167d1c86c1d28e7607c942fd989193 8e, last accessed 7 December 2007.

21. E. Carmel and P. Tjia, *Offshoring Information Technology: Sourcing and Outsourcing to a Global Workforce*, Cambridge University Press, 2005; P. Engardio, "The Future of Outsourcing," *Business Week* (3969), 30 January 2006, pp. 50–8; M. Minevich and F. Richter, "Top Spots for Global Outsourcing," *CIO Insight*, Vol. 1, No. 51, 5 March 2005, pp. 55–7.

22. S. Overby, "It's Cheaper in China," *CIO Magazine*, Vol. 18, No. 23, 15 September 2005.

23. Minevich and Richter, "Top Spots for Global Outsourcing."

24. https://www.cia.gov/library/publications/the-world-factbook/print/ch.html

25. http://www.witsa.org/press/DigialPlanetPressRelease_rev.doc

26. S. Bahl, J. Arora, and A. Gupta, "What's Happening in China," The Everest Group, ERI.2007, .2.W.0172, 2007.

27. www.fdimagazine.com/news/fullstory.php/aid/1868/Battle_of_the_bohemoths.html

28. *Ibid.*

29. In China, a family is considered middle class if they own assets valued from 150,000 to 300,000 yuan (US$18,072–36,144) according to the US Embassy. See http://www.china-embassy.org/eng/gyzg/t80880.htm

30. V. Couto, M. Mani, A. Lewin, and C. Peeters, "The Globalization of White-Collar Work: The Facts and Fallout of Next Generation Offshoring," research report by Booz, Allen, and Hamilton in cooperation with Duke School of Business, 2007.

31. Chillibreeze, *Top 10s in Outsourcing*, 2006, available at: www.chilli breeze.com

32. Brown-Wilson Group, *The Black Book of Outsourcing: State of the Outsourcing Industry: Results of Service Provider Buyers, Users, and Analysts*, 2007. While the sample included only 18 percent of IT buyers, it is certainly a surprising finding that South Africa was number one on the list of "countries of interest" beyond India. The next four "countries of interest as option to India" were Malaysia, Argentina, Costa Rica, and China.

33. G. Bruno, G. Esposito, L. Iandoli, M. Raffa, "The ICT Service Industry in North Africa," *Journal of Global Information Technology Management*, 2004, Vol. 7, No. 3, pp. 5–26.

34. S. Cagle, M. Reinsch, and X. Zhang, "IT in Developing Nations–A Look at Sub-Saharan Africa," University of Missouri, St. Louis IS5800 paper, 2006.

35. *Ibid.*

36. The plan is online at: http://www.uneca.org/aisi/NICI/country_pro-files/rwanda/rwanpap3.htm

37. W. Mwangi, "The Social Relations of e-Government Diffusion in Developing Countries: The Case of Rwanda," *ACM International Conference Proceeding Series*, Vol. 151, 2006, pp. 199–208.

38. Steffen, A., "Can Rwanda's Vision 2020 National Leapfrogging Plan Succeed?" available at: http://www.worldchanging.com/archives/004835.html

39. Mwangi, "The Social Relations of e-Government Diffusion in Developing Countries."

40. S. Ramanujam, "Nearshoring to Atlantic Canada: Is it the Smart Alternative to Offshore Outsourcing to India?" white paper, July 2005, available at: http://nearshoring.ca/whitepaper01.htm

41. Meyer, Nearshoring to Central and Eastern Europe.

42. C. Norris, "Move Over Rainforest, Save Rural America!" Worldnet-DailyNews, 25 June 2007 available at: http://worldnetdaily.com/news/article.asp?ARTICLE_ID=56338

43. Everest Research Group, *Business Process Outsourcing: Indian Supplier Landscape*, April 2007, ERI.2007.1.R.0160.

44. Evalueserve, Knowledge Process Outsourcing: Origin, Current State, and Future Directions, 16 July 2007.

45. *Ibid.*

46. A. Aggarwal, *Person-to-Person Offshoring,* Evalueserve Report, April 2007.

47. *Ibid.*

48. T. Friedman, *The World is Flat*, Farrar, Strauss, and Giroux, 2005.

49. http://www.cxoamerica.com/pastissue/article.asp?art=269068&issue=184

50. There are a number of recent articles addressing the trend of "virtual captive centers." See P. Allen, "Late to the Game of Offshoring? Take a Look at Virtual Captive Operations," 5 January 2007, available at: http://considerthesourceblog.typepad.com/consider_the_source/2007/01/late_to_the_gam.html; C. Foster and J. Funk, "The Offshore Solutions Spectrum: Getting the Best Fit," *Journal of Sourcing Leadership*, Vol. 3, No. 1, July 2006; Technology Partners International, *The Sourcing Leadership Exchange*, white paper, Spring 2006.

51. Brown-Wilson Group, *The Black Book of Outsourcing.*

52. Everest Research Group, *India Captive Center Market – Trends and Implications*, ERI, 2007.2.R.016, 2007.

53. M. Lacityand R. Hirschheim, *Information Systems Outsourcing: Myths, Metaphors and Realities*, Wiley, 1993.

54. For detailed case studies on DuPont and British Aerospace, see M. Lacity and L. Willcocks, *Global Information Technology Outsourcing: Search for Business Advantage*, Wiley, 2001.
55. The IT press has an informed and balanced view of offshoring and offshore outsourcing – it is the popular press that frequently portrays offshore outsourcing as harming Americans.
56. J. Searle, *The Construction of Social Reality*, Free Press, 1997.

References

Aggarwal, A., *Person-to-Person Offshoring,* Evalueserve Report, April 2007.

Aggarwal, A., and Pandey, A., *Offshoring of IT Services – Present and Future*, Evaluserve, 2004.

Allen, P., "Late to the Game of Offshoring? Take a Look at Virtual Captive Operations," 5 January 2007, available at: http://considerthe-sourceblog.typepad.com/consider_the_source/2007/01/late_to_the_gam.html

Bahl, S., Arora, J., and Gupta, A., "What's Happening in China," The Everest Group, ERI.2007, .2.W.0172, 2007.

Blackmore, D., De Souza, R., Young, A., Goodness, E., and Silliman, R., "Forecast: IT Outsourcing, Worldwide, 2002–2008 (Update)," *Gartner Report*, March 2005.

Brown-Wilson Group, *The Black Book of Outsourcing: State of the Outsourcing Industry: Results of Service Provider Buyers, Users, and Analysts*, 2007.

Bruno, G., Esposito, G., Iandoli, L., and Raffa, M., "The ICT Service Industry in North Africa," *Journal of Global Information Technology Management*, 2004, Vol. 7, No. 3, pp. 5–26.

Cagle, S., Reinsch, M., and Zhang, X., "IT in Developing Nations–A Look at Sub-Saharan Africa," University of Missouri, St. Louis IS5800 paper, 2006.

Carmel, E., and Tjia, P., *Offshoring Information Technology: Sourcing and Outsourcing to a Global Workforce*, Cambridge University Press, 2005.

Carr, N., "IT Doesn't Matter," *Harvard Business Review*, Vol. 81, No. 5, May 2003, pp. 41–9.

Chillibreeze, *Top 10s in Outsourcing*, 2006, available at: www.chillibreeze.com

Couto, V., Mani, M., Lewin, A., and Peeters, C., "The Globalization of White-Collar Work: The Facts and Fallout of Next Generation

Offshoring," research report by Booz, Allen, and Hamilton in cooperation with Duke School of Business, 2007.

Digital Planet/Global Insight, available at: www.itaa.org

E-business Strategies, "Offshoring Statistics: Dollar Size, Job Loss, and Market Potential," http://www.ebstrategy.com/Outsourcing/trends/statistics.htm, last accessed on 7 December 2007.

Engardio, P., "The Future of Outsourcing," *Business Week* (3969), 30 January 2006, pp. 50–8.

Evalueserve, *Knowledge Process Outsourcing: Origin, Current State, and Future Directions*, 16 July 2007.

Everest Research Group, *Business Process Outsourcing: Indian Supplier Landscape*, April 2007, ERI.2007.1.R.0160.

Everest Research Group, *India Captive Center Market – Trends and Implications*, ERI, 2007.2.R.016, 2007.

Foster, C., and Funk, J., "The Offshore Solutions Spectrum: Getting the Best Fit," *Journal of Sourcing Leadership*, Vol. 3, No. 1, July 2006.

Friedman, T., *The World is Flat*, Farrar, Strauss, and Giroux, 2005.

Hof, R., and Kerttetter, J., "Software: Will Outsourcing Hurt America's Supremacy?" *Business Week*, 1 March 2004, pp. 84–95.

Houghton, J., "ICT Adds 21bn to our Trade Deficit," *Information Age*, June 2007, available at: http://infoage.idg.com.au/index.php/id;673784999;fp;16;fpid;0

Krass, P., "The Dollars and Sense of Outsourcing," *Information Week*, No. 259, 26 February 1990, pp. 26–31.

Lacity, M., and Hirschheim, R., Information Systems Outsourcing: Myths, Metaphors and Realities, Wiley, 1993.

Lacity, M., and Willcocks, L., Global Information Technology Outsourcing: Search for Business Advantage, Wiley, 2001.

Lindsey, B., "Job Losses and Trade: A Reality Check," *Cato Institute Trade Briefing*, No. 19, 17 March 2004.

McCue, A., "Outsourcing Flops Blamed on Tunnel Vision," Silicon.com, published on ZDNet News: 22 June 2005, available at: http://news.zdnet.com/2100-9589_22-5757832.html

McGee, M., "Offshore Outsourcing Drags Down US Bonus Pay," *InformationWeek*, 25 August 2003.

Meyer, T., *Nearshoring to Central and Eastern Europe*, Deutsche Bank Research white paper, August 2006.

Minevich, M., and Richter, F., "Top Spots for Global Outsourcing," *CIO Insight*, Vol. 1, No. 51, 5 March 2005, pp. 55–7.

Mwangi, W., "The Social Relations of e-Government Diffusion in Developing Countries: The Case of Rwanda," *ACM International Conference Proceeding Series*, Vol. 151, 2006, pp. 199–208.

Norris, C., "Move Over Rainforest, Save Rural America!" WorldnetDailyNews, 25 June 2007 available at: http://worldnetdaily. com/news/article.asp?ARTICLE_ID=56338

Overby, S., "It's Cheaper in China," *CIO Magazine*, Vol. 18, No. 23, 15 September 2005.

Ramanujam, S., "Nearshoring to Atlantic Canada: Is it the Smart Alternative to Offshore Outsourcing to India?" white paper, July 2005, available at: http://nearshoring.ca/whitepaper01.htm

Ross, C., "Services Market Sizing Update: 2003 to 2008," Forrester Research Report, 27 April 2004.

Rothfeder, J., and Coy, P., "Outsourcing: More Companies are Letting George Do It," *BusinessWeek*, No. 3181, 8 October 1990, p. 148.

Searle, J., *The Construction of Social Reality*, Free Press, 1997.

Srivastava, S., "Could Rising Wages Diminish India's Outsourcing Edge?" News Report,

Siliconeer, 21 January 2005, available at: http://news.pacificnews.org/ news/view_article.html?article_id=167d1c86c1d28e7607c942fd989193 8e, last accessed 7 December 2007.

Steffen, A., "Can Rwanda's Vision 2020 National Leapfrogging Plan Succeed?" available at: http://www.worldchanging.com/archives/ 004835.html

Technology Partners International, *The Sourcing Leadership Exchange*, white paper, Spring 2006.

Tisnovsky, R., "IT Outsourcing in SME Businesses," an Everest Research Institute white paper, 2006. See www.everestresearchinstitute.com

Willcocks, L., and Lacity, M., *Global Sourcing of Business and IT Services*, Palgrave, 2006.

Zwieg, P., Kaiser, K. M., Beath, C., Bullen, C., Gallagher, K., Goles, T., Howland, J., Simon, J. Abbott, P., Abraham, T., Carmel, E., Evaristo, R., Hawk, S., Lacity, M., Gallivan, M., Kelly, S., Mooney, J., Ranganathan, C., Rottman, J., Ryan, T., Wion, R., "The Information Technology Workforce Trends and Implications 2005–2008," *MIS Quarterly Executive*, Vol. 5, No. 2, 2006, pp. 47–54.

INDEX

BRUNEL UNIVERSITY LIBRARY

Bannerman Centre,
Uxbridge, Middlesex,
UB8 3PH

Renewals: www.brunel.ac.uk/renew
OR
01895 266141

LONG LOAN

60 4249381 1